Southern Europe?

Martin Baumeister is Director of the German Historical Institute in Rome, Italy, and Professor of Contemporary European History at the University of Munich, Germany and *Roberto Sala* is a researcher at the Department of History, and Coordinator of the Basel Graduate School of History, University of Basel, Switzerland.

Martin Baumeister, Roberto Sala (eds.)

Southern Europe?

Italy, Spain, Portugal, and Greece from the 1950s until the present day

Campus Verlag
Frankfurt/New York

The publication of this present volume has been made possible through the generous support of the German Historical Institute in Rome (Deutsches Historisches Institut in Rom, DHI).

Distribution throughout the world except Germany, Austria and Switzerland by
The University of Chicago Press
1427 East 60th Street
Chicago, IL 60637

Bibliografic Information published by the Deutsche Nationalbibliothek.
The Deutsche Nationalbibliothek lists its publication in the Deutsche Nationalbibliografie; detailed bibliographic data are available in the Internat at http://dnb.d-nb.de

ISBN 978-3-593-50482-7 Print
ISBN 978-3-593-43257-1 E-Book (PDF)

Cover design: Campus Verlag GmbH, Frankfurt-on-Main
Printed on acid free paper.
Printed in the United States of America

For further information:
www.campus.de
www.press.uchicago.edu

Table of Contents

III. Modernity and Other Master Narratives

IV. Political Entanglements

Introduction

Martin Baumeister and Roberto Sala

In 2004, *The Economist* published, under the title "The Fit and the Flabby", a cartoon depicting three men in underpants.[1] The man at the center was remarkably obese and wore drawers in the colors of the German flag. At his sides, two slender bodybuilders—whose briefs had the colors of Spain and France—exhibited their fully oversized muscles. The message was clear. At that time, Germany was considered the 'sick man of Europe', as a country "facing its most serious stagnation in postwar history" (Hein and Truger, 2005). France, its traditional main concurrent, appeared to be in much better shape. The novelty was, however, the third counterpart: as Europe's new 'top performer', Spain appeared to match the two major economies of the continent. The Spanish economy represented a model envied by many that since the seventies had successfully managed the "transition from an agricultural society to a modern economy dominated by the service sector" (Mas and Quesada 2007, 87).

After the outbreak of the financial, the economic and eventually the debt crisis, a few years later the situation has fully changed. Not least thanks to its broad industrial sector, previously considered its weak spot, Germany has resurged and mutated from "Sick Man of Europe to Economic Superstar" (Dustman et al. 2014) while France has been hit by severe economic and social problems. Of the three, however, the main loser has been Spain, falling down from the economic miracle to a dramatic recession that has deeply affected the Spanish society as well as the cohesiveness of the European Union.

The rise and decline of Spain is paradigmatic for the area that—including also Italy, Portugal, and Greece—is usually called 'Southern Europe' in today's political and scientific discourse. Before the crisis, the international reputation of these countries was quite different. In comparison with other Western European states, Portugal and Greece were still regarded as less dy-

1 Anonymous (18/09/2004). The Fit and the Flabby. *The Economist*, 8393, 93–94.

namic economies that, nonetheless, were achieving remarkable results. On the contrary, Italy was said to be a country affected by stagnation and still living off the economic boom of the past. Nevertheless, all four Southern European countries were considered an integral part of the wealthy (Western) European economies. Also by leaving behind the past authoritarian regimes, they seemed to have mastered the deep economic underdevelopment still affecting them after World War II and become solid democracies and reliable members of the Western community.

After 2007 and especially 2010, the South has been at the center of public debates over the crisis. Although Ireland—as regards the debt crisis the second 'I' of the *PIIGS*—and partly France have shared common problems with these countries, it is undisputed that 'Southern Europe' constitutes 'the' European problem. In other words—as far as their economic and social emergencies are concerned—the near future of Italy, Spain, Portugal, and Greece appears to be decisive for the success or failure of the European integration project.

This book addresses the question of whether 'Southern Europe' is a useful concept for understanding the European present and recent past. Do Italy, Spain, Portugal, and Greece represent an area shaped by common paths and patterns of development as well as structural analogies? Or is 'Southern Europe' a misleading notion brought up by polarized political debates? From this perspective, following an interdisciplinary approach, the volume looks both at the current situation and considers its historical roots, back in the early post-war period.

While historiography has not dealt intensively with 'Southern Europe', in the last decades, disciplines such as economics, sociology, and political science have offered in-depth analyses of Italy, Spain, Portugal, and Greece in terms of a common area of development. A recurrent characteristic of these studies consists of highlighting the supposed deficits of 'Southern Europe' with regard to a European 'core'. A good example is a passage that Maurizio Ferrera—a renowned expert in the field of welfare state studies—wrote in 1996 and that retrospectively appears almost prophetic:

> "Within national debates, some voices have started to lament explicitly that perhaps the 'deeper and wider' European Union has arrived too early for the new southern Europe, which is therefore doomed to remain a second rate periphery. Others argue that the constraints posed by the integration process represent a good chance for a 'big' modernising 'bang', capable of finally aligning the still underdeveloped Medi-

terranean littoral with the more civilized European inland. The next decade is very likely to show which scenario will prevail." (Ferrera 1996, 34)

Even regarding the more technical aspects of his analysis of a Southern European welfare state, Ferrera focuses on insufficiencies of his 'Southern model', whose characteristics are its dualism, ineffectiveness, and particularistic clientelism, producing its permanent structural crisis (Ferrera 1996, 19, 25, 31). This tendency becomes especially evident in the *opus magnum* by Giulio Sapelli (1995)—one of the few historians dealing with this field—dedicated to the post-war history of Italy, Spain, Portugal, and Greece (as well as Turkey, which the author considers to be part of that area).[2] Adopting a Weberian perspective and examining both the economic and socio-political systems, Sapelli describes 'Southern Europe' as an area floating between *tradition* and *modernity*, i.e. as a region that—caught in archaic structures—has only partially achieved the features of a modern society. This development, in his opinion, is due to the fact that Southern European societies have experienced only a weak industrialization, changing almost directly from agricultural to service economies. Under these circumstances, the 'contractual system' and the 'market forces' shaping modern societies have not been able to develop fully. On the contrary, they have been slowed down by clientelistic and patronage structures both in economy and politics.

Without blaming their specific arguments, we can observe that Sapelli and Ferrera—like many other authors in the field—adopt a research framework dependant upon the normative narratives about the right or wrong path to European modernity. From this perspective, the volume is based on the assumption that both political debates and scientific research on 'Southern Europe' have been influenced by polarizing discourses reflecting internal European power hierarchies. To contextualize and historicize these discourses, however, does not mean rejecting the concept of 'Southern Europe' as a whole. It rather implies the necessity of identifying the danger of 'all-inclusive' interpretative paradigms, and of raising the question of to what extent this regional concept helps to understand Europe's present and recent past.

2 There are scholars who like Sapelli consider Turkey—as well as, in a similar logic, Cyprus–a part of 'Southern Europe' due to its reinforced 'Westernization' and 'Europeanization' in the post-war era. In this volume Turkey is largely left out of our discussion of the 'European South' according to the perspective of a good deal of research and the country's rather ambivalent position in political discourses about the mapping of Europe.

The volume consists of four sections. The *first section*, 'Southern Models?', surveys debates of the last three decades regarding the existence of 'Southern Europe' as an analytical category. In their chapter, *Martin Baumeister* and *Roberto Sala* examine the career and the potential of 'Southern Europe' as research agenda. They show that this concept is relatively young both in political and scientific discourses when referring to Italy, Spain, Portugal, and Greece. This category, as they show, almost ignored by historiography, has been increasingly employed since the seventies—in the specific context of the European integration as well as the Cold War and its aftermath—by social scientific studies. Although quite recent in its current use, the category of 'Southern Europe' has absorbed long-term normative discourses about the European South, especially those related to the idea of the 'Mediterranean'. *Baumeister* and *Sala* argue that both short- and long-term narratives underpinning the mental mapping of 'Southern Europe', rather than ignored, have to be examined as an expression of the economic, political and social structures. As an analytical tool to investigate the present and recent past, 'Southern Europe' has to focus on the relation of Italy, Spain, Portugal, and Greece with other parts of Europe. In this context, they see a potential useful framework in the 'center-periphery' perspective as it allows them to conceptualize structures of interdependence within Europe.

In his chapter, *Martin Rhodes* traces the concept as used in different perspectives and approaches since the eighties: firstly in international political economy, via world system theory (and its political-cultural variants), in which the area is located in the 'semi-periphery'; and secondly in comparative politics and political economy, where models of a Southern European 'variety of capitalism', or of a Southern European 'welfare state' have been proposed, sometimes as heuristic devices but also as empirical realities. *Rhodes* raises the question whether these theories and models can be useful for empirical analysis as well as for overcoming the theoretical inadequacy of historic-development approaches on Southern Europe, or whether they obfuscate as much as they reveal. The article also considers Italy, Spain, Portugal, and Greece in light of the recent financial crisis, and whether the causes and consequences of the crisis reveal similarities or deep contrasts across the region.

Focusing on a key sector of comparative research, *Claude Martin* analyzes the specific welfare regime that—in the opinion of many scholars—has shaped Italy, Spain, Portugal, and Greece. As he points out, in the nineties the existence of such a regime played a significant role within the discussion on Gøsta Esping-Andersen's three welfare state models (Esping-Andersen 1990). While some authors emphasized the specificities of those countries up to the point of building a fourth model, a 'southern ideal-type' beside the continental, liberal and universalist ones, others considered the southern configuration as a late development of a continental regime. *Martin* shows that this debate is still of great importance in spite of—or perhaps because of—the fact that the financial and debt crisis has deeply challenged the welfare state structures. He highlights the heuristic relevance of one characteristic attributed to the 'southern configuration', i.e. the central role of the family as a source of protection against risks and vulnerability. Examining family and gender structures can help to understand processes of change and the resilience capacity of the welfare systems, both in 'Southern Europe' and in many additional countries.

The *second section*, 'A European periphery?', adopts the center-periphery analytical framework as regards as the economic as well as socio-economic embedment of Italy, Spain, Portugal, and Greece within Europe. To analyze the interconnection of Western European industrial economies, *Annamaria Simonazzi* and *Andrea Ginzburg* define the 'center' as the first-comer industrializers (i.e. Germany and France) and the 'periphery' as the late-comers (Italy) or late-late-comers (Spain, Portugal, Greece). As they argue, most studies have regarded these clusters as two separate units without examining in depth the relations between 'core' and 'peripheral' countries. From their point of view, the analysis of center-periphery relations is crucial in evaluating the integration of European economies as well as their position within globalization processes in the last decades. In their opinion, the deep crisis that has hit the Southern European economies since 2007 cannot be understood without considering long-term roots to be traced back to the seventies on the one hand and the effects of economic policies promoted by the European partners, especially Germany, on the other. Simonazzi and Ginzburg show that catching-up processes of Italy, Spain, Portugal, and Greece have been less sustainable than commonly assumed as these countries were affected by an 'interrupted industrialization'.

As *Russel King* shows in his chapter, also migration movements from and to contemporary Italy, Spain, Portugal, and Greece give evidence of center-periphery dynamics. He distinguishes three main phases in post-war Europe. Firstly, King points to the impressive labor migration to countries such as Germany, France, and Switzerland; in the decades after the war, these flows involved millions of migrants from Southern Europe and resulted from its peripheral condition in comparison to the more advanced European industrial economies. Secondly, he looks at the transformation from mass emigration to immigration countries that shaped Southern Europe between the seventies and the nineties; due to flows from Asia, Africa, South America and Eastern Europe, Southern Europe became a 'semi-periphery' within global migration. Finally, King underlines that after the beginning of the economic crisis, Italian, Spanish, Portuguese, and Greece migrants are increasingly seeking job opportunities in the 'North'. Although they differ quantitatively and qualitatively from those in the past, these new flows are proof that center-periphery interdependencies within Europe are far from being overcome.

The *third section*, 'Modernity and other master narratives', looks in depth at discourses on the South. *Wolfgang Knöbl* illustrates that, against the background of the US-American cultural dominance after World War II, modernization theory significantly influenced sociological and anthropological analyses of single 'Southern European' countries, in particular Spain and Italy. On the one hand, these studies enhanced the persistence of archaic structures that would, for instance, affect political culture, on the other, they emphasized that those societies were experiencing modernization processes. As Knöbl shows, in the context of these studies, scholars developed a theoretical repertoire that, based on the diagnosis of a special path to modernity, has led to the concept of 'Southern Europe'.

In her chapter, *Patricia Hertel* emphasizes that there are not one, but different discursive connotations of 'Southern Europe'; although interwoven, these various narratives must be regarded in their peculiarity. As she shows, the 'backwardness discourse', which emerged in the 18th and 19th centuries, deeply shaped the transnational perception of 'Southern Europe' in the second half of the 20th century. By exoticizing those countries, France, Germany, or Great Britain could virtually consolidate their supremacy. However, cultural elites in the 'North' did not have the monopoly when it comes to employing the 'South' as a discursive device. On the one hand, in Italy as well as, to some extent, in Spain and Portugal, narratives of backwardness have emerged towards their own, economically weaker Southern regions. On the other hand, in the post-war period 'Southern European' countries had to renegotiate their discursive position towards Europe and the world. As Hertel analyzes with regard to Portugal, by relocating itself in Europe's South, the country could virtually compensate for the loss of power in the Atlantic sphere. Finally, she looks at the 'overshadowing' of the South in the context of the Cold War: due to the East-West divide, within Western Europe the differences between the 'South' and the 'North' remained in the background of public and political discourses, as shown through, for example, the little attention paid by international historiography towards 'Southern Europe'.

The *fourth section*, 'Political entanglements' raises the question as to what extent the concept of 'Southern Europe' has been shaped by international politics. As *Guido Franzinetti* illustrates, in the context of international relations, the tendency to perceive Italy, Spain, Portugal, and Greece (as well as, partly, Turkey) as a common area was an indirect consequence of Cold War and European Integration. The geopolitical upheavals leading to the formation of the 'Southern Flank' of NATO determined that Greece and Turkey were virtually absorbed into Western Europe, together with Italy that—in spite of being a founding member of the EEC and, at least formally, a stable democracy—had a precarious position in geopolitical terms. At the same time, after Spain had overcome the international isolation of the immediate post-war years, also the Iberian dictatorships began to be attracted by the Western sphere of influence. Against this background, due both to the progressive integration and the structural peripheral position in Western Europe of Greece and Italy on the one hand, and Spain and Portugal on the other, in the medium-term were perceived as parts of 'Southern Europe'. *Franzinetti* underlines that this way of thinking played an important role for democratization processes in Spain, Portugal, and Greece that, eventually, led to their admission into the European communities. As he shows, in the first years of the millennium, however, the concept of 'Southern Europe' partly lost importance: the end of the Cold War in the medium-term had caused a significant political instability in Italy and Greece, while Spain and Portugal continued to consolidate their reputation as solid democracies. It is after the beginning of the crisis that 'Southern Europe' became again a strong framework to locate these four countries within international relations.

In his chapter, *Massimo Piermattei* focuses on the specific interplay between 'Southern Europe' and European Integration. As he shows, the idea of 'Southern Europe' as a common area including the four countries under analysis constituted a conceptual framework closely connected with the expansion of the European communities and, eventually, the European Union. However, he argues, this concept was not simply a positive, undisputed reference resulting from the Southern enlargement. At the turn between the 20th and 21st centuries, alternative macro-regional concepts of Europe's South were also employed by other 'Southern' countries excluded from the Union and aspiring to become its members. Moreover, long before the debt crisis,

'Southern Europe' could be used as a negative reference within the conflicts between members states, as the negotiations for the monetary union in the nineties show.

The contributions of this book illustrate that indeed it can be useful to look at Italy, Spain, Portugal, and Greece from a common perspective—under three conditions. Firstly, it must be recognized that 'Southern Europe' has become a category that plays a decisive role within the struggles for resources between European countries. To employ it as an analytical framework, it is necessary to filter normative assumptions deriving from political and social discourses. Secondly, it is not enough to stigmatize and deconstruct these discourses as mere expressions of power hierarchies; they must be examined in depth as they are part of the European integration (or dis-integration) process. Thirdly, Southern European countries cannot be regarded as an isolated area; they rather must be examined with regard to their interconnection with Europe as a whole as well as to their position within global developments. Moreover, it makes sense to look at 'Southern Europe' as a common space to investigate several social, economic, and political processes as far as their present and recent past is concerned, without falling, however, into the traps of homogenization, essentialization, or determinism.

The analysis of Southern Europe can contribute to important theoretical and empirical achievements. Helping develop a differentiated approach towards (Western) European contemporary history, it shows not least that Europe cannot be regarded as a monolithic area within the globalization processes of the 20th and early 21st centuries. The category of 'Southern Europe' can serve as a useful agenda for comparative research, as a framework to discuss processes of negotiating, defining, and mediating relations of 'center' and 'periphery' in the continent. And it can also serve to contextualize Europe in wider settings and relationships.

As we are concluding the manuscript of this volume, negotiations about the Greek public debt are coming to their end. It is said that their success, or their failure, will decide whether Greece will continue to be part of the Eurozone, or be forced to leave it (as well as perhaps even the European Union). The 'Grexit' is much feared as it could initiate a chain reaction and provoke the contagion of other Southern European countries. Against the background of these dramatic upheavals, tense relations between 'South' and 'North' appear of no less importance than the emergence of a new 'East'-'West'-confrontation—which after the beginning of the crisis in the Ukraine might lead to a 'new cold war'. From this perspective, while apparently outdated mental maps are resurging from their graves to reflect on the 'South' plays a key role when it cames to understand Europe's recent history and its present.

Works Cited

Dustman, Christian, Bernd Fitzenberger, Uta Schönberg, and Alexandra Spitz-Oener (2014). From Sick Man of Europe to Economic Superstar: Germany's Resurgent Economy. *The Journal of Economic Perspectives*, 28:1, 167–188.

Ferrera, Maurizio (1996). The Southern Model of Welfare in Social Europe. *Journal of European Social Policy*, 1, 17–37.

Hein, Eckhard, and Achim Truger (2005). A Different View of Germany's Stagnation. *Challenge*, 48:6, 64–94.

Mas, Matilde, and Javier Quesada (2007). Spain: a Success Story Shadowed only by a Poor Productivity Performance. *National Institute Economic Review*, 200, 87–95.

Sapelli, Giulio (1995). *Southern Europe Since 1945. Tradition and Modernity in Portugal, Spain, Italy, Greece and Turkey*. London: Longman.

I. Southern Models?

A Long Road South. Southern Europe as a Discursive Construction and Historical Region after 1945

Martin Baumeister and Roberto Sala

"In the space we read the time": In this catchy book title the historian Karl Schlögel closely links space and history with a suggestive textual metaphor. He presents physical space as a written text, where one can read the traces of the human past (Schlögel 2003). There are not so many historians who follow Schlögel's motto of deciphering space as a man-made historical source. In the humanities and social sciences spatial categories, however, play a crucial role in defining units of research, whether villages or cities, states, nations, smaller or larger regions among others, as simple 'containers' or even as particular 'individualities'. The idea of a concurrence of space and history or culture respectively has been considered a self-evident truth in academic discourse for a long time. A wide range of disciplines in the field of area studies is defined by its regional focus, which generally implies some strong assumptions about particular features distinguishing one region from others as a cultural and historical entity. Nevertheless, some decades ago in light of the 'spatial turn' the idea of fixing history and culture in space was radically questioned by considering spatial categories basically as a product of cultural marking. Edward Said's critique of 'Orientalism' perhaps is the most famous case of deconstructing a major spatial concept as a result of explicit as well as implicit mental mapping, expressing claims to power and supremacy (Said 1978).

Even today, almost forty years after the publication of Said's seminal work, the divide has not been overcome between 'constructivists' who refer to spatial concepts as useful analytical tools and 'deconstructivists' who accuse 'spacing' of being a power game and therefore refuse to analyze spatial units as particular individual entities defined by common structures and cultural traits.[1] We can see this opposition for example in the dispute between two historians studying Southeastern Europe. Maria Todorova in an influ-

1 A survey of the debate is given by Macfie (2000). The further development of 'Orientalism' after Said is discussed by Burke III and Prochaska (2008).

ential book, published for the first time in 1997, analyzed the Balkans as a discursive construction, as a sample of predominantly negative stereotypical images closely intertwined with politics which, following Said, she called "Balkanism". Instead of considering the Balkans as a cultural or historical region of its own and in this way, as she warned, falling into the trap of essentialism, teleology and determinism, she proposed considering the role of "historical legacies" as perceived and referred to by concrete groups and individuals in order to define a region in specific historical and political contexts (Todorova 1997; 2002; 2005). Her colleague Holm Sundhaussen, however, defended the concept of the Balkans as a distinct historical-cultural region with a "unique, fascinating and sometimes dreadful profile" (Sundhaussen 1999, 651), formed, as he maintained, in a long historical process. For his part, he was convinced of the usefulness and legitimacy of studying historical regions, defined by patterns of common structures and interrelations.[2]

Looking at the Todorova-Sundhaussen controversy[3], there seems to be no middle ground between conceiving of spaces as discursive products or as structured entities. This general problem has to be kept in mind when it comes to reflect on another key concept related to Europe's South, i.e. 'Southern (Western) Europe'. On the one hand, contemporary Italy, Spain, Portugal, and Greece appear to share important analogies. On the other, as both a political and a scientific category 'Southern Europe' seems often to be affected by normative and moral assumptions.

To overcome the impasse that emerges from opposing structures and discourses, it must be realized that both perspectives are two sides of one coin—as this paper argues. Images of the South are, indeed, primarily an expression of power relations within Europe; in this context 'Southern Europe' is a relatively young (research) category that was deeply shaped by the political climate in the post-war period, and that, at once, has absorbed long-term narratives on Europe's South and the 'Mediterranean'. However, to contextualize 'Southern Europe' as a concept rooted in the struggles for supremacy between European societies does not mean, however, to get rid of Southern Europe as a field of enquiry; it rather confirms that (Western) European history must be read with regard to interdependencies between (changing) 'centers' and 'peripheries'. From this perspective, purged from normative assumptions, the question of to what extent Italy, Spain, Portugal, and Greece

2 For a similar position on 'historical regions' see Mishkova et al. 2013, Troebst 2003.

3 For further debates see Rutar 2014.

have shared similar paths can offer essential insights into Europe's present and recent past.

Southern Europe as a Category in Social Sciences and Historiography

'Southern Europe', contrary to Western or Eastern Europe among others, is not a particularly prominent paradigm in academic discourse. Mostly referred to as Italy, Spain, Portugal and Greece, it represents, however, an influential analytical category within social sciences. Since the seventies and eighties many studies in disciplines such as sociology, economics and political science have considered these countries as an area with common features and paths of development. At least four main thematic strands—widely tackled in this volume—shape this manifold field. Looking at Southern Europe, scholars have, firstly, examined the economic and political integration into the European Union (Gibson 2001; Holman 1996; Magone 2003; Simonazzi et al. 2013; Williams 1984). They have, secondly, discussed welfare state structures as well as social policy issues (Ferrera 2005, Rhodes 1997), and, thirdly, raised the question of whether these states share similar political cultures and experiences (Arrighi 1985; Diamandouros et al. 2001; Gunther et al. 1995; Gunther et al. 2006; Linz 1996; McLaren 2008). Fourthly, social science scholars have discovered new migration movements to that area, which for a century or so has been a classical region of emigration, as a key field of investigation (King et al. 2000). Moreover, Southern Europe has served as an analytical framework to deal with such different topics as international security politics and international relations, gender or welfare (Yachir 1989; González et al. 1999; Santos 2013).

These studies mostly offer interpretative models that, taking into account national and/or regional characteristics, do not approach Southern Europe in a reductionist way. Adopting a comparative perspective, several analyses rather enhance the specific experiences of single countries. However, the basic assumption that Southern Europe represents an area shaped by various analogies is never questioned. Political scientist Maurizio Ferrera, one of the most influential scholars within the field of studies on Southern Europe, writes:

"The nations of Southern Europe have followed a specific path to modernization (in the broad sense of the concept) and still share a number of common traits in their cultural backgrounds and political economies. There are, of course, significant differences between the four countries [i.e. Italy, Spain, Portugal, and Greece] of the region: the intra-area variation is certainly greater than in the Nordic context, though probably lower than in Central Continental Europe. It would be difficult to deny that the notion of 'Southern Europe' has not only a geographical, but also a substantive, cultural and politic-economic connotation." (Ferrera 2005, 3)

As an analytical category, the rank of Southern Europe within historiography is partly different. We cannot overlook that several historical studies have considered this area in a similar way as social sciences, i.e. to refer to Italy, Spain, Portugal, and Greece as a distinct cluster of countries within post-war Europe. Recently, in his social history of contemporary Europe, Béla Tomka has defined Southern Europe as a European region referring to these four countries and clearly distinguished from Western Europe, which "includes North Western Europe (United Kingdom/Great Britain, France, the Netherlands, Belgium and Ireland), Central Europe (Germany/FRG, Switzerland, and Austria) and Scandinavia (Sweden, Denmark, Norway, and Finland)" (Tomka 2013). Also monumental collective works such as the *Cambridge Economic History of Modern Europe* make systematic use of this regional macro-category (Broadberry and O'Rourke 2010).

Already in the eighties and nineties historians used Southern Europe as a strong conceptual framework. This is not only true for Giulio Sapelli's impressive study that conferred to the term historiographical deepness (Sapelli 1995).[4] Within the context of a broad social and economic history of Western Europe, Anthony Sutcliffe, for instance, described this area as "Europe's southern fringe [...] made up of three economic backwards countries—Spain, Portugal, and Greece—and a country which combined advanced and backward regions, Italy" (Sutcliffe 2014 [1996], 81). Moreover, in 1986, the influential historian of modern Spain Stanley G. Payne raised explicitly the question of whether Southern Europe represented a useful analytical perspective:

"In recent years a number of historians and social scientists have advanced the notion of the regional model of 'southern Europe' as a useful comparative frame of reference for understanding common features of modernization in Italy, Spain, Greece and Portugal. Though the concept has never been fully defined or gained common acceptance, it rests on the observation that the four southernmost countries of Europe

4 Sapelli belongs to the authors including Turkey in Southern Europe.

underwent generally similar changes along the path to political development and economic modernization, particularly during the late nineteenth and early twentieth centuries." (Payne 1986, 108)

Payne concluded his analysis by observing that, in spite of not offering a framework valid for all economic, political, and social processes, Southern Europe constituted a useful comparative category for key research issues such as the study of a common path of development (Payne 1986, 115). By raising similar questions, in 1992 Edward Malefakis looked at the career of what it still was at that time—a young concept:

"About twenty years ago, in the early seventies, a new term entered the academic vocabulary—Southern Europe. Occasionally the term included France, and sometimes Yugoslavia, Malta, Cyprus and even Turkey as well. But for the most part it referred to four countries—Portugal, Spain, Italy & Greece. It was logical that this should be so, because of the striking similarities in their recent development. All had been economically backward, socially divided and politically unstable countries. [...] The events of the past two decades have thus confirmed the usefulness of the idea of "Southern Europe," and converted it into one of the principle concepts through which we analyze the European experience of the present and future. But to what extent is it also viable in the past? [...] The concept of Southern Europe has gained currency among sociologists, anthropologists and above all political scientists; does it also merit adoption by historians?" (Malefakis 1992, 1)

Like Stanley Paine and—more recently—Effi Pedaliu (2013), Malefakis came to the conclusion that Southern Europe is a useful tool for research on contemporary European history (Malefakis 1992, 80). Most remarkable is the fact that Malefakis considered the concept a product of social sciences. By using it, historians would have adopted an analytical category developed by other disciplines.

This leads us to the question of whether Southern Europe, as a research category, has had similar success in historiography as it has had in social sciences. Besides the works cited above, further studies in modern and contemporary history have used the term to identify Italy, Spain, Portugal, and Greece, as regards both longer-time scales (Bock et al. 2003, Baumeister and Liedtke 2009; Taveres de Almeida et al. 2003) and the post-war period (Boulder 2002; Rizas 2012).[5] In comparison to the considerable social scientific production on the topic, however, historical studies appear not to have

5 Focusing on authoritarian regimes and democratization processes after 1945, some authors have associated Southern Europe primarily with the latter three countries (Del Pero 2011; Judt 2005 [2011]).

assumed Southern Europe to be a strong analytical framework for looking at these four countries. While social scientists have carried out intense debates on different issues, such as a Southern European model of welfare state (Rhodes 1997), only a handful of historians have proposed strong theoretical claims as far as common paths of Italy, Spain, Portugal, and Greece are concerned. Several historical studies often use the category Southern Europe in a more general—we might say geographical—way to indicate also a variety of additional countries, i.a. Austria (Grell et al. 2005) and France (Pacquette 2009). For historians influenced by Ferdinand Braudel's perspectives, the European South consists in the broad region reaching from the Iberian Peninsula to Northern Africa, from the Balkans to the Levant (Schenk and Winkler 2007); for scholars of the early modern, the Mediterranean area still represents a strong analytical framework (Piterberg 2010).

Statistical evidence helps illustrate to what extent Southern Europe has represented a relevant research category for the present and recent past. Using one of the largest databases of scientific journals, we have conducted a word frequency analysis on the words Southern Europe and Italy, Spain, Portugal and Greece. To determine an interpretative scale, we have calculated, with regard to five-year periods, in how many items these terms appear out of a thousand articles containing the word Europe in two different groups of journals: historical ones and others associated with three social scientific disciplines, i.e. economics, sociology, and political science.

Run for "Southern Europe", the word frequency analysis offers first interesting results. Until the eighties the frequency of this term was comparable in both groups. Afterwards, it has remained stable in historical journals, while it has increased remarkably in social scientific revues (see Graph 1). This appears to confirm that the category has gained more relevance in social scientific than in historical studies. In spite of reaching a difference of almost 50%, however, the gap between the frequency indexes does not allow for assuming the term "Southern" had a radically different status in the two groups.

Graph 1: Word frequency in scholarly journals: "Southern Europe"

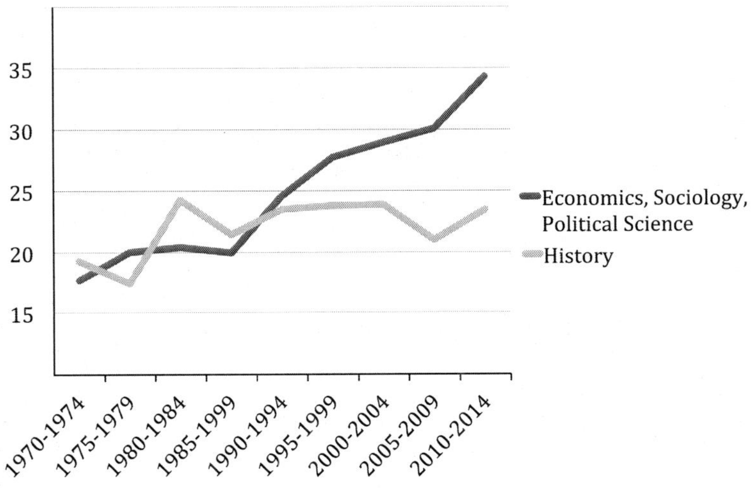

Source: Elaborations on Jstor.org data (accessed on March 23, 2015)

The word frequency analysis provides indisputable results if we search for articles containing both the terms Southern Europe and Italy, Spain, Portugal, and Greece, i.e. if we ask to what extent the former is related to the latter. At the beginning of the seventies, our frequency index amounts to approximately 1 both in historical and in social scientific journals (0,7 and 1,3 respectively, see Graph 2), i.e. these terms appeared only in one item out of a thousand articles containing the word Europe. With regard to historical studies, we can observe an increase up to the value of 2,6. However, as far as economics, political science, and sociology are concerned, the growth is rather significant. The index amounts to 5,6 in the early nineties, and reaches a value of almost 9,8 in the last period, more than five times more than in historical reviews. The figures are quite evident: As related to Italy, Spain, Portugal, and Greece, since the seventies the specific use of "Southern Europe" has gained more and more influence in social scientific studies, while it has remained in the background in historical research.

Graph 2: Word frequency in scholarly journals: "Southern Europe" in combination with Italy, Spain, Portugal, and Greece

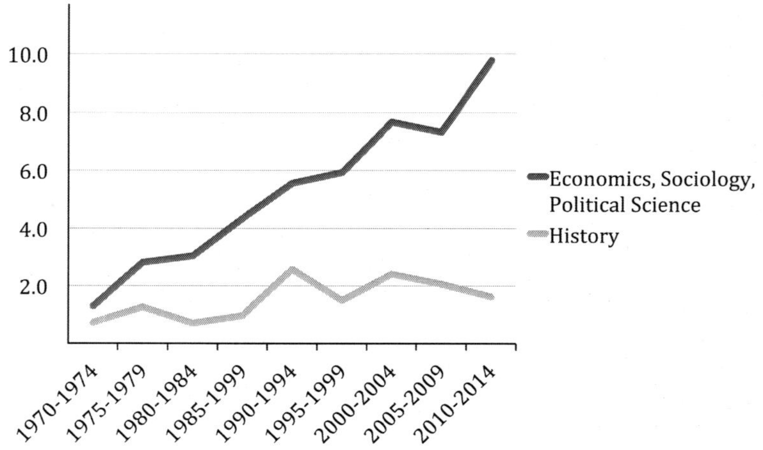

Source: Elaborations on Jstor.org data (accessed on March 23, 2015)

The analysis of scholarly journals raises the question of why the tendency of considering Italy, Spain, Portugal, and Greece as a common area has been predominant in social sciences and pretty marginal in historiography. The fact that social scientists have a strong tradition in area studies and international comparative research (Jacob and Hawkins 2011, 4), while historians—despite the "revolution" towards transnational history (Iriye 2013, 70) and the increasing attention to "historical regions" (Troebst 2003)—are still more inclined to focus on national developments, might have played a role; however, it does not offer a satisfying explanation.

These different trends are rooted in two interconnected dimensions: the Cold War and the European integration process. In the second half of the 20th century, "the very nature of bloc building had encouraged the search for historical narratives that legitimated such supranational alliance systems, therefore going beyond the national framework" (Berger 2007, 64). In other words, influenced by the East-West discourse, historiography tended to conceive Western Europe as a homogenous region; rather than neglecting them, it paid little attention to internal differences such as the contradictions between democratic and authoritarian regimes on the one hand, and between economic underdevelopment and material progress and wealth on the other. After the breakdown of the iron curtain, scholars have developed more differentiated approaches to contemporary (Western) European history (Judt 2005; Mazower 2000). Nevertheless, within the transnational historiographic canon, the recent past of Italy, Spain, Portugal, and Greece has still remained in the shadow of the 'core countries'. In a bibliography which records historiographical studies concerning post-war Western Europe, published in the mid-nineties, almost 250 works cited referred to France and (Western and Eastern) Germany, while only approximately 100 were related to Italy and Spain (Higbee 1996, 49–139). As a research category borrowed from the social sciences, Southern Europe has thus not been adopted but by a niche of historians, without advancing to a mainstream reference. This is true also after the financial and debt crisis, which does not appear to have evoked a major interest in the European South among historians, at least in the short term.

Not limited to studies on post-war Europe, the marginal position of these countries has tradition in international historiography. In the early nineties, Derek H. Aldcroft and Richard Rodger (1992) published one of the most complete historiographical bibliographies on European social and economic history, covering the period between 1700 and 1939. Remarkably, Southern Europe constituted one of the regions considered in the book. Works cited were however much fewer as regards "Southern European" compared to those regarding "Western European" countries. The former was employed in only one-fifth of the pages dedicated to the latter (see Table 1). While the bibliography on France and Germany contained 80 pages, the references to Italy and Spain did not reach even 15 pages. This disparity concerned also smaller countries such as Belgium and the Netherlands on the one hand, and Portugal and Greece on the other.

Cold War discourses deeply affected social sciences as well, one may think of the rise of modernization theory (Gilman 2003). However, present-oriented disciplines such as economics, sociology and political science found transnational objects partly situated beyond the East-West Conflict more easily. This is especially true for the "Mediterranean Enlargement" of the European Economic Community. Although the European integration process was deeply connected with the Cold War, as regards both the "hot" and the "détente" phases (Hanhimäki and Westad 2003, 313–346; Soutou 2007), it gained momentum independently from that major geopolitical controversy. When Greece, in 1981, and Spain and Portugal, in 1986, entered the European Economic Community, cold-war issues were not in the foreground

Table 1: Attention paid to single "Western Europe" and "Southern Europe" in the Bibliography of European Economic and Social History (Aldcroft and Roger 1992)

	Approx. number of pages
Western Europe*	95
France	42
Germany	38
Belgium	5
The Netherlands	9
Switzerland	2
Southern Europe	19
Italy	8
Spain	6
Turkey	2
Greece	2
Portugal	2
Malta	1

* Britain is not included in the analysis as the authors point to another bibliography, i.e. Chaloner and Richardson 1984.

(Preston 1997, 46–86). Rather socio-economic gaps between new and old members of the community were at the center of political debates (Kaiser and Elvert 2005, 75–138). The membership in the European Economic Community—and the preceeding negotiations that led to it—created a climate promoting social scientific research on these countries. While the hunger for studies on Spain, Portugal, and Greece became stronger, the concept of Southern Europe proved helpful in canalizing research. In this context, scholarship tended to identify these countries as an area to be distinguished from the rest of Western Europe. We might describe this tendency as an inclusion by exclusion: Greece, Spain, and Portugal were included into the social-scientific discourse on Europe by conceiving them as a separate group.

Italy was soon associated with that area because of its ambivalent status. In spite of belonging to the European communities from the very beginning and constituting a major industrial economy, the country has not conquered the deep inequalities between Northern and Southern regions, and appears to be in between a European core and its periphery (Demertzis 1997, 203).

By inserting Italy into a broader area, scholars have achieved a clear framework to situate the country within Europe, and at the same time strengthened the concept of Southern Europe. In this way—and in close connection with the political discourse—social sciences have coined a key category which reflects power hierarchies within contemporary Europe.

Discourses and Varieties of Mapping

Italy can serve as an example to illustrate the political implications of regional framing in academic research and public discourse. In its case, however, it would be difficult to find such a clear statement about the dialectics of the discursive construction of space as in the following affirmation by the Croatian writer Predrag Matvejević about another geographical and geopolitical concept used to include the Apennine Peninsula: "The Mediterranean and the discourse on it are inseparable from each other." (Matvejević 2007, 21) This affirmation without a doubt is particularly valid for the Mediterranean as a kind of symbolically overcharged imagined landscape, but it is certainly true also in the case of the Euro-Mediterranean area or, in other words, of the European South as spatial concepts which overlap and are entangled with the Mediterranean region in a larger sense. The fact that, contrary to Central or Eastern Europe, the history of Southern Europe does not exist as an established academic discipline or—with the exceptions discussed above—as a well-defined field of historical research has contributed perhaps to avoiding a critical revision or at least a serious reconsideration of what could be the meanings and consequences of the mental mapping of Southern Europe.

First of all, it seems almost trivial to observe, but has to be stressed that the South is a relational category. The idea of the European South as a historical and cultural region has a long-lasting and twisted history which is closely interrelated with the history of Europe as a physical space and a social and cultural construct. Moreover, its history is linked with that of other parts of Europe, such as Eastern and Southeastern Europe, which since the Age of Enlightenment, together with the South, were destined to become the periphery of a Western 'core' Europe along a double axis, a West-East and a North-South divide, marking a hierarchy of development, progress and power. Furthermore, like other subdivisions of Europe as well as the whole continent itself, the European South is a spatial category with rather fluid borders, which depend on the point of view of who is referring to it. It seems remarkable that the category of the South is not normally used by 'insiders' as a label for designating one's own origins or expressing one's sense of belonging, but is used by 'outsiders', from the 'West' or the 'North', for a rather wide range of countries and regions, generally including Portugal and Spain, Italy, Greece and sometimes even Turkey, as in the case of Giulio Sapelli's 'Southern Europe' (1995). The views of local people and the view from the outside can here diverge radically. Basques and Tuscans as well as Catalans and Lombards, to give only a few examples, would vehemently contest being labeled as 'Southerners'.

There are also some countries which reproduce the European North-South divide even within their own territory. In Spain it is Andalusia which often represents the quintessential South in images going back to European romanticism (e.g. Hoffmann 1961). In France, which as a whole is definitely not seen as a Southern country, but generally as the very essence of the European West, there is the *Midi* with main characteristics of the European South expressed in the idea of *méridionalité* (Borutta 2013). And in the case of Italy, the construction of a united nation state from the eighteen sixties onward was based on an explicit North-South dichotomy and the 'invention' of the *Mezzogiorno* as a defective and alien, if not hostile part of the body of the nation, a division which still continues to be considered a structural feature of Italian economy, society and politics today (Bevilacqua 2005; Petraccone 2000; Schneider 1998; Soriero 2014).

The spatial blurredness and ambiguous position of the European South is further enhanced by overlapping regional concepts, particularly the Mediterranean, generally reduced to its northern shores from a European point of view. The idea of a 'new Mediterranean' had emerged parallel to the rise of the concept of the European South since the second half 18th century and was in many aspects identical to it (Baumeister, 2015; Giaccaria and Minca 2010, 350–353). As far as the idea of a hegemonic 'West' was concerned, the South as well as the Mediterranean were expressions which, together with the East, were used to define peripheral zones lagging behind the West in its rush to modernity. We can't maintain that the North-South conflict is one of the constants of European history (Lepenies 2013, 11), but this divide certainly plays a significant role in the formation of what can be called a European or Western idea of modernity. The concept of the East from a Western point of view had already been used for a long time to refer to barbarous lands far from civilization and could easily be conflated with the quintessential European 'Other', Asia. The South, however, since the 18th century underwent a deep re-evaluation or devaluation, from a European core region, defined by its cultural pre-eminence, its economic wealth and political power in the case of Italy and Spain respectively, to a loser region on the borders of Europe, at best with a particular heritage of ancient greatness and splendor. In this tension between a glorious past and current misery, the South, by analogy to or as part of the Mediterranean, assumed a deeply ambivalent position on the reconfigured maps of a new Europe, marked by Orientalism and Classicism (Jirat-Wasiutyński 2007). That means on the one hand that this 'new' European South, increasingly marginalized after the shift of political and economic hegemony to the Atlantic West, was conceived in the context of euro-centrism, imperialism and colonialism, beginning with the Anglo-French struggle over the succession of the decaying Ottoman Empire in its former hegemonic position in the Mediterranean world. On the other hand, the South excelled as a unique place of origin by its role as the 'cradle' of Western civilization, located in ancient Greece and Rome, and by the attractions of an Arcadian nature and of artistic treasures as well as of pilgrimage and archaeological sites central to European identity.

While the Mediterranean in academic and public discourse, as expressed in Fernand Braudel's classic historical work, published in a first edition in 1949 (Braudel 1982), was imagined as a physical unity, held together by economic, social, cultural and political bonds, the European South remained a sample of national and regional cases, lacking contiguity and spatial coherence. All of these cases or elements, however, were considered to follow more or less similar dynamics and were associated with a common set of images and value judgements. This set of ideas emerged from what, according to Roberto Dainotto, was a radical shift in the rhetorical discourse of Europe, from an antithetical to a compensatory way of conceiving of the continent as an ethical category. While Europe had defined itself before in antithesis to a hostile 'Other', whether the kingdom of the Persians or the Muslim Orient, now alterity was assimilated by designating an intra-European 'Other', the South—and one might add the East—which in this way became a "symbolic formation of a displaced other", a "compensatory trope for a problematic modernity" (Dainotto 2000, 383, 387; Dainotto 2007). The European South was part of a "moral geography" which opposed the protestant North as the origin of capitalist and industrial modernity to the South as a zone of archaic immobility and backwardness.

After 1945 the political situation changed, however, and triggered another fundamental shift on the European mental maps. The European North-South divide was reduced considerably in the context of the Cold War, decolonization, an increasing European integration, and deep transformations of the Southern European countries from rural into predominantly urban societies, while a larger 'West', in contrast to the East in its hostile isolation behind the Iron Curtain, was absorbing first, post-fascist Italy, and then definitely after the fall of the respective dictatorships, Portugal, Spain and Greece. This change was sanctioned by the admission of the three countries into the European Community in 1981 and 1986, only a few years before things changed again completely after the dissolution of the Eastern bloc. The East-West divide of the Cold War was smoothening, while there was a role reversal between new members of the European Union and their Southern counterparts. Driven by the financial crisis from 2008 onwards, the old North-South divide resurged with new vigour (Ther 2014, 267–276). Even if the infamous PIGS acronym had been coined earlier on during the process of strengthening European integration (Dainotto 2007, 2; Pedaliu, 8) and the dark images of a problem-ridden South had never faded completely, it has been in the last years of a growing questioning of a European basic consensus, that old stereotypes of the contrasts between a virtuous North and a vicious South have appeared again in public debates as well as in political and economic analyses. Northern critics on Southern failure and misery, by re-cycling old stereotypes of a seemingly timeless European 'moral geography', are contested not only by appeals to question and deconstruct these stereotypes, but also by benevolent philo-southerners who answer negative with positive stereotypes, referring to the 'true' good essence of Southern thought and ways of life in contrast to the devastations of a merciless 'Northern' capitalism[6].

It is particularly in this context, where current debates about a 'problematic' South are intermingling and overlapping with the concept of the Mediterranean. Since Braudel's opus magnum, historians dealt with the 'interior sea' predominantly regarding the centuries prior to the French Revolution.

6 For German examples of presenting a stereotyped South see the cover story including the magazine's polemic cover: Die Armutslüge: Wie Europas Krisenländer ihre Vermögen verstecken. In *Der Spiegel*, nr. 16, 15.4.2013, instrumentalizing negative clichés; from a "philo-southerner" point of view: Max A. Höfer, Siempre la siesta. Südeuropa fühlt sich und die lateinische Lebensart bedroht. Absurd ist das nicht. In *Der Spiegel*, nr. 26, 24.6.2013, 128–129; Schoepp (2014); more nuanced Leggewie (2014).

The last impressive effort to revitalize the conception of the Mediterranean as an historical region beyond Braudel's structuralism has been presented by two British historians, a classicist and a medievalist, for a range of two thousand years, up to the end of the first millennium A.C. (Horden and Purcell 2000). A brilliantly written synthesis for a broader audience by the well known British medievalist David Abulafia covers the widest possible time range from the first human traces up to recent times, but presents more a panoramic view of history *in* the Mediterranean than a coherent analysis of the history *of* the Mediterranean, as expected by his colleagues Peregrine Horden and Nicholas Purcell (Abulafia 2011)[7]. For the history of the last two centuries, exactly the period when a new idea about the Mediterranean, which still continues to be ours, was rising in Europe, the Mediterranean Sea is not much more than a geographic indicator for historians (Borutta and Lemmes 2013). This is also true for the last decades, when the European South has become, as explained above, increasingly an object of research, at least in the social sciences. There are, after all, some cases in research about the era after 1945 where the 'Mediterranean' is used as a synonym for Southern Europe. This is what the Greek geographer Lila Leontidou does. Studying the period of rapid urbanization of Greece, Italy and Spain after World War II, she defines common structural features of what she calls the Mediterranean city. This type of city de facto refers to Southern European cities which she analyzes by distinguishing a Southern European form of urban development from a Northern one (Leontidou 1990).

Just when the transformations in the Euro-Mediterranean region analyzed by Leontidou were occurring, a whole generation of Anglo-Saxon ethnologist chose the 'interior sea' as their favourite area of research, shifting their fieldwork in the context of decolonization from overseas to circum Mediterranean regions. These scholars did not focus their attention on the rapidly expanding, continuously changing cities, but studied the Mediterranean as an essentially rural, archaic world, a sample of seemingly isolated village communities and small towns characterized by a value system of honor and shame, by "amoral familism" and patron-client relationships as the dominant mode of social integration (e.g. Davis 1977). Parallel to the Southern enlargement of the European Community in the eighties, anthropologists increasingly reduced their focus from a perspective encompassing the whole

7 This distinction between a history *of* from a history *in* the Mediterranean is made by Horden and Purcell 2000, 9 and passim.

Mediterranean region with its Northern, Southern and Eastern shores to simply Southern Europe (Driessen 2011). At the same time, however, in this relatively new academic discipline which conceived of the Mediterranean as a 'culture area', characterized by common social structures and values in open contrast to North-Western European modernity (Ben-Yehoyada 2014), a fundamental critique of using this spatial concept as an analytical paradigm arose, not because of its territorial reductionism, but more generally because of its basic legitimacy. Critics maintained that the Sea in Mediterranean studies, instead of being a physical reality, was a mere intellectual construction, deformed by its ideological content and political bias, informed, among other things, by colonialism and euro centrism (e.g. Horden and Purcell 2006, 725). Criticism culminated in the charge of 'Mediterraneanism', a term coined in analogy with 'Orientalism', as a form of essentializing, exoticizing and homogenizing of a culture area (Herzfeld 1984; 1987).

Certainly, many of the negative stereotypes targeted in discussions about Mediterraneanism are being revitalized in current debates about Southern vices and defects. There is, however, another type of Southern essentialism based on the older dialectic relationship of putting down the European South while at the same time emphasising its excellent qualities and values. This kind of Mediterraneanism positively spilled over into international media, when the philosopher Giorgio Agamben, in March 2013, published a polemic essay in Italian, quickly translated into other languages, calling for the creation of a "Latin empire" against the hegemony of nefarious Northern Protestant capitalism (Agamben 2013). A group of scholars, living and working mainly in Italy and France, among them most prominently the sociologist Franco Cassano, claim that what they call the 'South', a rather abstract Mediterranean region with an unmistakable European flavor, constitutes a physical, social and cultural reality, an "anchorage for a big common fatherland, a root of stone and sea which is stronger than the diversity, of that drift of continents, religions and ethnic pride from which incessantly arises the integralist temptation" (Cassano in Goffredo 2000, 19). They defend the diversity and peculiarity of the 'South', against the 'North Western' perspective, which considers it as its negative counterpart, as a deficient, pathological modernity, "the disease of the world" (Cassano 2001, 1). According to this "militant Mediterraneanism" (Giaccaria and Minca 2010, 355), the 'South' is more than a mere projection, more than a Northern invention. It is a subject of its own which must, however, "re-conquer its own outlook" and "learn to view itself independently" in open contrast with the 'North' (Cassano 2001,

2). Cassano and his peers turn 'classical' Mediterraneanism upside down and call for "re-attributing to the Mediterranean the role of a new center, a paradoxical center, because it is situated on the borderline" (Cassano 2001, 7). The essence of this 'South' is 'Southern thought' which is characterized by its rejection of all kinds of fundamentalism and hegemonic universalism, by its insistence on "slow time" against capitalist acceleration and its profound "sense of measure" (Cassano 2011; Fogu 2010, 14). For militant Mediterraneanists the "smaller" South, the Italian *Mezzogiorno,* Southern Europe and the Mediterranean, are closely connected with all other Souths of the world (Cassano 2011, IX), that is to say that for them *il sud* is part of the 'global South'.

The advocates of 'Southern thought' argue against a hegemonic 'Northern' project of modernity and progress, where terms as "the modern Mediterranean" and "Mediterranean modernity" appear "debatable if not outright oxymoronic" (Ben-Yehoyada 2014, 107). Cassano and his followers, in contrast, interpret the 'South' as including the Mediterranean, as "an invaluable source of inspiration for the experience of 'alternative modernities'" (Giaccaria and Minca 2010, 346). The anthropologist and sociologist Iain Chambers sees Naples, a quintessential 'Southern', Mediterranean city, as a configuration of a modern life of its own, as the opposite to the "modern myth of the rational organization of urban space, production, labor and profit" which in this city "continues to be interrupted, decomposed, and deviated by innumerable pockets of social resistance, mercantilism, barter, corruption, and crime" (Chambers 2008, 74, 73). For him, the city under the volcano is the expression of a "porous modernity", capable of soaking up external elements, of embodying and incorporating foreign elements and external pressures while maintaining its initial form:

> "Naples proposes an interruption and interrogation of our inherited understanding of urban life, architecture and planning. Participating in progress without being fully absorbed in its agenda, Naples, as a composite space, reintroduces the uneven and the unplanned, the contingent, the historical." (Chambers 2008, 81)

Chambers presents Italy in its ambiguous position between 'modern West' and the 'South' as a case of a "composite modernity", not as a late-comer, but as a country between 'North' and 'South' with its own, diverse trajectory to European modernity (Chambers 2010, 3). Accordingly, in a critical distance to normative teleological concepts of modernity and modernization, some scholars refer to Shmuel N. Eisenstadt's notion of "multiple modernities" in order to tackle the contradictory realities and developments of Southern Europe or, in a wider sense, of the circum-Mediterranean cultures (Welz 2004).

Beyond Discourses?

Debates about 'modernity' and 'modernization' have been at the origins of conceiving of the 'European South' as a region characterized by common structures and dynamics of development in the post-war era. The concept of 'Southern Europe' is closely connected with the idea that those countries have followed a special path to modernity, i.e. that they are supposed to have achieved only an incomplete modernization in comparison with Europe's 'core'. These arguments about the peculiarities of the 'South' have a different historical depth. While disciplines such as economics, sociology, and political science look at Southern Europe from a short-term perspective, by referring to assumed long-term special features, there are some attempts by historians to explain a particular Southern European path to modernity in a long-term view, going back to the caesuras of the French Revolution and the Napoleonic era. Stanley Payne, in his assessment of "common dilemmas of economic development or social structure and change" of Southern European countries, considered two periods of "maximum convergence" in contemporary history, "between about 1860 and 1915, when structures and sequences were most clearly parallel to each other" and again since 1975, "when Spain, Portugal and Greece all joined Italy once more in the ranks of democracy while pursuing somewhat similar policies of social democracy and more rapid modernization within the EEC and the Nato alliance" (Payne 1986, 115). Edward Malefakis, while using metaphors of trauma and pathology,[8] shares Payne's *longue durée* approach and his interpretation of the two last centuries of the history of Southern European countries as an arduous way to modernity, crowned by a positive final outcome. Southern Europe, according to his interpretation, at the beginning of the 19th century, belonged fully to the Western mainstream only in its aspirations: "A beginning had been made toward political modernization, but it was a traumatic beginning, one

8 For metaphors of a defective South, more concretely European Southwest, comprising Italy, Portugal, and Spain, in moral terms see Tortella (1994, 4), who in order to investigate its "common political and economic sins" wants "to study what was wrong with the bodies and the souls of our Latin countries".

that left deep wounds which would affect Southern Europe's further evolution" (Malefakis 1992, 19). For Malefakis, the "decades from the 1790s to the 1870s witnessed the agonizing birth of a new and seriously deformed Southern Europe" (1995, 76). The "curse of Southern Europe" (1992, 35), of a delayed, if not failed catch up with Western Europe could be lifted only in the quarter-century between 1950 and 1975, due to a unique mix of external and domestic factors, when the region "witnessed an astonishing reinvigoration […] which carried it well beyond the thresholds of sickness around which it had hovered for the preceding two centuries and one which seemed to assure it a more or less normal future" (1995, 76).

In historical analyses concentrating on the post-war development of Southern Europe we find key elements of Payne's and Malefakis's arguments regarding "normalization", i.e. "Europeanization" and the catching up of Southern Europe, pushed along by 'Western' influence since the fifties. At first look, however, there seem to be considerable differences between such works as those by Giulio Sapelli (1995) and Tony Judt (2005 [2011]). While Sapelli is mostly committed to economic and social history, Judt argues rather from the point of view of political history. Adopting a Weberian perspective, Sapelli analyzes Southern Europe as an area split up between tradition and modernity. By linking up economic, social and political developments, he identifies the common features that, in his opinion, shape Southern European countries, like for instance, a weak industrialization (63–90) and a clientelistic political culture (114–122). Enhancing the persistence of traditional structures, Sapelli points to the deficits affecting Southern Europe, i.e. its incomplete modernization (10–13). From a quite different point of view, Judt focuses on Southern European dictatorships and their position within Europe. He underlines that Spain, Portugal and Greece were integrated into the so-called Western block long before the dictatorships collapsed. Only on this basis, in his eyes, modernization and economic development accelerated when they joined the Economic European Community and received significant financial as well as political stimuli. According to Judt, writing in 2005, between the sixties and the nineties these countries had thus got through an enormous catching up process, and achieved a social and economic standard not far from that of continental Europe (Judt 2005 [2011], 516–529).

The authors' different approaches apparently lead to almost opposite results. Inspired by the ideal types of Western modernity, Sapelli enhances economic and social structures. From this perspective, Southern Europe appears as an area affected by multiple deficits, unable to get over the gaps separating it from the European core. On the contrary, Judt looks primarily at politics, i.e. he regards economic and social developments as a result of the geopolitical framework. He believes that the Spanish, Portuguese, and Greek societies and economies could catch up to those of other European countries especially thanks to the political integration within Western Europe. While Sapelli focuses on the persistence of differences, Judt emphasizes integration processes. Paradoxically, both perspectives can be combined. Placing sharp boundaries on Western Europe, the geopolitical context of the Cold War and European integration significantly influenced the economic and social development of those countries. As they had to belong to the capitalist societies politically, their integration into the 'Western' economies constituted an important policy issue within international relations—this applies also to Italy and its regions affected by economic underdevelopment (Bouchard and Ferme 2013, 5). In that context, moreover, Greece had been virtually included in the West: until the present day, it is generally said to belong to Southern Europe, i.e. *Southwestern Europe*, and not to Southeastern Europe, in spite of having close cultural, geographical and historical linkages to the other Balkan countries (Augustinos 2003).

With its unsteady pace, the European integration process has indeed deeply shaped the notion of Southern Europe both in the political and academic discourse. As it joined the 'West' and the European Union only after the end of the Cold War, a country like Bulgaria is usually not numbered among the Southern European states. On the contrary, some scholars—such as Giulio Sapelli (1995)—do regard Turkey as part of Southern Europe. This results from the country's political "Westernization" and "Europeanization" since the fifties (Müftüler-Bac 1997)[9], that—in spite of not having led to a full membership in the European Union—keeps on raising the normative question of Turkey's place within Europe or, in other words, between "tradition and modernity" (Kramer 2000, 11–23). Suggesting—as underlined above—both inclusion and exclusion, Southern Europe expresses the country's ambivalent position within the European hierarchy.

Within that transnational space, however, socio-economic development has gone beyond the integrative dynamic that resulted from the geopolitical order. The interconnectivity characterizing Western Europe has depended

9 For similar reasons, also Cyprus and Malta—which, in spite of having joined the European Union not until the beginning of the 21st century, belonged to the "Western block" within the post-war order—are often mentioned as Southern European countries (Verney 2011).

not only on similarities, but also and especially on different levels of social and economic structures. By focusing on this aspect, the question of whether 'Southern European' countries have shared common paths becomes sharper. A valuable example in dealing with inner European interdependence dynamics is international labor migration. Between the fifties and the seventies, millions of labor migrants left Italy, Spain, Portugal, and Greece: "labour migrations divided Europe into a northern in-migration region and a southern out-migration regions" (Bade 2003, 219). Within a short time, they all developed from emigration to immigration countries, sharing as such quite similar features (Reyneri and Baganha 2001). From this perspective, it seems hardly possible to neglect a Southern European path as regards international migration (King et al. 2000).

By broadening the perspective, however, the existence of a "Southern European migration system" (Mau and Verwiebe 2010) appears less evident. With Thomas Hammar (1985, 3), for instance, we can describe post-war labor migration until the seventies, instead of a movement from south to north, as one from the periphery to the center (see Map 1). Hereby, we can observe that Ireland and Finland were subject to mass emigration to more industrialized areas. Moreover, besides to some extent northern African countries, Turkey and Yugoslavia participated significantly in that phenomenon. Migration flows from Italy, Spain, Portugal, and Greece thus have to be inserted into the broader context of post-war labor mobility that concerned both other Western European countries as well as those only partially integrated into the capitalist bloc. Among them, several ones turned into immigration areas.

Starting from processes such as migration, it makes sense to adopt a center-periphery perspective[10], as it has been developed particularly by political economists with regard to the interdependence among more and less advanced capitalist societies (Arrighi 1985). This approach can help to solve a main dilemma concerning the concept of Southern Europe, i.e. the danger of interpreting common dynamics in terms of an area sharing all paths of development. In his social history of Europe in the second half of the 20th century, historian Hartmut Kaelble (2013) offers a good example of this approach, referring to the interplay between a 'rich center' and 'poor periphery' as the analytical framework of his book. This applies to the relation between Western and Eastern European countries on the one hand, and to the inter-

10 See the chapter by Russell King in this volume.

action between more and less developed regions within Western Europe on the other. In Kaelble's opinion, after the Second World War, countries both in the North—Finland and Ireland—and in the South—Italy, Spain, Portugal and Greece—belonged to a scarcely industrialized Western European periphery. From this perspective, he reconstructs various analogies that have shaped the recent past of these states as regards different fields such as education, migration, urbanization, labor, welfare, secularization, civil society, and consumption. Kaelble, however, is far from depicting this 'periphery' as a homogenous space. He rather looks at the convergence dynamics that, triggered by Europe's economic and social (as well as political) integration, have involved several countries, but with different rhythms and partly different results. In his book, whose first edition was published in 2007, shortly before the financial crisis, he observes that at the beginning of the 21st century Finland, Ireland, and (as a whole) Italy had fully achieved the social and economic standards of the European 'core', while Spain, Portugal, and Greece—similarly to Slovenia, Estonia and Latvia—were still, but rapidly catching up.

Map 1: Schematic representation of post-war labor migration, 1950–1973

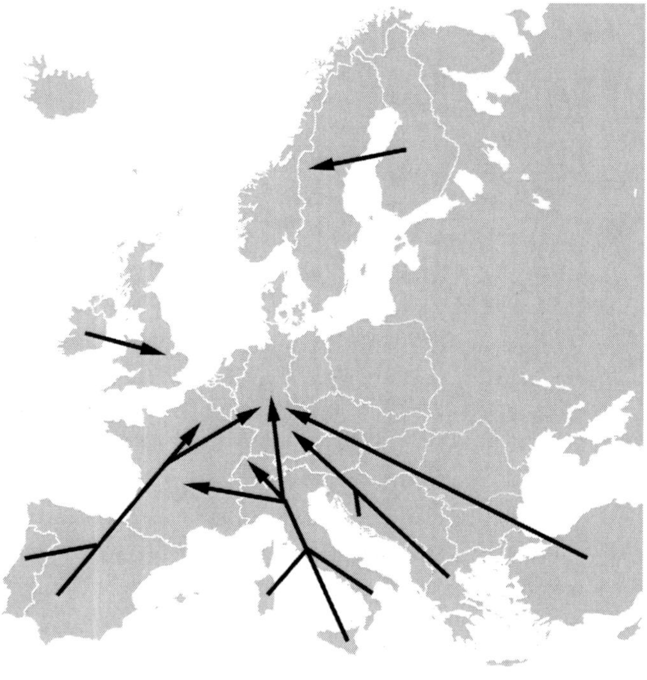

As employed by Kaelble, the center-periphery perspective bears the danger of conceiving monolithic areas, leading to exhaustive interpretative models as well as introducing by the backdoor normative conjectures we see in the modernization paradigms used by scholars such as Payne, Malefakis or Sapelli. This risk can be avoided if we consider the interrelation between more or less 'advanced' European economies and societies as one (mighty) dynamic that interacts, however, with more specific national, regional, and transnational configurations. In other words, we can look for analogies characterizing certain groups of countries in different fields without assuming the existence of one unique path of development.

With these 'precautions', the center-periphery perspective can contribute to pondering the several similarities shared by Italy, Spain, Portugal, and Greece, independently from the fact of whether we define them as 'Southern Europe' or not. As concerns the welfare state, for instance[11], we can observe that these countries' social policies had to face similar challenges without hiding the important differences that—due to specific national settings—partly led to divergent solutions. From this point of view, the general interpretations of Southern Europe's recent past and present proposed by Edward Malefakis and Giulio Sapelli should be revisited by eliminating their Weberian all-encompassing pretensions and re-scaling them according to the respective research agenda.

Conclusions

The idea of the European South as a cultural and historical region is deeply rooted in the continent's 'moral geography'. It cannot be detached as an 'objective' autonomous physical-cultural entity from processes of mental mapping which, in addition, up to now have undergone profound shifts and reconfigurations influenced by changing geopolitical situations. In the decades after 1945, dominant factors have been the Cold War, European Integration, the (supposed) end of the East-West-confrontation, and recently, the financial and economic crisis. The Cold War and the great transformation of 'Southern' countries starting in the fifties after the turmoil of the Second

11 See the chapters by Claude Martin and Martin Rhodes in this volume for an exhaustive analysis of the debate on a Southern European model of welfare state.

World War had contributed to forging a 'new South' as an integral part of the 'West'. The formation of the European community, democratic consolidation and the socio-economic catching-up process gave new visibility to the 'South' as a model of successful development and a reliable European partner, which in the nineties appeared even more dynamic and promising than problem-ridden, unified Germany. After 2007, however, the ghost of a 'bad South' re-emerged and with it a whole bundle of seemingly old outdated stereotypes of Southern sins and failures.

The 'South' as a geographical unit dealt with in social sciences and history is not independent from these shifting constellations and political trends. Academic interests and perspectives are rather clearly interrelated with them and are imbued with assumptions and value judgments deriving immediately from the discursive construction of the region. We can observe this dependency in central paradigms used with regard to the changing destinies of Southern European countries such as progress and backwardness or modernity and modernization. Revisiting, or better, relocating the 'South' in this perspective means to deconstruct highly normative assessments, often expressed in a moralizing or medical language, of sins and pathologies. It is not appropriate to narrate recent developments of the European South as a 'long road West'—as imagined for Germany by Heinrich August Winkler (2006–2007)— with the final menace of breaking away from it. It might be legitimate and useful to reconstruct the history of the 'South' as a literary-artistic idea (Richter 2009)—an attempt which, notwithstanding all the differences in approach and scope, has some parallels with Winkler's highly ambitious monumental study of the history of the 'West' as a political-cultural project unfolding from Greco-Roman antiquity up to our present (Winkler 2009–2015). At the same time, however, it is necessary to review critically a spatial category which is transformed too easily into rather abstract ideas and principles. In this way, it might be possible to overcome the impasse between 'constructivists' and 'deconstructivists' as manifest in the Todorova-Sundhaussen controversy we mentioned initally. Studying the 'South' on the mental maps might be an important task for understanding internal hierarchies, power relations and the logics of defining 'core' and 'periphery' in Europe, but a critical re-evaluation of this category could also be a first step in reconsidering the 'South' as a research agenda without falling into the trap, inherent in every concept of a historical region, of essentialization, homogenization and teleological determinism.

With this in mind, one can start again from the rich agenda developed by social sciences studying 'Southern Europe' as a composite region with common political, economic and cultural convergences and structures. This approach has been particularly fruitful for the analysis of periods of profound transformations in these respective countries, looking at dynamic processes more than at apparently immutable, timeless structures. The 'European South', however, may not serve only as a sample of cases for this kind of comparative study. The 'South' is also an essentially relational category, both in a European and an extra-European perspective. This becomes evident also in recent developments. Under the impact of the financial and economic crisis, the 'South' is being considered a 'new East' (Ther 2014, 253–264). Many recent EU member states in Eastern and Central Eastern Europe seem to be recovering more successfully from the effects of the crisis than their Southern counterparts, which are dropped back to levels of the early sixties when the process of economic and social convergence was starting. An imbalance, already perceptible before 2007, is currently aggravated by the effects of the crisis, as one can deduce from statistics concerning public debts, (youth) unemployment, increasing regional disparities and declining spending power. Growing prosperity of most of the new EU members and economic decline in the 'South' have caused a role reversal when politicians and economic experts praise Eastern and Central Eastern countries for their economic "successes" in the context of a globalizing neoliberal order while blaming the economies of Southern PIGS. These are serious indications of a deep re-configuration of European mental maps. (Ther 2014, 267–276).

At the same time, the 'South' in its Mediterranean extension has a strong transregional and even intercontinental dimension, passing European borders. There has always been a certain overlapping of the two distinct concepts of the Euro-Mediterranean and an all-encompassing circum-Mediterranean region. In the current geopolitical situation, when hundreds of thousands of refugees are trying desperately to cross the Sea and fears of international terrorism are spreading, the idea of the Mediterranean as a zone of connectivity, of contact and struggle reemerges, gaining, however, new meanings, in many ways opposite to the values of peace, security and prosperity proclaimed in the so-called Barcelona declaration of 1995 which was intended to create a new Euro-Mediterranean partnership (European Union. External Action n.d.; Euro-Mediterranean Conference 1995).

The current crises with their global backgrounds and dynamics show clearly how 'Southern Europe' is not only a testing ground for the future of

Europe, but also for understanding its past and present, as its borders, internal hierarchies, the relations between 'core' and 'periphery' and its political and cultural identity are concerned. Looking at the 'South' one can reevaluate Europe's mental maps, one can discuss basic assumptions about the development of European societies in a comparative perspective, and one can contextualize Europe in broader settings and relationships. That is why it is worth the effort to reconsider and relocate the 'South' beyond familiar stereotypes and preconceived expectations.

Works Cited

Abulafia, David (2011). *The Great Sea. A Human History of the Mediterranean*. London: Allen Lane and Penguin Books.

Agamben, Giorgio (2010). Se un impero latino prendesse forma nel cuore d'Europa. *La Repubblica*, March 15.

Aldcroft, Derek Howard, and Richard Rodger (1992). *Bibliography of European Economic and Social History*. Manchester: Manchester University Press.

Arrighi, Giovanni (ed.). (1985). *Semiperipheral Development. The Politics of Southern Europe in the Twentieth Century.* Beverly Hills: Sage.

Augustinos, Gerasimos (2003). Greece and the Balkans Between the World Wars: Self-identity, the Other, and National Development. In Dēmētrēs Tziobas (ed.). *Greece and the Balkans. Identities, Perceptions and Cultural Encounters since the Enlightenment*, 84–98. Aldershot: Ashgate.

Bade, Klaus J. (2003). *Migration in European History*. Malden, Massachusetts: Blackwell.

Baumeister, Martin (2015). The Return of Ulyses. Varieties of the 'New Mediterranean' between Mediterraneanism and Southern Thought. In Achim Lichtenberger and Constanze von Rüden (eds.). *Multiple Mediterranean Realities. Current Approaches to Spaces, Resources and Connectivities*, 259–272. Paderborn: Wilhelm Fink and Ferdinand Schöningh.

Baumeister, Martin, and Rainer Liedtke (eds.). (2009). Städte in Südeuropa. IMS–*Informationen zur modernen Stadtgeschichte*, 1/2009.

Ben-Yehoyada, Noam (2014). Mediterranean Modernity? In Peregrine Horden and Sharon Kinoshita (eds.). *A Companion to Mediterranean History*, 107–121. Chichester: Wiley Blackwell.

Berger, Stefan (2007). Writing National Histories in Europe: Reflections on the Pasts, Presents and Futures of a Tradition. In Konrad Jarausch and Thomas Lindenberger (eds.). *Conflicted Memories. Europeanizing Contemporary Histories*, 55–68. Oxford: Berghahn Books.

Bevilacqua, Piero (2005). *Breve storia dell'Italia meridionale: dall'Ottocento a oggi.* Rome: Donzelli.

Bock, Gisela, and Anne Cara (eds.). (2003). *Écrire l'histoire des femmes en Europe du Sud XIVe–XXe siècles / Writing Women's History in Southern Europe. 19th–20th Centuries.* Oeiras: Celta Editoria.

Borutta, Manuel (2013). De la Méridionalité à la Méditerranée. Le Midi de la France au temps de l'Algérie coloniale. *Cahiers de la Méditerranée*, 87, 385–402.

Borutta, Manuel, and Fabian Lemmes (2013). Die Wiederkehr des Mittelmeerraumes: Stand und Perspektiven der neuhistorischen Mediterranistik. *Neue Politische Literatur*, 58, 389–419.

Bouchard, Norma, and Valerio Ferme (2013). *Italy and the Mediterranean. Words, Sounds, and Images of the Post-Cold War Era.* New York: Palgrave Macmillan.

Braudel, Fernand (1982). *La Méditerranée et le monde méditerranéen à l'époque de Philippe II,* 2 volumes 5th edition. Paris: Armand Colin.

Broadberry, Stephen, and Kevin H. O'Rourke (eds.). (2010). *The Cambridge Economic History of Modern Europe: Volume 2. 1870 to the Present.* Cambridge: Cambridge University Press.

Burke III, Edmund, and David Prochaska (2008). Introduction: Orientalism from Postcolonial Theory to World Theory. In Edmund Burke III and David Prochaska (eds.). *Genealogies of Orientalism. History, Theory, Politics*, 1–71. Lincoln: University of Nebraska Press.

Cassano, Franco (2001). Southern Thought. *Thesis Eleven*, 67, 1–10.

Cassano, Franco (2011). *Il pensiero meridiano*, 4th edition. Rome: Laterza.

Chaloner, William H., and Roger C. Richardson (1984). *Bibliography of British Economic and Social History.* Manchester: Manchester University Press.

Chambers, Iain (2008). *Mediterranean Crossings. The Politics of an Interrupted Modernity.* London: Duke University Press.

Chambers, Iain (2010). Another Map, Another History, Another Modernity. *California Italian Studies,* 1, 1. URL: http://escholarship.org/uc/item/7vp210p4 (accessed 15 May 2015).

Costa Pinto, António, and Nuno Severiano Teixeira (eds.). (2002). *Southern Europe and the Making of the European Union, 1945–1980s.* Boulder and New York: Social Science Monographs.

Dainotto, Roberto M. (2000). A South with a View. Europe and its Other. *Nepantia: Views from South*, 1:2, 375–90.

Dainotto, Roberto M. (2007). *Europe (in Theory).* Durham: Duke University Press.

Davis, John (1977). *People of the Mediterranean: An Essay in Comparative Social Anthropology.* London: Routledge & Kegan Paul.

Del Pero, Mario (2011). The United States and the Crises in Southern Europe. In Guilia Migani and Antonio Varsori (eds.). *Europe in the International Arena During the Seventies*, 301–316. Bruxelles: Peter Lang.

Demertzis, Maria et al. (1997). Does a Core-Periphery Regime Make Europe into an Optimal Currency Area? In Paul J. J. Welfens (ed.). *European Monetary Union Transition, International Impact and Policy Options*, 161–234. Berlin: Springer.

Diamandouros, P. Nikiforos, and Richard Gunther (eds.). (2001). *Parties, Politics, and Democracy in the New Southern Europe*. Baltimore: Johns Hopkins University Press.

Driessen, Henk (2011). Shifting Boundaries. Ethnography, Community, and Area in the Mediterranean. In Gisela Welz et al. (eds.). *Epistemische Orte. Gemeinde und Region als Forschungsformate*, 45–54. Frankfurt: Institut für Kulturanthropologie und Europäische Ethnologie der Johann Wolfgang Goethe-Universität.

Euro-Mediterranean Conference (1995). *Barcelona Declaration*. URL: http://ec.europa.eu/research/iscp/pdf/policy/barcelona_declaration.pdf (accessed 15 May 2015).

European Union. External Action (n.d.). *The Barcelona Process*. URL: http://eeas.europa.eu/euromed/barcelona_en.htm (accessed 15 May 2015).

Ferrera, Maurizio (ed.). (2005). *Welfare State Reform in Southern Europe. Fighting Poverty and Social Exlusion in Italy, Spain, Portugal, and Greece*. London and New York: Routledge.

Ferrera, Maurizio (2005). Welfare States and Social Safety Nets in Southern Europe. In Maurizio Ferrera (ed.). *Welfare State Reform in Southern Europe. Fighting Poverty and Social Exclusion in Italy, Spain, Portugal and Greece*, 1–32. London and New York: Routledge.

Fogu, Claudio (2010). From *Mare Nostrum* to *Mare Aliorum*: Mediterranean Theory and Mediterraneanism in Contemporary Italian Thought. *California Italian Studies*, 1, 1. URL: http://escholarship.org/uc/item/7vp210p4 (accessed 15 May 2015).

Gibson, Heather D. (ed.). (2001). *Economic Transformation, Democratization and Integration into the European Union. Southern Europe in Comparative Perspective*. Basingstoke and New York: Palgrave.

Giaccaria, Paolo, and Claudio Minca (2010). The Mediterranean Alternative. *Progress in Human Geography*, 35:3, 345–65.

Gilman, Nils (2003). *Mandarins of the Future. Modernization Theory in Cold War America*. Baltimore: Johns Hopkins University Press

Goffredo, Giuseppe (2000). *Cadmos cerca Europa. Il Sud fra il Mediterraneo e l'Europa*. Torino: Bollati Boringhieri.

González, María José et al. (eds.). (1999). *Gender Inequalities in Southern Europe. Women, Work and Welfare in the 1990s*. London: Frank Cass.

Grell, Ole Peter et al. (eds.). (2005). *Health Care and Poor Relief in 18th and 19th Century Southern Europe*. Aldershot: Ashgate.

Gunther, Richard et al. (eds.). (1995). *The Politics of Democratic Consolidation. Southern Europe in Comparative Perspective*. Baltimore: The Johns Hopkins University Press.

Gunther, Richard et al. (eds.). (2006). *Democracy and the State in the New Southern Europe*. Oxford: Oxford University Press.

Hammar, Thomas (1985). Introduction. In Thomas Hammar (ed.). *European Immigration Policy: A Comparative Study*, 1–13. Cambridge: Cambridge University Press.

Hanhimäki, Jussi M., and Odd Arne Westad (eds.). (2003). *The Cold War. A History in Documents and Eyewitness Accounts*. Oxford: Oxford University Press.

Herzfeld, Michael (1984). The Horns of the Mediterraneanist Dilemma. *American Ethnologist*, 11, 439–54.

Herzfeld, Michael (1987). *Anthropology through the Looking-Glass. Critical Ethnography in the Margins of Europe*. Cambridge: Cambridge University Press.

Horden, Peregrine, and Nicolas Purcell (2000). The *Corrupting Sea. A Study of Mediterranean History*. Oxford: Blackwell.

Higbee, Joan Florence (1996). *Western Europe Since 1945. A Bibliography*. Lanham, Maryland: Scarecrow Press.

Hitchcock, William I. (2003). *The Struggle for Europe. The Turbulent History of a Divided Continent, 1945–2002*. New York: Doubleday.

Hoffmann, Léon François (1961). *Romantique Espagne. L'image de l'Espagne en France entre 1800 et 1850*. Paris: Presses Universitaires Françaises.

Holman, Otto (1996). *Integrating Southern Europe. EC Expansion and the Transnationalisation of Spain*. New York: Routledge.

Horden, Peregrine, and Nicolas Purcell (2000). *The Corrupting Sea. A Study of Mediterranean History*. Oxford: Blackwell.

Horden, Peregrine, and Nicolas Purcell (2006). The Mediterranean and the "New Thalassology". *The American Historical Review*, 111, 722–40.

Iriye, Akira (2013). *Global and Transnational History. The Past, Present, and Future*. New York: Palgrave Macmillan.

Jacob, W. James, and John N. Hawkins (2011). Setting the Global Education Policy Stage: Shifts, Trends, and Perspectives. In John N. Hawkins and W. James Jacob (eds.). *Policy Debates in Comparative, International, and Development Education*, 3–11. New York: Palgrave Macmillan.

Jirat-Wasiutyński, Vojtěch (2007). Modern Art and the New Mediterranean Space. In Vojtěch Jirat-Wasiutyński with the assistance of Anne Dymond (eds.). *Modern Art and the Idea of the Mediterranean*, 3–33. Toronto: University of Toronto Press.

Judt, Tony (2011 [2005]). *Postwar. A History of Europe Since 1945*. London: Pimlico.

Kaelble, Hartmut (2007). *Sozialgeschichte Europas: 1945 bis zur Gegenwart*. Munich: C.H. Beck.

Kaelble, Hartmut (2013). *A Social History of Europe, 1945–2000. Recovery and Transformation after Two World Wars*. New York: Berghahn Books.

Kaiser, Wolfram, and Jürgen Elvert (eds.). (2004). *European Union Enlargement. A Comparative History*. London: Routledge.

King, Russell et al. (eds.). (2000). *Eldorado or Fortress? Migration in Southern Europe.* Basingstoke: Macmillan.

Kramer, Heinz (2000). *A Changing Turkey. The Challenge to Europe and the United States.* Washington, DC: Brookings Institution Press.

Leggewie, Claus (2014). *Zukunft im Süden.* Hamburg: Körber Stiftung.

Leontidou, Lila (1990). *The Mediterranean City in Transition. Social Change and Urban Development.* Cambridge: Cambridge University Press.

Lepenies, Wolf (2013). *Ost und West. Nord und Süd. Der europäische Himmelrichtungsstreit.* Halle: Universitätsverlag Halle-Wittenberg. URL: http://www.universitaetsverlag-halle-wittenberg.de/media/upload/file/Kapitel_Vorworte/0635_Lepenies.pdf (accessed 15 May 2015).

Linz, Juan J., and Alfred Stepan (1996). *Problems of Democratic Transition and Consolidation. Southern Europe, South America, and Post-communist Europe.* Baltimore: Johns Hopkins University Press.

Linz, Juan J. (1996). *Problems of Democratic Transition and Consolidation. Southern Europe, South America, and Post-communist Europe.* Baltimore: Johns Hopkins University Press.

Lucarelli, Sonia, and Claudio M. Radaelli Lucarelli (eds.). (2005). *Mobilizing Politics and Society? The EU Convention's Impact on Southern Europe.* London and New York: Routledge.

Macfie, Alexander L. (2002). *Orientalism. A Reader.* London: Longman.

Magone, José M. (2003). *The Politics of Southern Europe. Integration into the European Union.* Westport, Connecticut: Praeger.

Malefakis, Edward (1992). Southern Europe in the 19th and 20th Centuries: An Historical Overview. *Working papers. Instituto Juan March de Estudios e Investigaciones, Centro de Estudios Avanzados en Ciencias Sociales,* 35.

Malefakis, Edward (1995). The Political and Social Contours of Southern European History. In Richard Gunther et al. (eds.). *The Politics of Democratic Consolidation. Southern Europe in Comparative Perspective,* 33–76. Baltimore: The Johns Hopkins University Press.

Matvejević, Predrag (2007). *Breviario mediterraneo.* Milan: Garzanti.

Mau, Steffen, and Roland Verwiebe (2010). *European Societies. Mapping Structure and Change.* Bristol: Policy Press.

Mazower, Mark (2000). *Dark Continent. Europe's Twentieth Century.* New York: Vintage Books.

McLaren, Lauren M. (2008). *Constructing Democracy in Southern Europe. A Comparative Analysis of Italy, Spain and Turkey.* London: Routledge.

Mishkova, Diana, Bo Stråt, and Balázs Trencsényi (2013). Regional History as a "Challenge" to National Frameworks of Historiography: The Case of Central, Southeast, and Northern Europe. In Matthias Middell and Lluis Roura (eds.). *Transnational Challenges to National History Writing,* 257–314. Basingstoke: Palgrave.

Müftüler-Bac, Meltem (1997). *Turkey's Relations with a Changing Europe*. Manchester: Manchester University Press.

Paquette, Gabriel B. (ed.). (2009). *Enlightened Reform in Southern Europe and its Atlantic Colonies, c. 1750–1830*. Farnham, Surrey: Ashgate.

Payne, Stanley G. (1986). The Concept of 'Southern Europe' and Political Development. *Mediterranean Historical Review*, 1:1, 100–116.

Pedaliu, Effi (2014). The Making of Southern Europe: An Historical Overview. In *A Strategy for Southern Europe. LSE Ideas. Special Report*, October 2014, 8–14. URL: http://www.lse.ac.uk/IDEAS/publications/reports/pdf/SR017/Pedaliu.pdf (accessed 15 May 2015).

Petraccone, Claudia (2000). *Le due civiltà. Settentrionali e meridionali nella storia dell'Italia dal 1860 al 1914*. Bari: Laterza.

Piterberg, Gabriel et al. (eds.). (2010). *Braudel Revisited. The Mediterranean World, 1600–1800*. Toronto: University of Toronto Press.

Preston, Christopher (1997). *Enlargement and Integration in the European Union*. London: Routledge.

Reyneri, Emilio, and Maria Baganha (2001). Migration and the Labour Market in Southern Europe. *IMIS-Beiträge*, 17, 33–53.

Rhodes Martin (1997). *Southern European Welfare States: Between Crisis and Reform*. London and New York: Routledge.

Richter, Dieter (2009). *Der Süden: Geschichte einer Himmelsrichtung*. Berlin: Wagenbach.

Rizas, Sotiris (2012). *The Rise of the Left in Southern Europe. Anglo-American Responses*. London: Pickering & Chatto.

Rutar, Sabine (ed.). (2014). Beyond the Balkans. Towards an Inclusive History of Southeastern Europe. Zurich and Berlin: Lit.

Said, Edward (1978). *Orientalism*. New York: Pantheon Books.

Santos, Ana Cristina (2013). *Social Movements and Sexual Citizenship in Southern Europe*. Basingstoke: Palgrave Macmillan.

Sapelli, Giulio (1995). *Southern Europe Since 1945. Tradition and Modernity in Portugal, Spain, Italy, Greece and Turkey*, London: Longman.

Schenk, Frithjof Benjamin, and Martina Winkler (eds.). (2007). Einleitung. In Frithjof Benjamin Schenk and Martin Winkler (eds.). *Der Süden. Neue Perspektiven auf eine europäische Geschichtsregion*, 7–20. Frankfurt: Campus.

Schlögel, Karl (2003). *Im Raume lesen wir die Zeit. Über Zivilisationsgeschichte und Geopolitik*. Munich: Hanser.

Schneider, Jane (ed.). (1998). *Italy's "Southern Question": Orientalism in One Country*. Oxford: Berg.

Schoepp, Sebastian (2014). *Mehr Süden wagen. Oder wie wir Europäer wieder zueinander finden*. Frankfurt: Westend.

Simonazzi, Annamaria et al. (2013). Economic Relations between Germany and Southern Europe. *Cambridge Journal of Economics*, 37:3, 653–675.

Soriero, Giuseppe (2014). *Sud, vent'anni di solitudine*. Rome: Donzelli.

Soutou, Georges-Henri (2007). The Linkage between European Integration and Détente: the Contrasting Approaches of de Gaulle and Pompidou, 1965 to 1974. In N. Piers Ludlow (ed.). *European Integration and the Cold War. Ostpolitik-Westpolitik, 1965–1973*, 11–35. London: Routledge.
Sundhaussen, Holm (1999). Europa balcanica. Der Balkan als historischer Raum Europas. *Geschichte und Gesellschaft*, 25, 626–53.
Sutcliffe, Anthony (2014 [1996]), *An Economic and Social History of Western Europe*. Abingdon and New York: Routledge.
Tavares De Almeida, Pedro et al. (eds.). (2003). *Who Governs Southern Europe? Regime Change and Ministerial Recruitment, 1850–2000*. London: F. Cass.
Ther, Philipp (2014). *Die neue Ordnung auf dem alten Kontinent. Eine Geschichte des neoliberalen Europa*. Frankfurt: Suhrkamp.
Todorova, Maria (1997). *Imagining the Balkans*. New York: Oxford University Press.
Todorova, Maria (2002). Der Balkan als Analysekategorie: Grenzen, Raum, Zeit. *Geschichte und Gesellschaft*, 28, 470–92.
Todorova, Maria (2005). Spacing Europe: What is a Historical Region? *East Central Europe/L'Europe du Centre-Est*, 32:1–2, 59–78.
Tortella, Gabriel (1994). Patterns of Economic Retardation and Recovery in South-Western Europe in the Nineteenth and Twentieth Centuries. *The Economic History Review*. N.S. 47:1, 1–21.
Troebst, Stefan (2003). Introduction: What's in a Historical Region? A Teutonic Perspective. *European Review of History*, 10:2, 173–188.
Venturini, Alessandra (2004). *Postwar Migration in Southern Europe, 1950–2000. An Economic Analysis*. Cambridge: Cambridge University Press.
Verney, Susannah (ed.). (2011). Euroscepticism in Southern Europe: A Diachronic Perspective. *South European Society and Politics*, 16:1, 1–29.
Welz, Gisela (2004). Transnational Cultures and Multiple Modernities. Anthropology's Encounter with Globalization. In Günter H. Lenz et al. (eds.). 'Between Worlds': the Legacy of Edward Said. *Zeitschrift für Anglistik und Amerikanistik*, 52:4, 409–422.
Williams, Allan (ed.). (1984). *Southern Europe Transformed. Political and Economic Change in Greece, Italy, Portugal and Spain*. London: Harper & Row.
Winkler, Heinrich August (2006–2007). *Germany. The Long Road West*, 2 volumes. Oxford: Oxford University Press.
Winkler, Heinrich August (2009–2015). *Geschichte des Westens*, 4 volumes. Munich: C.H. Beck.
Yachir, Faysal (1989). *The Mediterranean. Between Autonomy and Dependency*. Tokyo: United Nations University.

Southern Europe in Social Science. A 'Southern European Model'?

Martin Rhodes[1]

The most recent crisis of European economies, assuming its most acute form in Southern Europe, demands a reappraisal of the ways in which the region has been analyzed by social scientists and the use of the concepts they have developed as lenses for examining the current situation and outlook. The aim of this paper is to explore the ways in which 'Southern Europe' has been categorized and analyzed in several key areas of social science—notably in a historical and comparative political economy. This discussion proceeds in several steps. In part one I look at the analysis of Southern Europe in historical-developmental terms, before turning to part two to look at three perspectives on the region based on heuristic frameworks: 'world-systems' analysis, which locates Southern Europe in the capitalist 'semi-periphery'; the analysis of Southern Europe's different productive systems as a particular 'variety' of European capitalism; and the analysis of Southern Europe's redistributive systems as a particular 'variety' (or perhaps sub-variety) of the European welfare state. In part three, before concluding, I bring those perspectives together to look at the longer-term problems of the region revealed and compounded by the recent financial and economic crisis.

There are two key threads running through the analysis. The first concerns when it does and does not make sense to speak of an identifiable Southern European 'region', 'model' or (less politely) a Southern 'syndrome', 'anomaly', or even 'curse'. This chapter does not seek to settle the debates on this topic, but rather to set out their various elements as either complementary or competing hypotheses. The second concern of the paper, stemming from the first, is to make some tentative propositions about how we might use the insights of the debates regarding Southern Europe to illuminate the nature of the recent (and ongoing) economic crisis in the region.

1 I would like to thank Roberto Sala and Martin Baumeister for their very useful comments on an earlier draft of this chapter.

The Analysis of Southern Europe in Historical-Developmental Terms

The analysis of Southern Europe in historical-developmental terms is of great utility for social scientists in providing us with a set of hypothesized pathways to (and possibly a theory of) incomplete modernization. Giulio Sapelli (1995)—a key contributor to this literature–has outlined and examined the core features of what he calls a "distinct and specific socio-economic formation" and "personality" in Southern Europe driven by two 'master' independent variables differentiating Southern Europe from the rest of Continental Europe and the British Isles: late industrialization coupled with a state that was as interventionist as it was administratively weak; and the low degree of political institutionalization, together with the disintegrating consequences of clientship. There is also a dependent variable—a "lack of synchrony between social structures and productive structures" or "modernization without development".

According to Sapelli, the southern European formation has five core developmental characteristics with powerful legacies from "centuries-old structures" (1995, 20):

1. the social continuity of "anthropological relationships typical of rural societies in a world which has undergone rapid changes";
2. a road to industrialization in which there was a rapid transition from agricultural to service sector employment, with little solidity of production or employment among small and medium-sized firms, and the absence of state regulatory systems able to promote evenly-spread and coherent economic development;
3. an advent of 'social democracy' alongside democracy, but in the form of a welfare state that divided society into groups rather than unifying it through mechanisms of solidarity: instead of horizontal relationships, hierarchical ones persisted;
4. a specific and common form of modern authoritarianism that rose from the contrasts between the land-owning classes on the one hand and the agrarian and industrial labor force on the other; and
5. an 'anomic division of political work'—i.e., a distinctive and common incapacity to institutionalize politics whereby the norms and democratic procedures of "negotiation, compensation and regulation regulate the di-

verse interests of the various political groups", leading to the persistence of patronage and weak and personalistic political parties.

As politics became more simplified and centrist, argues Sapelli, the clientship and 'spoils' system persisted, leading to a 'balkanization' of a non-Weberian state and administrative apparatus—a legacy of the fact that the two most widespread pre-existing forms of politics in Southern Europe were liberalism and *caciquismo* (clientelist practices by local notables or *caciques*). Southern Europe's capacity to shake itself free from these legacies is ultimately questionable in Sapelli's treatment of the topic.

Examining patterns of retardation in the 19th century versus catch up in the 20th century, Gabriel Tortella (1994) concludes like Sapelli that there exists a South-Western European group (Italy, Portugal, Spain) identified by their "culture and geographical endowment". For Tortella, that endowment has numerous components. On the geographic side, the most important is the long-term legacy of late agricultural modernization, creating a stagnant agricultural sector that failed dismally (with the partial exception of Northern Italy) as a market for industrial products and as a supplier of capital for modernization. This stagnation had a series of consequences (Tortella 1994, 5ff): no surplus population to flock to the cities and factory work in clear contrast to Britain (since the mid-18th century) and Germany (since the mid-19th); a low level of urbanization throughout the 19th century (it was only the external shock of foreign competition in grain, and the 'agricultural depression' of the last quarter of that century, that pushed peasants and farmers into the cities and overseas); and a very low ratio of foreign trade to the size of the economy, except for Italy in the final decades of the 19th century when a modernizing agricultural sector contributed to the development of exports.

Also like Sapelli, Tortella notes "surprising affinities between our three Latin countries". Four such affinities across Southern Europe are identified:

1. all three were ruled by dictators during long periods of the twentieth century, indicating for Tortella similar socio-political reactions to the problems of economic modernization;
2. chronic budget deficits plagued Italy, Portugal and Spain during the second half of the 19th century, with similar effects—"destabilizing the currency, damaging monetary policies, driving up interest rates, crowding out private borrowers, causing serious problems to the management of the public debt, hurting the international rating of the state and the pri-

vate borrowers alike in international financial markets, and pushing governments into nationalizing and selling off church and municipal properties" (p. 10). The similarities with the late 20th and early 21st centuries are rather striking;
3. the pattern of land tenure, Tortella argues, is a third common feature—i.e., "the twin problems of latifundia and minifundia, absentee ownership, and widespread sharecropping (mezzadria, aparcería, parçaria)";
4. literacy rates well below those of most other European nations are a fourth common feature: at the turn of the 20th century, nearly 50 per cent of the adult population in Italy and Spain were unable to read and write (the Portuguese rate was even lower), while in Belgium (one of the least educated of the 'developed' European countries), only 19 per cent of the adult population was illiterate.

Although unspecified in his analysis, these characteristics are assumed to leave important legacies for subsequent processes of 'catch-up' between North and South. Striking educational and skills deficits, for instance, still distinguish the Southern European countries from their Northern counterparts today.

Andrew Janos (1989; 2000) adds non-materialist components to these arguments, links them explicitly with problems of economic 'catch-up' and extends them to a much broader geographic area, that includes East-Central Europe (ECE) as well as Southern Europe in a revisionist interpretation of center-periphery relations. Janos adopts a variant of world system theory (e.g. Wallerstein 1979—explored below in section 2a) and builds into it elements of Thorsten Veblen's theories of consumption and need. He thus produces his own theory of an 'international demonstration effect', in which peripheral states seeking to 'catch-up' with the core strive for commensurate material consumer conditions ahead of underlying productive capacity. In an interesting hybrid argument of cultural-economic causation, Janos concludes that the "first, and perhaps foremost, factor underlying the region's backwardness was psychological: it was an endemic sense of relative deprivation generated by images of the material progress of the countries of the advanced West" (Janos 2000, 414). Feelings of relative deprivation were compounded by close cultural, religious and geographical proximity to the successful, core countries.

According to Janos, elites in the periphery did not just emulate consumption in the core: they also envied and emulated its constitutions, parliaments and bureaucracies, but did so in countries where the requisite social and political transformations that accompanied the agricultural and industrial revolutions of the European Northwest had not yet occurred: i.e., the opening of new cleavages and conflicts, as well as their resolution, not just between bourgeoisie and aristocracy but between 'modern elements'—"the bourgeoisie, the bureaucracy and the mass of common people 'entering' the political process" (Janos 1989, 329). Institutional development was therefore also contorted by the mismatch between political ambitions in the periphery and its underlying 'backward' socio-economic conditions.

The current Central and Eastern Europe and Southern Europe (including both Southwestern and Southeastern Europe) are in Janos's periphery, and according to his theory—which echoes the analyses of Sapelli and Tortella–will have registered the longest delays in development along three dimensions: "(1) the capacity to produce surplus and the subsequent risk-taking entrepreneurship; (2) the increasing complexity of the social division of labor, and the attendant pressures for more rationalized and elaborate systems of administrative regulation; and (3) new forms of social consciousness, especially a sense of personal efficacy, among ever larger segments of societies" (Janos 1989, 329).

In thinking about the durability of these developmental factors identified by historians, a parallel literature by political scientists also argues that there is a mismatch between political ambitions and retarded economic development in Southern Europe, but is more attentive to contemporary change. As Edward Malefakis remarks (1992, 19), with affinities to Janos's 'international demonstration effect': "Southern Europe during the early 19th Century belonged fully to the Western Europe mainstream *in its aspirations, but not in other ways* [my emphasis]. A beginning had been made toward political modernization, but it was a traumatic beginning, one that left deep wounds which would affect Southern Europe's future evolution".

Those 'deep wounds'—once again with strong echoes of Sapelli and Tortella–are revealed by Malefakis to be:

1. a deep factionalism among ruling elites and the political movements they led, producing Italian 'trasformismo', Portuguese 'rotativismo' and Spanish 'caciquismo'—systems of assuring peace among the ruling classes that could only be sustained through massive corruption in electoral politics and the politics of everyday life;
2. a backward society with very high levels of illiteracy and low levels of working class organization;
3. against this background, political liberalism—dishonest and corrupt—became increasingly discredited and rejected, and "because no true lib-

eralism had evolved in Southern Europe in the 19th Century, it would be difficult for stable democracy to emerge in the region in the 20th century";

4. a common economic cycle: boom conditions in the 1870s and 1880s, crisis in the 1890s and even prosperity after 1900 that "in turn affected the political patterns of the 1870–1914 period" (1992, 29);
5. foreign policy disasters at the end of the 19th century (revealing perhaps the failure to successfully emulate British imperialism) "which seriously undermined the already weak legitimacy of the existing regimes";
6. bitter struggles across the region between liberalism and neo-conservatism; and
7. a fierce conflict between capital and labor that became deeply rooted as revolutionary working class movements continued to grow (1992, 25–38)

The implicit causal argument here is one of failed political and economic catch-up with the rest of Western Europe despite the opportunity provided by periods of economic prosperity in the late 19th century. Malefakis calls this "the curse of Southern Europe" at the turn of the 20th century, with a major part of the blame attributed to "the sterility and ineptness of the governing classes during the preceding decades" (1992, 35). In the early 20th century, he argues, each country goes through a full-scale social and political crisis in the interwar period as the lack of "brilliant triumphs" prevented the "healing of wounds" and the forging of a new consensus after the First World War. In particular, new democratizing forces could not achieve hegemony; a leftist ascendancy could not transform itself into a powerful force able to instill its vision in society; and, above all, the utter ineffectiveness of pre-existing liberal regimes to govern effectively created enthusiasm for new dictatorships, and left a legacy of an overwhelming number of unresolved problems, extreme factionalism, and a conflictive political culture permeated by violence and corruption.

Yet the latter part of the 20th century, argues Malefakis, saw Southern Europe transformed, and the consequences of the "deep wounds" of the past reduced to residual status. The moderation of the democratic transitions and consolidations of the latter part of the 20th century, and the purported end of Southern Europe's 'anomalous position' in the European continent, are essentially explained by Malefakis by the 'new ecology' of membership (and influence from) the broader community of democratic European nations. His conclusion is optimistic (1992, 81): "Remnants of past debilities survive, of course, but the future sorrows and joys of the region will no longer be so especially its own, but will be shared with most of the rest of Europe".

The 'curse of Southern Europe' had apparently been lifted. But looking back more than twenty years later makes that optimism seem rather misplaced—and the "sharing of sorrows" between Southern European countries and their Eurozone counterparts in the current period limited to difficult and divisive debt bailouts.

In considering further the extent to which the past is still visible in the social, political and economic topography of the European south, the 'Southern Europe joins the European mainstream' argument is articulated more fully by Gunther et al. (2006a) who argue that historical legacies and 'leapfrogging' are both manifest in the contemporary period. In a statement that could have been written by Andrew Janos, Gunther et. al. write that "Since southern Europeans were historically and culturally close to the dominant nations of Europe, they fervently wanted to follow in the paths set by Britain, France and Germany and had many fewer mental reservations than those held by non-European societies […] Therein lies the source of the frustration and despair so characteristic of Southern European history in the nineteenth and much of the twentieth centuries […] Even though a great deal was accomplished […] their distance from those who had once been their equals or inferiors could not but torment them" (2006a, 24).

And yet, Gunther et. al. subsequently argue (2006a, 27) that under the combined impact of transformative processes—socio-economic development, democratization and Europeanization—Greece, Italy, Portugal and Spain have each, in their own way, "succeeded in shedding their old 'exceptionalist' identity as constitutive parts of a region regarded as the 'backwater of Europe'. They have thus assumed the characteristics of modernity, "approximating the general attributes associated with the advanced (post)-industrial societies and democracies in Western and Northern Europe." This is also true, they argue, for the state which, although in the past both 'heavy' and 'weak', leading to 'impaired functionality' (2006a, 10), has undergone such extensive transformation since the seventies "as to gradually alter most aspects of the ideal type derived from its traditional organization of behavior" (2006a, 27). Overall, they stress that, "This dimension of macro-level change implies a clear rupture with the traditional conceptualization of Southern Europe as a palimpsest or even as a museum where all layers of facets of the distant and more recent past survived intact or, at the very least, remained visible, coexisting with structures of the present" (2006b, 362).

Political change, Gunther et. al. insist, has been "so sweeping that no significant vestiges" of predecessor authoritarian regimes or more distant political traditions survived into the democratic period. 'Leapfrogging' trajectories of change can be identified in the political parties, campaign politics and related patterns of electoral behavior that have allowed Southern European countries "to skip over developmental stages" characteristic of other democracies earlier in the 20th century (2006b, 360). There is not much scope here for Sapelli's 'anomic division of political work'. Socio-economic change has been less far-reaching, they argue, but European integration has forced economic sectors to liberalize and become more efficient—creating a similar rupture to the past found in the political realm. And yet they do find "unanticipated time lags" in efforts to reform the bureaucracy, labor law and the structure of social welfare, arguing that "Archaic and dysfunctional features of state structures or policies have proven difficult to dislodge or reform" (ibid.). But they also maintain (2006b, 358–361) that, due to important differences among the four countries, "there is no longer a single 'model' of the Southern European state that can be regarded as a valid description of structures and practices today".

This brief survey of the historical-developmental approach to studying Southern Europe leaves us with roughly convergent views (Sapelli, Tortella and Malefakis) regarding the tortuous path taken by the countries of the region to what one could call 'incomplete modernization', but disagreement regarding the nature of the destination. Sapelli (1995) sees the legacies of the past manifest in weakly-developed political parties, plagued by patronage and 'personalistic' (e.g., factionalized) organization, as well as in the perpetuation of a 'non-Weberian state', in which legal-rationalism has been hard to enshrine. Yet Tortella, Malefakis and Gunther et al., consider that the path-dependent and highly problematic modernization of the region has been broken by socio-economic development, the end of dictatorship in Spain, Italy and Greece and by Europeanization under EU membership. From this perspective then, the puzzle remains as to the extent to which path-dependence or path-departure prevails in these political and economic systems. Part of the problem lies in the absence of a theory that would help avoid ad hoc assessments and establish more precisely the nature of continuity and change.

The work of José María Maravall helps illuminate the conceptual path forward. Like Janos (1989) Maravall (1997) compares southern and central-eastern European political and economic transitions in their respective periods of democratization. His analysis of Southern Europe looks at background commonalities (their legacy of late development); differences (e.g.

the contrasts between the economic growth of Italy after the 1950s compared to the sclerosis of the autarkic dictatorship economies of Portugal and Spain); their differential but equally poor adjustment to the post-oil shock economic crisis of the seventies; the joint enterprise of 'modernization' that all southern countries engaged in under Socialist parties in the eighties and nineties but which in all cases were founded on the contradictions of southern 'neo-corporatism' (i.e. negotiating the modernization of the economy and demands for redistribution with fragmented interest organizations), particularly pernicious tradeoffs between the search for economic efficiency and the reduction of inequality, and the problems afflicting the political parties themselves—i.e., internal divisions, corruption and weakening support from an increasingly mistrustful public. The issue, then, is how to identify the origins of what Maravall (1997, 139–146) describes as the 'Southern European syndrome'—i.e., the economic, social, cultural and political conditions that confront and constrain projects of modernization in Southern Europe much more so than in the continent's north.

Theorizing Southern European Socio-Economic Systems

The following analysis cannot cover the entire spectrum of factors that have prevented a completion of the modernization projects discussed by Maravall, but in discussing some rather complementary theoretical approaches, one can begin to place the study of the region in a framework that allows the identification of some of the critical common variables at play. If theory and the hypotheses it generates are consistently and systematically deployed it will allow for successive iterations of empirical investigation that, in turn, can help build out and even revise the framework. In this section I outline several attempts to provide greater conceptual clarification to the question of Southern European political and economic development—using Emmanuel Wallerstein's World System Theory, the 'Varieties of Capitalism' approach developed by Peter Hall and David Soskice, and analysis in the theoretical tradition of Gøsta Esping-Andersen's 'Worlds of Welfare Capitalism'.

World-System Theory and 'Semi-Peripheral Development'

Interestingly, in the seventies and eighties, studies of relations between the 'center and periphery' in the Marxisant political economy tradition of World-System theory (e.g., Wallerstein 1979) reached similar conclusions regarding development lags in Southern Europe to the historical perspectives of Sapelli, Tortella and Malefakis. Thus, although contributors to Arrighi's (1985) group study of Southern European 'semi-peripherality' (i.e. its middle position between the developing, or peripheral, and developed, or core, capitalist worlds) could not agree on whether Southern Europe existed as an analytical category, with an over-arching form of political-economic development, they did come up with some useful observations. While Gunther et al. reject the idea that Southern Europe is somehow semi-peripheral, Arrighi et al make the following points that (a) coincide with some of the key arguments made by economic historians and (b) translate well into the other theoretical models discussed below:

1. That within their semi-peripheral location vis-à-vis the 'core', each of the four countries (Italy, Portugal, Spain and Greece) has undergone a form of political and economic development with substantial internal hierarchies, unevenness and economic disequilibria—or dualism–that has deepened over time.
2. That one of Southern European semi-peripherality's most distinguishing characteristics has been the dependency of its uneven forms of economic development on foreign capital. Outside of Italy's and Spain successful industrial regions, much of Southern Europe has the industrial development of third-world countries, with poor long-term growth prospects, creating a peripheral/semi-peripheral divide within the region and within the countries that comprise it. Uneven and dependent industrialization has failed to provide solid foundations for employment creation, and has generated migrant labor flows northwards and flows of capital investment southwards from the core. The legacies of that form of industrialization can still be found today;
3. That in the process, an important political and economic divide developed between traditional land-owning and commercial classes, oriented towards mercantilism and authoritarian rule, and 'modern' commercial and industrial capitalists increasingly interlocked with international capital; and

4. That the slow and incomplete transition from 'immature' to 'mature' capitalism has seen the persistence of territorial dualism, a high proportion of small firms in all Southern European countries, and the continued importance of sub-sectoral and clientelistic, economic linkages between the state and economic actors.

The limits of the analysis in this volume (and a source of disagreement among its contributors) are found in its failed attempt to draw clear links between developments in the political economy of the region and political organization and behavior. But the focus on political-economic linkages between the European periphery, or 'semi-periphery', and the core remains useful, first, in understanding the underlying reasons for ongoing uneven development in the region, and second for the hypotheses it raises–still quite pertinent today–regarding the nature of the relationship between 'northern' and 'southern' European capitalism. I will return to this point below. But first, the insights of a more recent contribution to the study of comparative political economy—the 'varieties of capitalism' approach—can help refine what we know about Southern European political economies.

'Varieties of Capitalism' and 'Mixed-Market Economies'

The 'varieties of capitalism' approach (or VoC) (Hall and Soskice 2001) develops a model of two ideal-type national economic systems (liberal market and coordinated market economies—or LMEs and CMEs for short), with rather precise logics underpinning them, and provides a heuristic device for analyzing both those economies that closely approximate the ideal types as well as those that depart from them in significant ways—including what Molina and Rhodes (2008; 2011—from which the following draws) have referred to as the 'mixed-market economies' (MMEs) of Southern Europe. In addressing the particular characteristics of Southern European 'mixed-market economies' I will make reference to various insights derived from the various literatures discussed above.

One of the core insights of the 'varieties of capitalism' school of analysis is that the institutions of a nation's political economy will tend to encourage investment by firms and other actors in particular kinds of assets—specific or co-specific assets (dependent on cooperation and strategic interaction) in coordinated market economies and more flexible, switchable assets in liberal market economies (Hall and Soskice 2001). Actors will become committed to the continuation of a given activity where such assets are applied: actors that have invested in particular institutional arrangements are likely to mobilize more readily to protect their investment by opposing change or pursue incremental changes that maintain a high return on those investments.

These forms of actor interaction are well understood for liberal and coordinated market economies. The capacity to defend specific or co-specific investments is determined to a large extent by the organizational characteristics of core interest groups, i.e., trade unions and employer organizations. In coordinated market economies, well-organized socio-economic actors have invested in institutions that produce a range of collective goods. An example is Germany's co-determination system and sectoral industrial relations framework, the resilience of which is underpinned by the strength of the labor movement and an employer-employee, cross-class consensus and coalition. Both employers and employees share an interest in protecting their comparative institutional advantage and maintaining the complementarities it produces for firms. Neo-liberal de-regulation will be resisted. By contrast, in liberal market economies (such as the United Kingdom), weaker employer and union organizations cannot produce as easily the collective goods or autonomous forms of coordination that support investment in specific assets. Complementarities come instead from the opportunity structures of more fluid markets. Coalitions in favor of higher levels of institutional regulation find it hard to mobilize support, and reform is more likely to be driven by a market-making logic.

However, mixed-market or 'hybrid' political economies–such as those Molina and Rhodes argue are found in Southern Europe–will typically combine both market and non-market forms of coordination. While unions and employers in Southern European mixed-market economies tend to have stronger organizational structures than in liberal market economies, they tend to be more fragmented and weaker than in coordinated market economies. Thus, while they are unable to deliver the same coordinated market-type collective goods, or create strong autonomous forms of coordination (in collective bargaining, for example), they frequently do have the power to veto change and/or demand compensation from the state. Maravall (1997) refers to this phenomenon as a particular Southern European variety of 'neo-corporatism' rendered problematic by internally divided and numerically weak—but symbolically powerful–labor movements across the region.

The centrality of a 'heavy but weak' state in such systems (given equal attention, despite their differences, by Sapelli, Tortella and Malefakis) is critical in defining the core characteristics of the Southern European economies. The form of state, and the reaction to, and involvement in it, of organized interests in Southern European capitalism is quite distinctive and important for understanding complementarities (i.e. institutional relationships that facilitate economic development) and non-complementarities (institutional relationships that impede it) in these systems:

1. in Southern Europe's 'semi-peripheral' development the exertion of strong veto powers by organizationally weak socio-economic interests has limited investment in either specific or co-specific assets (e.g. training and skills provision) and has contributed to serious coordination failures—in wage bargaining, the regulation of the work place and the management of social and employment protection;
2. since coordination failures have often been met by (weak) state intervention, processes of adjustment are typically dependent on the gate-keeping role of the state, much more so than in, say, Germany's more coordinated market economy;
3. although the incentives for specific and co-specific asset investment are limited, there have been strong incentives to invest in one kind of asset—political power—creating strong clientelistic links or mutually-supportive relations between political parties and their flanking organizations, including trade unions; and
4. the state's role in correcting for coordination deficits will therefore often be accompanied, and sometimes subverted by, 'compensation' (subsidies, protection) demanded by interest organizations in return for cooperation (rather than the much more difficult to achieve coordination).

Semi-peripheral development has also had a legacy for these countries' social systems that remain distinct–despite important policy convergence on those of Northern European countries in recent decades. Thus, disparities of income, labor market and educational opportunities–and life chances as a whole–are often acute in these countries, as reflected, for example, in the highly unequal distribution of employment and unemployment between the Italian *Mezzogiorno* and the regions of the center and north, and between different regions in Spain. As Maravall (1997, 190–192) argues, although successful in expanding welfare provision in the eighties in all Southern European countries, the Socialist parties in government during the period (and their left and center-right successors thereafter) faced enormous problems in rectifying the kinds of labor-market dualism and consequent inequalities that continue to characterize the region.

These reform-resistant economic disparities are linked to the political, cultural and class disparities that persist in these countries of uneven growth, which to some extent also coincide with contrasts between pre-industrial and increasingly post-industrial areas and populations. These disparities lie, for example, behind a particular southern type of social exclusion, linked to lower average incomes, higher income inequality, a higher poverty rate and a greater reliance of households on social protection transfers which, nonetheless, tend to be less effective in alleviating poverty than in Northern Europe (Ferrera 1996). At this point, another research agenda—influenced heavily by Esping-Andersen's 'Three Worlds of Welfare Capitalism' approach—becomes pertinent for deepening our understanding of the ways in which Southern European production systems and social systems interact.

Southern Europe's Social Systems

The development of social policies of various types—ranging from social security and health care to employment promotion—has arguably occurred against a particular background–one of social heterogeneity, territorial disparities–and in the context of resource constraints and inadequately institutionalized state structures. Though with substantial variation across the countries of Southern Europe, clientelistic rather than 'rational-bureaucratic' forms of administration have undermined the effectiveness of policy and helped fuel undisciplined spending. Partly as a result of this type of uneven, interrupted and incomplete welfare state development, traditional 'pre-industrial' forms of welfare—provided by the family and charitable institutions—remain much more important than elsewhere and remain essential for filling certain important welfare protection gaps (see, for example, Ferrera 1998; Rhodes 1997a, 1997b).

The heuristic framework provided by Gøsta Esping-Anderson's (1990) 'Worlds of Welfare Capitalism' (WWC) assists in our understanding of production system-social system interaction in the South. Like the varieties of capitalism approach, Esping-Anderson's WWC analysis allows the Southern European welfare states to be located in relation to a broader theoretical framework. The core argument in WWC is that various welfare systems can be assessed in terms of their levels of de-commodification (the extent to which a welfare state separates insurance against individual risk of poverty, sickness, loss of work and 'social exclusion' from the market) and the ways in which welfare programs 'stratify' a society via rules of access and entitlement. The heuristic framework identifies three 'worlds of welfare' that combine these characteristics in different ways: the liberal, social democratic and continental-conservative systems—with Southern Europe seen as part of the continental cluster.

The Southern European group of Italy, Spain, Portugal, and Greece clearly does resemble the Continental family (especially in its Bismarckian system of social insurance), but with specific institutional traits (Ferrera 1996; 1998: the following summary comes from Hemerijck, Keune and Rhodes 2006). Thus, benefit coverage reflects a mixed orientation: Bismarckian in income transfers, with especially generous pensions, but Beveridgean (typically a feature of liberal welfare states such as the UK) in health care, with fully universal national health services in both Italy and Spain. The social safety net of basic benefits is under-developed. Social charges (i.e., taxes on employers and employees) are widely used, but general taxation is becoming more important in financing social services. The family is still a significant source of care and support, and makes up for deficits in the welfare system, but has adverse implications for the position of women in the household and the labor market. Inadequate administrative capacities reinforce poor social policy implementation and, in some cases, clientelism.

Like continental countries, Southern European countries also suffer from low employment rates, especially among young people, women, and older men, and are under pressure to transform their pay-as-you-go pension systems—which they have gradually been doing (and have been forced to do during the financial and economic crisis), though the political obstacles are many. Job stagnation is partly related to payroll-based social insurance financing which encourages high productivity and low employment-creating investment.

These problems also have adverse consequences for fertility, labor supply and ultimately welfare state viability. Low birth rates are linked to the difficulties facing young people seeking work and affordable housing and childcare. Women are thus forced to choose between careers and forming families and young people experience protracted dependence on their parents. Higher female employment rates are needed to counteract population aging, reduce household poverty risks and underpin the financial sustainability of the southern welfare systems.

With demographic shifts (population aging) and relatively early retirement across the region (until very recently) fewer workers have to support a growing number of inactive benefit recipients—thereby creating a serious 'inactivity trap' which reinforces traditional patterns of social exclusion and dualistic divisions between well-protected 'insider' workers and underprivileged 'outsiders' in the production system, including young people and women.

This kind of dualism spanning the production regime and the social protection system is a particularly strong example of the 'negative complementarities' found in Southern European capitalism. Intervention by a 'weak but heavy state' has tended to perpetuate such divisions. Poor state regulation will tend to perpetuate long-term inefficiencies because of the collective action problems that ensue. In the absence of mechanisms for collective goods provision, or a state too independent and powerful to resist vested interest demands, actors will tend rationally to pursue their independently-defined interests. 'Positive complementarities'—the outcome of coordination between freely-contracting actors–are extremely difficult to build.

A Southern European Logic of Socio-Economic Adjustment

The Southern European-specific logic of socio-economic adjustment is therefore very different from that found either in liberal or coordinated market economies. Liberal market economy reform can be rapid due to majoritarian political systems and the relative absence of veto players. In coordinated market economies, institutional change–even when exogenously induced—will proceed slowly and incrementally to accommodate veto constraints and recalibrate institutional sub-systems, tending to produce a 'bottom-up' accommodation of political preferences into the macro-level tier of national policy making. But in Southern European economies, the weaker (and less productive) linkages between institutional sub-systems of the economy (wage bargaining systems; industrial training; employment policy; unemployment support) make them more vulnerable to the disruptive effects of exogenous shocks (such as the oil price shocks of the seventies, and the financial crisis of 2008–10) and reduce the likelihood of concerted efforts to manage them.

The weakness of foundations for coordination at the micro- and meso-levels of the economy impedes the formation of stable cross-class alliances either across or within sectors. Sporadic concertation provides a mechanism for governments and socio-economic actors to resolve certain forms of distributive conflict, partially compensating for coordination deficits and increases, the overall governability of the system—though arguably to a greater extent in Spain and Italy than in Greece (Rhodes 2008).

Critically for economic development, it can be argued that the 'hybridity' of the Southern European mixed-market economies, combining some liberal market and coordinated economy characteristics, with features of their own derived from a common process of late and highly uneven industrialization, has some serious consequences for economic performance and adjustment to external shocks. This is where the consequences of 'negative complementarities' can be most clearly detected—as in the following chain of institutional and organizational characteristics that perpetuate collective action problems:

- fragmented or weak employers and union organizations (and the latter's syndicalist tradition) forestall cooperation both in and above the firm;
- the large universe of micro-firms also prevents sectoral coordination beyond the large-firm sector (e.g. in Italy's industrialized north;
- (weak) state intervention to foster human capital development is therefore unsupported by inter-firm networks;
- and compliance with labor law is also undermined by the same factors, producing large unregulated 'underground' parts of these economies.

The resultant collective action deficits prevent not just the autonomous creation of cross-firm 'club goods', notably in systems of training and investment in human capital formation, but also state-driven solutions—contributing to long-term productivity problems, as manifest in very poor levels of multi-factor productivity growth in the last two decades across the Southern European countries.

The Recent Financial and Economic Crisis and its Aftermath: *Crónica de una Muerte Anunciada*?

In the contemporary period, the collective action deficits discussed above have led to one of the most critical common problems facing the Southern European economies—poor long-term productivity performance and declining competitiveness vis-à-vis the core European economies, especially

Germany, but also perhaps vis-à-vis the emerging, semi-peripheral 'dependent' market economies of Central and Eastern Europe.

The consequences of weak competitiveness, low levels of collective action capacity and inadequate social and employment policy have been revealed across the multiple economic crises that have confronted European economies since the seventies: Southern European countries' responses to the oil price shocks of the seventies (producing unemployment and high inflation), the crisis of the early nineties (which pushed up unemployment) and the recent financial and economic crisis (triggering low growth and high unemployment) have all been less successful than in the Northern European countries. In the most recent crisis, while the coordinated market economies to their north (notably Austria and Germany) could rapidly elaborate working hours reduction schemes to modulate responses to a decline in demand, protecting both firms and their workers from labor redundancies and disruptions, in the south only in Italy was there a partial and functional equivalent found in the concerted expansion of the existing system of unemployment support for workers in large firms (*cassa integrazione guadagni*) to smaller-firm sectors (Perez and Rhodes 2015).

Since the late nineties, Southern European productive systems, fiscal systems (spending and taxing), redistributive systems (welfare states) and labor markets have all been affected by (a) the process of bringing debts, deficits and inflation levels into line with the EMU membership criteria, (b) by the consequences of closer integration with the core European economies, and (c) by the impact of the financial and economic crisis since 2008.

The consolidation of membership of 'Europe' by joining the Eurozone was seen by many among Southern Europe's cosmopolitan elites as the ultimate guarantor that the 'remnants of past debilities' would be removed once and for all, and that their 'joys and sorrows' would be shared with the rest of Europe, to cite Malefakis (1992, 82). Giulio Sapelli (1995, 15) articulates that aspiration for a 'rescue by Europe' thus: "The common market could perhaps produce exogenous shocks for social and state rationalization through the diffusion of meritocratic and contractual systems that those nations were unable to express by themselves". But the transformative power of EMU turned out to be a delusion—one arguably due to hubris, over-optimism, and perhaps also to inattention among European political and economic elites to the path-dependent characteristics of the 'Southern European model'.

How can we link—provisionally at least—those path-dependent characteristics to the problems facing the Southern European economies in the wake of the recent crisis? First, echoing Janos's historical analysis of what he calls the 'international demonstration effect' in consumption (Janos 1989; 2000), Costas Fernandes and Mota (2011; 2013) argue that the domestic roots of the financial and economic crisis in Southern Europe are to be found in the 'non-mature nature' of Southern European democracies–or more precisely in the predisposition of individuals, families and governments to emulate the behavioral patterns of their more affluent counterparts in the North, building up high levels of both private and public debt in the process: "the attainment of higher education levels by a population long repressed by previous dictatorships in their ability to follow other countries' consumption patterns has pressed for high government expenditures, as opposed to the conservative fiscal preferences exhibited by the more developed and mature countries" (Costas Fernandes and Mota 2013, 300). The problem with this hypothesis is that it is hard to falsify; and across the region one finds high household savers (Italians), and thrifty governments (Spain) as well as undisciplined spenders.

Nevertheless, some evidence can be found for this thesis. As Barry Eichengreen (2010) argues regarding the timing and origins of the imbalances and competitiveness problem in the southern Eurozone, there was evidence of real exchange rate appreciation and real overvaluation in the euro-area periphery already in 2002—evidence that differential inflation rates exceeded what could be explained by Balassa-Samuelson (i.e., economic catch-up) effects. Meanwhile savings seemed to decline in the countries of the euro-area periphery more rapidly than the positive wealth effect of lower interest rates and the positive income effects of faster growth due to the availability of foreign finance could explain.

Second, real exchange rate appreciation in the face of capital inflows, which clearly damaged Southern European competitiveness, should not distract us from the combined consequences of some of the factors referred to in the schematic, model-based analysis of Southern Europe above. The expansion of the small firm sector (sometimes, as in Italy, to evade labor market regulation) and the use of low-skilled labor, has adversely affected productivity gains, while low levels of spending by firms on training across the region (except for very large firms), a lack of capacity for collective goods provision, and large informal labor markets, all sustain a bias towards low-skill and low-tech activities. As Silva and Teixeira (2012) explain, Italy, Portugal and Spain experienced a decline in productivity growth after 1995 which was far more intense than at the broad European level, while growth accounting exercises show that poor multifactor productivity growth was the main source of the productivity slowdown. This is the key structural problem—the result of the 'negative complementarities outlined above–underlying weak Southern European economic performance. Italy—the most industrialized of the Southern European economies–has seen its specialization increase in lower value added, lower-skilled sectors, since the nineties (Buti 2009); and processes of reform over the last two decades have failed to put in place the foundations for a different kind of future growth (Simoni 2012).

The longer-term weaknesses of the Southern European economies—as revealed by their declining export performance—have, it is true, been exacerbated by external factors, in particular the adverse effects of financial flows to the southern Eurozone preceding the crisis, with consequences that these countries have been institutionally ill-equipped to respond to. As Chen et al (2013) argue, "while trade shocks [in the late nineties and early two thousands] would have required real effective exchange rate depreciations in debtor countries to restore external sustainability in the long run, intra-eurozone capital inflows and the trend in the euro nominal exchange rate contributed instead to further real appreciation, which further affected export performance". They also note the effect of "credit booms, with increases in domestic prices and unit labor costs inconsistent with underlying productivity gains and with the external budget constraint". A major consequence of these shifting terms of competitiveness was that the rise of China (and more generally of emerging Asia) displaced Southern European countries' exports from some of their traditional foreign markets. Rapid growth in China (and other emerging market economies) boosted the demand for goods, such as machinery and equipment, exported by Germany, and by some other core European economies, but had much more limited benefits for southern European countries' exporters.

Of course, being coupled closely inside a single currency zone with Germany—a 'Mercedes Benz economy', with extraordinary adjustment capacities, as argued by Hancké (2013)–is a large part of the problem. Contemporary adjustment of Germany and the other core European economies have altered the dynamics and interdependencies between them and the European semi-periphery, with some positive results for some of the Central and East European economies, but with less positive ones for the South.

As Guerrieri and Esposito (2012) explain, a good part of the post-crisis imbalances in the Eurozone are related to the pre-crisis international reorganization of the German (coordinated market) production system. Outsourcing to Eastern Europe has been a central part of this production restructuring, and the consequential reduction of costs has been coupled with German wage restraint (internal devaluation), enhancing the competitiveness of German firms and increasing its trade surplus with the Southern European semi-peripheral countries. Given the weaker adjustment capacities of the latter, as explored above, those countries were unable to pursue a similar strategy, and their firms' capacity for innovation has been further damaged by the consequences of the crisis (Archibugi and Filippetti 2011; Simonazzi, Ginzburg and Nocella 2013).

Importantly, as the World Bank has noted (see Raiser and Gill 2012), the kind of foreign direct investment (FDI) flows that Southern Europe expected from closer integration with the core European economies has now been supplanted by the growth of investment flows from Europe's core economies, especially Germany, to the Central and Eastern European Economies. As a result, although still poorer on many measures than the more developed parts of Southern Europe, Central and Eastern European 'semi-peripheral capitalism' is beginning to look preferable in some ways its Southern European version. As indicated by the preliminary 'varieties of capitalism' analysis of Southern European mixed-market economies above, the Southern semi-peripheral economies are lacking in some of the core complementarities that benefit both their liberal and coordinated market economy counterparts—making them less than ideal locations for foreign direct investment. Low levels of investment in both human capital formation and in fixed capital (with particular deficits in information and communications technologies) distinguish Spain, Italy, Portugal and Greece both from coordinated-market Germany and the Nordic social market economies, as well as from the liberal-market UK, which while also low in human capital investment in manufacturing, excels in both low and high-skilled services and ICT fixed capital investment (Sakamoto 2012).

Recent studies of the CEE countries reveal that Southern Europe seems also to lack the kinds of complementarities now to be found on Europe's Eastern 'semi-periphery', that are making some of its countries very attractive to inward investors–and not just to Germany which has incorporated significant parts of those economies into its industrial supply chains. Nölke and Vliegenthart (2009) describe these assets as "institutional complementarities between skilled, but cheap, labor; the transfer of technological innovations within transnational enterprises; and the provision of capital via foreign direct investment". In a supply- and demand-side analysis, Bert van Ark et. al. (2013) contrast the dynamism of the German-Austrian-CEE 'outward-looking', globally-oriented, supply chain system with that of the structurally weak and 'inward-looking' Mediterranean group, that includes France. European peripheries in competition—just one more problem, and a very serious one, for the Southern European variety of capitalism.

Conclusions: The 'Southern Model' in Social Science

The aim of this chapter has been to examine historical and comparative political economy approaches to the study of Southern Europe, and to identify some background developmental factors and their contemporary manifestations. The various approaches discussed are complementary to one another and an exploration of their potential as explanatory 'models' (by which I mean their systematic identification of the key characteristics shared by these counties) provides the critical first step towards understanding the institutional, political, and socio-economic nature of the region. They do not provide all the answers, or even the correct answers to questions regarding the existence of what Sapelli (1995, 19) purports to be "distinct and specific socio-economic formation" and "personality" in Southern Europe. But they do provide us with a framework for seeking answers to those questions, and in my analysis above I have pointed to some useful (preliminary) explanations.

The utility of these approaches is that, once adapted for the analysis of Southern Europe, they have a specific and purposefully limited heuristic ambition: to identify inductively certain kinds of system 'logic' that can then be used to generate hypotheses for subsequent deductive investigation. If those hypotheses are not confirmed in sufficient number, then the model can be revised. A common response, however, is to deny that utility based on the following criticisms: either that a model is deficient if it cannot describe, explain and account for all of the detail in the arena under analysis; or that a 'model' (as in 'the Southern model') fails because it purports to show that all countries in the region are identical—which is clearly not true, and something no one would claim was the case. This misunderstanding stems from methodological confusion. The real intent behind the construction of a 'model' is to create a point of departure for analysis, not to finalize the analysis itself.

Not all of the elements in these approaches can be combined or integrated with one another. Sometimes in social science concepts (and the existence of a 'Southern European model' appears to be one of them) are "essentially contested"—in other words there is no final resolution to the debates. Yet those contested concepts continue to retain heuristic value. The solution to competing notions in social science is not necessarily the fusion or integration of theories: it is the creation of competing hypotheses that are then investigated in opposition to one another. Following from that point, it has not been my intention–in this chapter at least–to extract elements from these debates and reject some in favour of others. I do not have a 'thesis' regarding the existence of a 'Southern model' beyond stating that the hypotheses that emerge from the debates surrounding it have a continued salience and therefore provide heuristic value, but only if they are treated with skepticism and used for the purposes of conducting analysis, not for leaping to unjustified conclusions. To the extent that it is useful to have a 'model' at all, this is one in which there is a cluster of hypotheses which take us closer to some kind of 'truth', without necessarily ever getting there. The journey is more important than reaching the destination.

Works Cited

Archibugi, Daniele, and Andrea Filippetti (2011). Is the Economic Crisis Impairing Convergence in Innovation Performance across Europe? *Journal of Common Market Studies*, 49:6, 1153–1182.

Arrighi, Giovanni (ed.). (1985). *Semiperipheral Development: The Politics of Southern Europe in the Twentieth Century*. Beverly Hills, California: Sage Publications.

Buti, Marco (ed.). (2009). *Italy in EMU: The Challenges of Adjustment and Growth*. Palgrave: Macmillan.

Chen, Ruo, Gian Maria Milesi-Ferretti, and Thierry Tressel (2013). Eurozone Imbalances. *Economic Policy*, January, 101–142.

Costa Fernandes, Abel L., and Paulo R. Mota (2011). The Roots of the Eurozone Sovereign Debt Crisis: PIGS vs Non-PIG. *Panoeconomicus*, 5, 631–649.

Costa Fernandes, Abel L., and Paulo R. Mota (2013). "The Euro Zone Peripheral Countries" Sovereign Debt Crisis: Also a Case of Non-Mature Democracies? *Panoeconomicus*, 3, 291–310.

Diamandouros, P. Nikiforos, Richard Gunther, Dimitri A. Sotiropoulos, and Edward E. Malefakis (2006). Introduction: Democracy and the State in the New Southern Europe. In Richard Gunther, P. Nikiforos Diamandouros and Dimitri

A. Sotiropoulos (eds.). *Democracy and the New Southern Europe*, 1–41. Oxford: Oxford University Press.

Eichengreen, Barry (2010). Imbalances in the Euro Area. mimeo, University of California, Berkeley, November. URL: http://emlab.berkeley.edu/~eichengr/Imbalances_Euro_Area_5–23–11.pdf

Esping-Andersen, Gøsta (1990). *The Three Worlds of Welfare Capitalism*. Princeton, New Jersey: Princeton University Press.

Ferrera, Maurizio (1996). The "Southern Model" of Welfare in Social Europe. *Journal of European Social Policy*, 6:1, 17–37.

Ferrera, Maurizio (1998). The Four Social Europes: Between Universalism and Selectivity. In M. Rhodes and Y. Mény (eds.). *The Future of European Welfare: A New Social Contract?* Palgrave: Macmillan.

Guerrieri, Paolo, and Piero Esposito (2012). Intra-European Imbalances, Adjustment, and Growth in the Eurozone. *Oxford Review of Economic Policy*, 28:3, 532–550.

Gunther, Richard, P. Nikiforos Diamandouros, and Dimitri A. Sotiropoulos (eds.). (2006a). *Democracy and the New Southern Europe*. Oxford: Oxford University Press.

Gunther, Richard, and P. Nikiforos Diamandouros (2006b). Conclusion. In Richard Gunther, P. Nikiforos Diamandouros and Dimitri A. Sotiropoulos (eds.). *Democracy and the New Southern Europe*, 338–362. Oxford: Oxford University Press.

Hall, Peter, and David Soskice (2001). *Varieties of Capitalism: The Institutional Foundations of Comparative Advantag*e. Oxford: Oxford University Press.

Hancké, Bob (2013). *Unions, Central Banks and EMU: Labour Market Institutions and Monetary Integration in Europe*. Oxford: Oxford University Press.

Janos, Andrew C. (1989). The Politics of Backwardness in Continental Europe, 1780–1945. *World Politics*, 41:3, 325–358.

Janos, Andrew C, (2000). *East Central Europe in the Modern World: the Politics of the Borderlands from Pre- to Postcommunism*. Stanford, California: Stanford University Press.

Malefakis, Edward (1992). Southern Europe in the 19th and 20th Centuries: An Historical Overview. Center for Advanced Study in the Social Sciences, Juan March Institute, Madrid.

Malefakis, Edward (1995). The Political and Socioeconomic Contours of Southern European History. In Richard Gunther, P. Nikiforos Diamandouros and H-J. Puhle (eds.). *The Politics of Democratic Consolidation: Southern Europe in Comparative Perspective*, 33–76. The Johns Hopkins University Press.

Maravall, José María (1997). *Regimes, Politics and Markets: Democratization and Economic Change in Southern and Eastern Europe*. Oxford: Oxford University Press.

Molina, Oscar, and Martin Rhodes (2008). The Political Economy of Adjustment in Mixed Market Economies: A Study of Spain and Italy. In B. Hancké, M. Rhodes and M. Thatcher (eds.). *Beyond Varieties of Capitalism: Conflict, Contradiction and Complementarities in the European Economy*, 223–252. Oxford: Oxford University Press.

Molina, Oscar, and Martin Rhodes (2011). Spain: From Tripartite to Bipartite Pacts. In S. Avdagic, M. Rhodes and J. Visser (eds.). *Social Pacts in Europe: Emergence, Evolution and Institutionalization*, 174–202. Oxford: Oxford University Press.

Nölke, Andreas, and Arjan Vliegenthart (2009). Enlarging the Varieties of Capitalism: The Emergence of Dependent Market Economies in East Central Europe. *World Politics*, 61:4, 670–702.

Perez, Sofia, and Martin Rhodes (2015). The Evolution and Crises of the Social Models in Italy and Spain. In Jon Erik Dølvik and Andrew Martin (eds.). *European Social Models, Inequality and Employment in the Era of Monetary Integration: From Crisis to Crisis*, 117–213. Oxford: Oxford University Press.

Raiser, Martin, and Indermit S. Gill (2012). *Golden Growth: Restoring the Luster of the European Economic Model.* Washington, DC: World Bank. URL: https://openknowledge.worldbank.org/handle/10986/6016

Rhodes, Martin (ed.). (1997a). *Southern European Welfare States: Between Crisis and Reform.* London: Frank Cass.

Rhodes, Martin (1997b). Southern European Welfare States: Identity, Problems and Prospects for Reform. In Rhodes (ed.). *Southern European Welfare States: Between Crisis and Reform*, 1–21. London: Frank Cass.

Rhodes, Martin (2008). Desperately Seeking Consensus: Policy Reform in Greece in Comparative Perspective. In M. Carlos (ed.). *The Challenge of Social Policy Reform in the 21st Century: Towards Integrated Systems of Social Protection*, 333–361. Athens: Kritiki Publishing.

Sakamoto, Takayuki (2012). Three Worlds of Productivity Growth: Human Capital Policy Profiles and Productivity Growth Outcomes. URL: http://ssrn.com/abstract=2150552 or http://dx.doi.org/10.2139/ssrn.2150552

Sapelli, Giulio (1995). *Southern Europe Since 1945. Tradition and Modernity in Portugal, Spain, Italy, Greece and Turkey.* London and New York: Longman.

Schneider, Ben Ross (2013) *Hierarchical Capitalism in Latin America: Business, Labor, and the Challenges of Equitable Development.* Cambridge and New York: Cambridge University Press.

Simoni, Marco (2012). *Senza alibi: Perché il capitalismo italiano non cresce più.* Venezia: Marsilio Editore.

Tortella, Gabriel (1994). Patterns of Economic Retardation and Recovery in South-Western Europe in the Nineteenth and Twentieth Centuries, *Economic History Review*, 47:1, 1–21.

Silva, Ester G., and Aurora A.C. Teixeira (2012). In the Shadow of the Financial Crisis: Dismal Structural Change and Productivity Trends in South-Western Europe over the Last Four Decades. WWWforEurope: Workshop on European Governance and the Problems of Peripheral Countries, July 12 and 13, Vienna. URL: http://www.foreurope.eu/fileadmin/documents/pdf/Ester_Silva_and_Aurora_Teixeira_Paper.pdf

Simonazzi, Annamaria, Andrea Ginzburg, and Gianluigi Nocella (2013). Economic Relations between Germany and Southern Europe. *Cambridge Journal of Economics,* 37:3, 653–675.

Van Ark, Bart, Vivian Chen, Bert Colijn, Kirsten Jaeger, Wim Overmeer and Marcel Timmer (2013). Recent Changes in Europe's Competitive Landscape and Medium-Term Perspectives: How the Sources of Demand and Supply Are Shaping Up. *European Economy,* Economic Papers No. 485, April. European Commission: Directorate-General for Economic and Financial Affairs.

Wallerstein, Immanuel (1979). *The Capitalist World-Economy.* London: Cambridge University Press.

Southern Welfare States. Configuration of the Welfare Balance between State and the Family

Claude Martin

Since the mid-nineties, following the publication of Esping-Andersen's seminal book, "The Three Worlds of Welfare Capitalism" (1990), a discussion has developed about the hypothesis of a fourth welfare regime: a Southern European one, i.e. a common model shared by Italy, Spain, Portugal and Greece. Some authors argued that common traits justify the existence of a Southern or Mediterranean ideal-type beside the continental, liberal and universalist ones,[1] while others considered the Southern configuration as a late development of a continental regime, possibly with some historical, institutional and cultural specificities (Katrougalos 1996).

After having reached its acme in the nineties, this discussion was rediscovered recently, on the occasion of the 25th anniversary of the publication of Andersen's crucial and inspiring book. The debate still concerns the characteristics and specificities, the significant differences and gaps in Southern Europe compared to other welfare state regimes. In other words, the main question is the following: to what extent does the Southern configuration add anything relevant to the previous main dimensions of Esping-Andersen's model, in terms of social stratification, decommodification of the labor force and nexus of protection in the triptych–state, family and market? Looking back, it seems as if this debate arose only due to the discussion related to Esping-Andersen's model; a discussion which, in the end, seems weakly connected to the broader literature on the historical making of Southern Europe.

However, unquestionably, the historical context of this scientific debate has changed drastically in the last three decades. Just to give an idea of this huge variation of context, we could, for example, distinguish between, first, the period of integration into the European Economic Community (EEC) of Greece (1981) Portugal and Spain (1986), which were just democratizing after having lived through a long period of dictatorships and autocratic regimes, when Italy was already considered one of the classical Bismarckian

1 See table 1, p. 84 below for the characterization of this typology.

welfare states; second, the spectacular modernization of these four countries in the nineties which leads to a debate concerning the "New Southern Europe" with "the crucial role played by welfare state programs in the anchoring of democratic institutions and in promoting social cohesion and economic growth" (Ferrera 2010, 617); and finally, the current situation where these four Southern countries are qualified PIGS[2] in Europe—a terrible acronym used once again in economics, finance and media since 2008—and some of them have been taken over by the Troïka since 2010. These variations over time explain different contradictory comments addressed to Southern European countries depending on the period: "Portugal as Europe 'star pupil'" in the beginning of the nineties, or the "success of Spanish economy" in the early two thousands; comments which contrast peculiarly with the current picture of these countries.

Is it still useful to reactivate this academic discussion about the relevance of another welfare state model in the South in 2015? It could seem a bit superfluous when considering the tremendous impact of the 2008 financial crisis on Europe and particularly on Southern European countries; an impact which may lead to the risk of Europe dismantling like an area suffering the retorts of an earthquake. Do we still need a confirmation of a Southern configuration when looking at the social and economic conditions of European citizens in Greece, Portugal, Spain and Italy, or the situation of the health and pension systems or social services in these countries?

I argue that the 2008 financial crisis spurs the revisiting of that discussion, not the scrapping of it. But more than a pure reproduction of the debate initiated 25 years ago, it is necessary to consider national trajectories or, to put it differently, to abandon the discussion concerning ideal-types and prioritize the processes of change and capacities of resilience of the different welfare systems. Southern European welfare states are under radical threats and some media and political comments suggest that they are just imploding. But it is crucial to consider that this extremely negative economical context affects all Europe without exception. This means that we are in a very different or even reverse situation compared to the eighties and nineties: the one where continental countries, like France in particular, could follow the Southern European track, as many other Mediterranean countries such as

2 Some comments in newspapers add Cyprus and Ireland (a quasi-Southern liberal state), and also sometimes France and the UK, to this stigmatized group.

Cyprus, Malta or even Turkey or Israel already do, an "extended family of Mediterranean Welfare states" (Gal 2010).

In the first section of this paper, we propose to come back and synthesize the main arguments of this debate since the nineties and argue that this discussion is crucial, not only for academic or theoretical concerns, of course, but also to think of the present of Europe and offer a guide for understanding the general process of restructuring European welfare states. On the one hand, as stated by Luis Moreno (2008), one has to consider that the changes in Southern European countries during the last twenty years were such that some of these countries, like Spain, followed a 'Nordic path', which means that changes overthrew the initial configuration of the ideal-type. But, on the other hand, the analysis of the Southern configuration is also useful beyond the South to figure a Southern path or trajectory which could be followed by other countries (like France, at least) under certain conditions. Among them, and following Kees Van Kersbergen and Philip Manow (2009), we consider that religion and churches are crucial in welfare framing as they explain particular political coalitions which are still at stake at the moment. This theoretical orientation could serve social scientists in interpreting some current phenomena and trends.

In the second part, we focus on one of the characteristics of Southern configuration underlined in the nineties: the central role of the family as a source of protection against risks and vulnerability, or a social bumper. The question nowadays is not only the transfer of responsibility for social problems from the state, or even local authorities, to the family in a shedding process but the careful investigation of, first, the transformation of the family itself in the meantime and also of the emergence of new social risks which are challenging caring capacities of our societies. Families have transformed substantially in all European countries, particularly due to the increasing number of women in the labor market, but also as Luis Moreno and Pau Mari-Klose argue, due to the succession of generations which radically transform social expectations and practices (Moreno and Mari-Klose 2013). This revolution of the gender division of labor hugely modifies the question of care, caring task, care workers, respective roles of formal and informal carers, etc. This variable plays a crucial role in understanding simultaneously the process of change and the capacity of resilience of welfare systems in the South but also in many other nations.

Lessons from the Welfare State Discussion Concerning the South of Europe

Inclusion or Exclusion of the South in the Welfare State Modeling Business

At the risk of being too simplistic, one could identify different and main phases in the welfare state comparisons that will progressively become a "welfare state modeling business" (Abrahamson 1999). The first one (from the Second World War to the late eighties) was mainly concerned with a historical, developmental and/or genealogical perspective, as the main issue, for many analysts, was to understand how industrialization was progressively accompanied by different systems of regulation and protection against some risks due to a "huge transformation" (Polanyi 1944). In Polanyi's terms, this process was less a functional link between industrialization *per se* and a growing need for social policies, but rather the necessity to compensate the development of a full-fledged market where human society became an "accessory of the economic system" (Polanyi 1957 [1944], 73). Here comes the idea that labor became a commodity in a self-regulating market as well as, even if not expressed as such by Polanyi,[3] the necessity to decommodify it to avoid the destructive impact of the economic market logic on traditional forms of protection: bonds of kinship, family ties and guilds.

Robert Castel adopts a similar perspective. In his seminal book *Les métamorphoses de la question sociale*, Castel proposes a genealogy of the "salariat" (the salary system), following its transformation since the *ancien régime*, to show the protecting role of social and labor laws, which allowed an alternative form of property, a "social property", for those without material property to protect themselves against life's risks (Castel 1995). Castel also put emphasis on the interconnected role of employment contract and protection of relatives in the individualization process of modern societies. As he stated himself: "No individual without supports". (Castel 2009, 443).

According to this perspective, many authors insisted on the tempo of modernization and its effects on the process of definition of the welfare systems (Rimlinger 1971; Wilensky 1975; Flora and Heidenheimer 1981). In this process, steps of development and a large series of variables were identified: institutional and economic variables, historical events, configurations

3 Polaniy's terms were more to "domesticate the market".

of actors and coalitions, political mobilization, circulation of ideas, learning processes, etc. Two main matrixes were also underlined: a Bismarckian and a Beveridgian one in two different historical contexts: revolutionary menace of the working class and fear of the development of the International socialist movement in Prussia at the end of the 19th century; adaptation of the British welfare system in the context of the warfare economy at the request of Ernest Bevin, Minister of Labor under Winston Churchill in 1940, to prepare the post-War reforms. One of the limits of this genealogical angle of understanding was probably its insistence more on common mechanisms and instruments, whatever the political and institutional background of each nation state, than on differences. As Kees van Kersbergen stated: "The prime explanatory problem for these theories concerns the very existence of, rather than the variation among, Western welfare states" (van Kersbergen 1995, 10).

These matrixes and the description of their national variations across Europe opened a second period, which ended at the end of the 20th century. The main issues concerned comparative frameworks and propositions of ideal-types. Following some pioneers, like Richard Titmuss (1974), this new phase gave rise to a very rich discussion about the characteristics and number of ideal-types. Esping-Andersen's seminal book, *The Three Worlds of Welfare Capitalism*, synthesizes brilliantly this discussion as it reviews the main arguments in the academic literature, builds a specific theoretical framework and defends a typology which provoked an intense discussion all at the same time. It is precisely in this context of intense debate about typologies that the idea appeared to distinguish a "Latin rim", "Mediterranean", "Catholic", "southern" type of welfare system, but also some other "families of nations" (Castles 1993) from the Post-Soviet to Asian and Confucian nations (Jones 1993). But the comments on this seminal book did not focus only on the number of ideal-types, but also on other crucial issues like gender, which changed the global picture of national differences drastically (Lewis 1992; Sainsbury 1994).

A new phase has developed since the turn of the last century, when research focused on the process of change at stake, qualified in various ways by the ideas of dismantling, downgrading, and recalibrating welfare systems and sometimes also converging and liberalizing them (Pierson 1994; Svallfors and Taylor-Gooby 1999; Esping-Andersen et al. 2002). The question of the level of change becomes central (Hall 1993). Taking into account a series of reforms since the end of the nineties, this literature questions the capacity of governments to adapt their respective welfare systems. Contrarily to Esping-Andersen's initial diagnosis, which insisted on the inertia of Bismarckian's original pact which made it a "frozen welfare regime", many authors suggest nowadays that a progressive, but very deep change has finally occurred even in the frozen landscape (Palier 2010; Palier & Martin 2008). This new phase has also given rise, since the 2008 financial crisis, to a new crucial issue concerning the resilience of these societies and nations, their capacity for adaptation confronted by common threats and challenges (Hall and Lamont 2009; Hall and Lamont 2013; Crouch 2015).

Main Arguments to Consider a Southern Model

Esping-Andersen's typology in the *Three worlds of Welfare Capitalism* generated many critiques and comments; at least two main types of comments: first about the capacity of this typology to include all the national welfare systems in Europe and more largely in developed countries, a discussion which also raised the question of the adequate number of ideal-types; and second, more fundamentally, about the gender issues and the limits of Esping-Andersen's theoretical framework to catch gender inequalities, caring issues and defamilialization of caring tasks (see the seminal paper by Jane Lewis 1992).

Maurizio Ferrera (1996) and Martin Rhodes (1996) are among the first who exposed the arguments for a specific Southern European welfare regime (see also Moreno 1996). In his 1996 paper, Ferrera noted that: "unfortunately, the academic debate has so far largely neglected the study of the south European Welfare states" (Ferrera 1996, 18). Mainstream literature during the eighties and nineties indeed treated Southern European countries generally as "late-comers on the same path as that followed by other continental, 'conservative-corporatist' nations" (ibid.) or argued that these countries only "reflected the delay in the construction of the welfare state and more generally the relative economic underdevelopment of the Mediterranean South" (Katrougalos 1996, 43). Only a few authors insisted on the specificities of these "Latin rim" countries: the rudimentary character of the welfare programs, the influence of Catholicism on their framing and the prominent role of the family as a social bumper, but hesitated to define these specificities as an ideal-type (Leibfried 1992; Castles 1993).

In his first attempt, Ferrera tried nevertheless to compile a preliminary descriptive list of features, without expecting *a priori* to formulate a real ideal-type. Looking at the four main Southern European countries (Italy, Spain,

Portugal and Greece), he developed some hypotheses to explain these specificities, not by underdevelopment or delay, but with a historical-institutionalism perspective. The first feature of this "Latin rim" regime concerns the cash benefits which are highly fragmented and corporatist-driven (mainly pensions), in particular in Italy and Greece (which is also the case in France, a partly Southern and Mediterranean country as well), but also very dualistic with a clear opposition between overprotected insiders (the "citadels of *garantismo*": the regular white-collar labor force, public employees, and the labor force of large enterprises) and outsiders (irregular workers, traditional services, agriculture, but also the female labor force and youth). Both Ferrera and Rhodes mentioned "peaks of generosity" and "gaps of protection". A second feature, quite counter-intuitive for a continental Bismarckian orientation, is the adoption of a universal health care system: national health services (since 1976 in Portugal, 1978 in Italy, 1983 in Greece, and 1986 in Spain), a circumstance which justifies the expression of a "hybrid" model. But this turn to universalism appears to hide paradoxes like a public/private mix of services, which resulted in an enormous waste of public money; an incomplete shift of funding from contributions to taxes; a dual structure of services as these national health services are in fact mainly targeted to the most vulnerable groups; etc.

Compared to the continental welfare regime, the Southern configuration has other specificities, for instance the role of political discretion, which is very different from the administrative or professional discretion role and comes close to "electoral manipulation of welfare benefits" (Ferrera 1996, 25). The absence of a long tradition of technocracy (compared to France, for example), "the weakness of state institutions, especially in terms of bureaucratic professionalism and autonomy, the failure to modernize the civil service in a 'Weberian' sense prior to the mass expansion of welfare programmes has offered a fertile ground for the persistence of clientelistic relations" (Ferrera 1996, 30), which may justify using this qualification for the ideal-type. Ferrera and Rhodes also insist on the necessity of distinguishing between Northern and Southern regions at least in Italy and Spain, as these Northern regions are closer to the conservative/ continental/ corporatist regime than to the respective Southern regions; "the persistence of backwardness in many 'South of the South'" (Ferrera 2010, 617).

In summary, these authors mentioned a series of characteristics: strongly gendered labor markets; a substantial shadow economy with the important role of the informal labor market; the weakness of state intervention; the absence of a state technocracy; clientelism or persistence of "patronage systems" to distribute cash subsidies to political client groups; important territorial disparities; and last but not least, the expansion of these systems at a time when other continental welfare states were already confronted with the need to restructure. This accumulation of features finally demonstrated the necessity of complementing the three classical worlds of welfare (see Table 1).

Table 1: Four Welfare State Regimes

Welfare state regimes	Liberal minimalist	Southern clientelist	Conservative corporatist	Social democratic universalist
Aim of the system	Regulation of poverty; needs' satisfaction through the market	*Dualistic cover of social risks (over-protection of core /regular workers and under-protection of vulnerable and atypical workers)*	Social protection of male workers	Universal access to high level of benefits and services to all citizen
Norms of access	Means-test	*Work and citizenship (in principle)*	Work	Citizenship
Financing	Taxes (+) & contributions (-)	*Contributions (+) and taxes (-)*	Contributions	Taxes
Regulation	Central state	*Clientelist local state*	Unions	Decentralized state
Nexus of solidarity	Market	*Family*	Family	State
Level of decommodification	Weak	*Weak*	Medium	High
Level of defamilialization	+	– –	– –	+ +
Level of social protection	Weak	*Moderate*	High	High

Various authors (Andreotti et al. 2001; Karamessini 2008) developed some additional features and hypothesis: the weight of small-scale farming and the role of migrations. As far as social stratifications are concerned, Southern Europe seems also characterized by the weight of the self-employed and small farmers in particular, even after the democratic transition. The self-employed and small landholders are not generally considered defenders of collective agreements and social protection systems, at least in South and Western Europe.[4] A weaker position of the state, a toleration of tax-evasion and informal labor, self-reliance and family solidarity could be the results of the weight of the self-employed in the social structure, a group which had a weaker voice in the political arena.

Andreotti et. al. (2001) also insist on the impact of migration, an important flux of male population toward Northern countries in the fifties and sixties which provoked a real hole in the work force. For Andreotti et. al., migration and a low level of proletarianisation represent two major elements to explain the Southern Europe configuration:

> "Waves of emigration helped to slow the process of proletarianisation. By removing labor from local market, migration allowed a smooth transition from agriculture to an industrial economy. The relatively low level of proletarianisation, and conversely, the persistently high level of self-employment are both important characteristics of the south European model, as they have heavily influenced its structure" (Andreotti et al. 2001, 44).

Karamessini even argues that "emigration policy may be viewed as a functional equivalent of employment policy until the mid-1970s", as it prevented mass unemployment (Karamessini 2008, 521). One can also understand emigration as a determinant factor to explain the "weak industrialization" in the South of Europe, underlined by Sapelli (1995), or a heavy price to pay during the transition to modernity.

Centrality and weakness of the state go hand in hand with strength and marginality of the family and the third sector, that is to say with the weakness of civil society and all its consequences like the weakness of universalistic principles or strength of corporatism, clientelism and specific arrangements with the rules. With such a social structure and configuration, Southern European welfare systems are less the result of social movements and mobilization and often preceded democratization.

These aggregated factors generated important disparities and a particular "southern type of poverty linked to lower average incomes, higher income inequality and a higher poverty rate" (Rhodes 1996, 8). But, as Rhodes stat-

4 Nordic countries offer another configuration with powerful agrarian parties defending universalist flat-rate social policies. "Agrarian parties in the north voice resistance against the income-differenciated social benefits that Social Democrats favored. Instead, they preferred universalist, flat-rate benefits because many small landholders had no long history of steady income and therefore feared that they would actually be unable to benefit from welfare entitlements that were contribution financed with contributed-related benefit levels" (van Kersbergen and Manow 2006, 27).

ed: "Perhaps more important than economic disparities as such are the quite different political, cultural and class disparities that persist in these countries of uneven growth, which to some extent also coincide with contrasts between pre-industrial and increasingly post-industrial areas and populations" (ibid.).

In their first insights, Ferrera's and Rhodes' gave priority to developmental factors and explained the Southern road from a politico-institutional perspective. Even if it seemed possible at first glance to subsume Southern European countries under the continental/conservative regime, they argued that "the 'socio-political etiquette' which inspires their functioning is hugely different" (Ferrera 1996, 29). First, because of the traces or even stigma of authoritarian regimes and rules, which may explain at the same time the resilience of institutional traditions, like corporatism, a traditional atrophy of civil society, but furthermore, the radicalization of a Left excluded from government for significant periods of time, remaining in this way rigid defenders of their political clienteles in the work force, even at the expense of more vulnerable workers.

And here come the crucial arguments concerning political conflicts and coalitions and their specific combination in Southern Europe, linked to the fight between the state and the Catholic church. Following van Kersbergen's work about Christian democracy and the link between religion and the welfare state (van Kersbergen 1995), Kees van Kersbergen and Philip Manow (2009) gave particular attention to the crucial role of the electoral and political party systems, considering that "countries cluster on policy because they cluster on politics" (Shalev 2007, 289). They intend to explain the difference between Social Democrats and Christian Democrats when looking at the role of religion in Western welfare states framing. They reveal two different coalitions in each configuration:

"The Social Democratic generous welfare states, which we find in the Nordic countries, have been the result of a coalition between Social Democratic parties and parties of agrarian defense (red-green coalition). One important precondition for this coalition has been the absence of a strong religious cleavage in the Scandinavian countries. On Europe's continent, in turn, we find welfare states that are the product of a coalition between Social and Christian Democracy (red-black coalition). This is due to the fact that the second cleavage represented in the party systems of continental Europe, besides the dominant left-right or labor-capital cleavage, has been the religious cleavage, a cleavage inherited from the state-church conflicts in the wake of the national revolution in which Liberal states' elites challenged the church in its former domains such as education or poor relief" (Van Kersbergen and Manow 2009, 22).

This perspective is very relevant to catching Southern European welfare state specificities. In a recent paper, Philip Manow goes further and argues:

"The fundamental character of the political conflict reveals the explanatory limits of an argument based *solely* on socio-economic analysis. In these conflicts, religion becomes relevant, first in the explanation of the totalitarian episodes of the southern countries—since religion renders coalitions between workers and peasants impossible and thereby fosters the fascist path. These totalitarian episodes are then, second, an important explanatory factor for the persistence of political polarization in the postwar period, inter alia manifested in the fragmentation of the left in their party systems" (Manow 2015, 37).

For this author, this combined religious/political factor is crucial in each mono-confessional Southern country, as it explains at the same time the radicalization on the right and on the left side of the political arena: the reactionary and anti-republican Catholicism since the 19th century, the rift between a reformist and a radical left wing, and finally the "spiral of fear and mutual repulsion backed by violence until each side feels its very existence endangered by the other" (Martin, 1978, 17), which explains the war "à l'outrance", to use David Martin's expression to describe this "Latin pattern" and the violent shock between massive secularism and massive religiosity, between a clerical right and an anticlerical left.

"The split between communist and social-democratic parties in the countries of southern Europe (Italy, Spain and Portugal, but also France)… is closely related to the decidedly anti-republican position held by the Catholic church in the mono-denominational Catholic countries of Europe's South, since the deep divide between a sharp anticlerical labor movement and pious farmers under close tutelage of the church left the political left without allies for a reformist strategy" (Manow 2015, 33).

These religious and political factors explain, much better than the economic one, the difference between Nordic, Continental and Southern countries, all of them concerned with a late industrialization. When a political alliance between small-holding farmers and workers was possible in the Northern (Protestant) countries, it was clearly rejected, "due to non-economic reasons" (Manow 2015, 40) in the Catholic South, marked by the violence of the confrontation between pious rural classes and the Marxist workers' movement.

Family as a Nexus of Solidarity

Among the specificities of the Southern welfare state regime, a consensus emerged concerning the role of the family as a central nexus of solidarity. Maurizio Ferrera underlines "the importance and resilience of the family as a sort of clearing house for the welfare of its members—with significant implications in terms of gender" (Ferrera 2000, 168).

Many authors insist on this feature of the Southern configuration (see Flaquer 2000, Naldini 2003; Ferrera 2010; Gal 2010), which draws a specific familialist care regime:

"In Southern Europe, it is taken for granted that it is up to households to provide for the welfare of their members and therefore no emphasis is placed on family policy. This is why citizens in these countries give the family the top priority on their value scale. Their levels of well-being depend more on family arrangements and connections than on the provisions of welfare state institutions. This is what causes at the same time the force of kith and kin and the reproduction of a system based on a limited amount of family-friendly public measures" (Flaquer 2000).

"The family has historically been the cornerstone of South European societies, functioning as an effective 'social shock absorber' and welfare broker for its members and responding to a wide range of risks and needs, from childcare to unemployment, from care for the elderly to disabled and housing" (Ferrera 2010, 622).

But the interpretation of this phenomenon, or the hypothesis to explain it, is a controversial issue. On one side, some argue that family is "culturally" a nexus of protection in the South in the sense that people develop a peculiar sense of family and mutual solidarity based on legal obligations within the kinship. But on the other hand, it seems more appropriate to consider that family solidarity is precisely a result of this Southern (political more than anthropological) configuration itself, and not so much one of its foundations. And if it is so, what could be the impact on the Southern welfare model of the huge transformations of family structures and practices, of the evolution of gender roles, of new private expectations, of individual claims, etc.?

Familialism took a particular orientation in Southern Europe that Saraceno and Keck named "familialism by default" or "unsupported familialism" (Saraceno and Keck 2010).[5] Effectively, the absence or weakness in public in-

5 We can mention that "familialism by default" concerns a larger group of countries than the four Southern European countries under scope in this discussion, including Poland and Bulgaria (Saraceno and Keck 2010).

terventions, subsidies and services to support families in their caring activities and responsibilities is a specific sort of familialism; a very different one compared to "supported familialism" developed in some other countries, and even more clearly a different choice than the one adopted in countries which give priority to "defamilialization" of caring tasks by supporting households to externalize part of these tasks to services and professionals, but also to employees in the formal or informal labor market. In a comparative perspective, it is clear that de-familialization is one of the main conditions which promote female employment, and thus female social citizenship.

We argue with these authors that (large) family solidarity or protection by close relatives (what we have called in French the "protection rapprochée", Martin 2000) is thus a result of this absence of support in the long run. Without these supports, families are *forced* and *required* to assume many caring responsibilities towards children, youth and elderly, but also towards many other vulnerable groups like handicapped or chronically ill people. They *have to do so* as there is not any real alternative. This family nexus of solidarity also explains the relatively marginal role of social assistance and, of course, also the high level of poverty, as family solidarity is certainly not a way to reduce inequalities, but rather a factor which increases them (Martin 2004).

This configuration was effectively dominant in Southern Europe until recently. And it was clearly the case in the eighties and the beginning of the nineties, when the literature on welfare regimes developed. But wasn't this family nexus of solidarity also dominant in many other Western and Nordic countries just after the Second World War, which pleads for the hypothesis of an effect of long-term change more than of national variations?

In Southern Europe, this family responsibility had also drastic secondary impacts on family reproduction and gender, as underlined by Maurizio Ferrera:

> "The lack of external supports and opportunities as regards housing, transfers and services has started to restrict the range of choices for young people and to act as a clear obstacle for family formation (marriages) and family expansion (children)… a problematic syndrome is emerging in this area: an institutional configuration originally built to serve the family is now working to erode its own foundations by discouraging, precisely family reproduction" (Ferrera 2000, 172).

Such a configuration put care obligations and the care work/burden on the shoulders of women, which means that "familialism by default" is also a typical gender model based on the "male breadwinner—female perfect housewife" contract. To figure this arrangement and its consequences and pathologies, Ferrera speaks of a "southern syndrome" characterized by: "Low rates of female employment, especially in Spain, Italy and Greece, and partly also the dramatic decline of fertility among women sandwiched between heavy home duties and unfriendly labour markets" (Ferrera 2010, 623).

But the main impact concerns intra-familial dependency, a gender and generational dependency. Family can be considered as a cornerstone of South European societies, as welfare is organized as a specific arrangement between the state, local authorities and households. The important thing seems to be to guarantee a minimal income to the household (or sometimes a network of households) by the access for at least one member (generally a man) of a family network to a permanent protected job and status, while the others remain dependent of this main male breadwinner. Even informal economy is connected to this "arrangement", when it allows working families to earn additional incomes through marginal activities and avoid taxes on the second income. Of course, this arrangement has had many negative consequences and generated a vicious circle in terms of insiders and outsiders, but also in terms of family trajectories:

> "In this pattern, rigid labor laws protected male workers who were heads of the family (male breadwinner model), undermining the possibilities of employment for women and young people. The direct consequences have been low adult male unemployment rates and high rates of female and youth unemployment. Their exclusion from the labor market has been functional to maintaining the system and reenforced the familial culture" (Andreotti et al. 2001, 54).

We argue, however, that this arrangement is not a "cultural trait", but rather a way or a strategy for the members of families to face adversity and compensate, as best as they can, for the absence of public support. It reveals a private and collective mechanism which corresponds probably to the famous family bumper against life's risks.

> "Under these conditions, crossing the formal / informal divide constitutes part of an array of family strategies to pool resources, and thus 'informality' does not absolutely reflect a rigid insider / outsider divide in labor market terms. It is mostly in respect of the steadily new forms of atypical work (i.e. short-term contract) in southern Europe, and the influx of immigrants lacking the capacity to benefit from family, kin support (and clientelistic ties) that the insider / outsider divide became more pronounced in labor market terms, requiring new policy measures" (Petmesidou 2013, 185).

From our perspective, the specific role of families in Southern European welfare regimes does not result from a common "cultural" heritage, but from the general institutional framework. In other words, we do not need to assume the existence of a "Southern European family model" in terms of a long-term cultural heritage.

The main victims of this state /household and family arrangements are unmistakably women and young people, particularly confronted with dependence from their parents and the necessity to accommodate in a context where the access to permanent jobs is almost impossible. The level of intergenerational cohabitation is one of the indicators of this phenomenon, very frequent in Southern European countries (Van de Velde 2008).

But this centrality of the family does not mean only conservative reproduction of gender roles or intergenerational domination. At the same time, as Trifiletti (1999) argues, considerable changes have occurred in Southern societies and emancipation of women and young people is also developing, but in a very different way: an emancipation 'within the family'. Andreotti et al. observe in this regard:

> "This does not mean that women are not emancipated. While in northern Europe, women emancipate from the family, finding their place mainly *outside*, in paid—very often part-time—employment, in southern Europe women emancipate *within* the family, doing the same care work, in the same professional way, with the only difference that they do it for their families. In this sense, women in southern European states represent the link between the family and the state, as they deal with modern public democracy (i.e. hospitals, schools, public administration) and family needs" (Andreotti et al. 2001, 51).

A Rapid Public and Private Revolution: but a Stop and Go Process

The threats to the future of the Southern European welfare system were clearly exposed almost twenty years ago. Martin Rhodes put it this way already in 1996:

> "The coming years will be critical ones for the southern European countries, as they adjust their economies, administrative cultures and welfare states to pressure from

beyond their borders—including the consolidation of the single market, EMU[6] convergence and greater competition in more open world markets. To some extent, these pressures will lead to greater conformity, in terms of budgetary disciplines, the rationalization of bureaucracies, the reduction of clientelism and attacks of anomalies in taxation and benefits … None of this means that the basic features of the 'southern syndrome' will disappear over night " (Rhodes 1996, 19).

Taking the current economic indicators, looking at the present situation in Greece, Spain or Portugal, it seems that the threat is just becoming a reality. But such a shortcut would minimize the enormous demographic, sociological and economic changes that occurred in the meantime, between the end of the nineties and the financial crisis of 2008. Taking these changes into account, we could consider more the half-full rather than the half-empty glass and insist on positive aspects like the adaptability and the capacity to recalibrate the Southern welfare systems.

Indeed, many major reforms were adopted and implemented in the meantime: reduction of the generous guarantees (especially in the field of pensions) for the privileged occupational groups; improvement of minimum income and social benefits; adoption of safety-nets; expansion of childcare and elderly care services to support families; development of family policy measures that were almost inexistent previously (like parental leaves, for example) ; promotion of gender equality; measures against the black economy (that previously represented between 15 to 30% of the GDP) and tax evasion; reform of labor market legislation; development of social dialogue in industrial relations; rapid tertiarization of the labor market; reduction of self-employment, etc. Thus, despite their characteristics and handicaps, Southern European countries have changed radically.

Maurizio Ferrera recently confirmed this process of change:

"Welfare state building has followed a distinct path, characterized by weak Fordism, dualistic social insurance, and faulty and fragmented social assistance. However, under the spur of European integration, the 1990s and 2000s have witnessed substantial efforts to recalibrate and further modernize the welfare state, with the view to achieving more efficient and equitable labor markets, more sustainable and internally more homogeneous social insurance systems and a more effective and inclusive safety-net" (Ferrera 2010, 627).

And, in parallel, public opinion about family life but also about family practices has changed drastically (Moreno and Mari-Klose 2014). Once again,

6 Economic and Monetary Union criteria.

it is not a process of change per se, just coming from the inside of the family. Family change and modernization are directly connected to the transformation of the labor market but also to educational attainment: increase in literacy rates; rise of the number of university graduates, development of women's employment rates; development of the number of bi-active households in accordance with EU norms and incentives and centrally generational change. And this evolution impacts feed-back on the Southern welfare state model deeply, generating new demands and expectations, new claims but also disappointments.

Looking at the Southern Europe employment model, Karamessini argues: "From the beginning of the eighties onwards, a transition towards a dual-earner family model can be identified accompanied by a spectacular upward trend in female activity and employment" (Karamessini 2008, 522). Indeed female employment rates increased in the four main Southern European countries: from 40% in 1983 to 60% in 2007 in Greece; from 38,8% to 59,3% in Italy; from 58,8% to 75,3% in Portugal and from 29,4 to 63,7% in Spain. These changes still vary between countries (more effective in Spain and Portugal than in Italy and Greece) and of course also between regions. When comparing the changes in Italy and Spain, Naldini and Jurado (2012) argue, for example, that "Spain is moving towards a dual earner family model, while in Italy the family kinship solidarity model is still prevalent". Moreno also argues that the Spanish welfare state already followed the 'Nordic path' (Moreno 2008).

These changes during the nineties and the first decade of the 21th century, compared to Western Europe, indicate a clear convergence. We can even argue that this process of modernization is close to the one that characterized many other Western and even Nordic countries at another phase of their respective development and modernization. The process is unique, but the track, the pace, the direction and the conditions of this transformation vary depending on the countries, from the core of capitalism to the semi-periphery of it. The challenge nowadays concerns the impact of the economic crisis on this deep generational change. As Luis Moreno and Pau Mari-Klose put it: "Since recent times, the Mediterranean welfare regime, and in particular its capacity to perform as a social 'shock absorber' and a generous supplier of welfare activities in the informal domain, is facing challenges generated by new lifestyles and emerging social needs of young generations" (Moreno and Mari-Klose 2014, 494).

Concluding Remarks: Lessons from the South

One of the main lessons of this discussion about welfare state ideal-types is certainly the complex interaction between familial protection versus state and collective protection, i.e. "the balance sheet of the critical nexus between family and welfare" to use Ferrera's terms. Recent events and official reports underline this balance shift between state, market and family. Just to give an example: "The 'White Paper on Welfare' issued by the Italian Labor Ministry in mid-2009 clearly resonates the retrenchment of public provision by stressing that 'the current balance between state, market and family should be shifted in favour of more market, more family, and less state'" (Petmesidou 2013, 191).

The financial crisis since 2008 has amplified this challenge. And we argue that in such a context, Southern Europe's experience (i.e. Italy, Spain, Portugal and Greece), with this stop and go process, could be a guideline for learning, not only for many other Southeastern countries (such as Romania, Bulgaria, Albania, Croatia, Macedonia and even Turkey), which share many similarities with their Southern counterparts,[7] but also for the rest of Europe confronted with the development of "new social risks", which don't fit with the anterior social pact and the insurance mechanism built up after the Second World War.

But one can also consider that the Southern European experience could be helpful in considering the huge transition that most if not all European welfare systems are facing in order to adapt themselves to what has been called "new social risks". Peter Taylor-Gooby defines theses new risks as: "the risks that people now face in the course of their lives as a result of the economic and social changes associated with the transition to a post-industrial society" (2004), for example, supporting a frail elderly parent in a context of rapid aging of the population; long-term unemployment and long-standing exclusion from the labor market; raising children as a single parent; difficulties in conciliating work and care, etc. All European welfare systems are confronted with these new social risks and the adaptation or recalibration of the previous welfare systems is difficult everywhere.

7 Ferrera is defending such a position concerning the Southeast of Europe when he argues: "Given many similarities, it can be suggested that South-Eastern Europe is likely to embark upon a path to welfare state building which will bear many resemblances with that followed in the past by Greece, Italy, Spain and Portugal (probably in this order)." (Ferrera 2010, 628).

For example, most European countries are developing long-term care policies and in particular "cash for care" schemes with different ways of financing (payroll taxes, taxes, private insurances) and also with the recourse to informal care work and sometimes development of a migrant workforce (Bettio et al. 2006; Le Bihan et Martin 2010 and 2012; da Roit and Weicht 2013). The rapid aging of the population and the considerable increase in fragility and vulnerability of the 'older olds' are challenging our welfare systems.

Gender and generational inequalities are becoming main issues in this respect and it seems quite obvious that the previous system of actors and interest groups (social classes, professional corporations) which were managing the 'old social risks' are not used to these new challenges and it seems difficult to identify a new set of actors capable of representing the new population's needs and claims. Moreover, such inevitable reforms are challenging all the welfare systems which are used to social agreements and the issue of decommodification when the new challenges impose the consideration of recommodification and flexibility.

In their process of change, we argue that Southern European countries have at least demonstrated important capacities of adaptation and that many lessons could be learned from their situation. Taking just an example of the way we could use this debate to analyze another national case, let's turn to the French configuration. According to Philip Manow's perspective, France is clearly one of these Southern countries. The current political and media scene gives many examples to confirm this diagnosis: weakness and unpopularity of the current social-democratic government caught between a growing extreme-right movement, a radical shift to the right wing (*droitisation*) of the French population, and victim once again of the split of the left; or the radical Catholic mobilization against same-sex marriage used to reactivate the war between church and state. So, according to Manow's perspective, economically, politically France seems to run on the Southern track. But, of course, the pace of this movement is still uncertain. The balance sheet between state and family is very different from other Southern European countries, as the state is still supporting households with public services, at least in childcare. But this equilibrium is unstable and France could be obliged to prove its resilience in case of accentuation of the economic crisis and rise in unemployment; one of the worst indicators being the level of youth unemployment and the not-held promise of the current President of the French Republic to give priority to young people in his political agenda—a promise which must be kept before the end of the Presidential mandate in 2017.

Following Moreno and Mari-Klose, we argue that all European countries are involved in this paramount mechanism for prompting social change: the succession of generation. As they put it for the South: "The long-standing claim that the family remains the Alpha and Omega institution shaping all prospective scenarios for Southern European welfare is being shacked by unforeseen 'collective impulses' of a new generation" (Moreno and Mari-Klose 2014, 511). Let's keep in mind the role of the generational variable in analyzing the next step for Europe.

Finally, this Southern European welfare model discussion, which complements many other lines of reflection about Southern European specificities seems to be heuristic. Not confusing ideal-types with reality, we recognize the crucial inputs of this discussion and its capacity to help us to understand a complex process of transformation. Even if it is nowadays less important to confirm or not the permanence of the Latin rim regime, this discussion and concept were clearly helpful all along the last three decades in conceptualizing the transition and the process of change. Isn't it precisely the finality of concepts that temporarily help us to think and understand reality? But it is also true that these concepts or questions have to be regularly adapted or revisited in order to follow the process of social change we want to understand (see Castel and Martin 2012).

Works Cited

Abrahamson, Peter (1999). The Welfare Modeling Business. *Social Policy and Administration,* 33:4, 394–415.

Andreotti, Alberta, Soledad Marisol Garcia, Aitor Gomez, Pedro Hespanha, Yuri Kazepov, and Enzo Mingione (2001). Does a Southern European Model Exist? *Journal of European Area Studies*, 9:1, 43–62.

Baglioni, Simone, and Louis F. O. Mota (2013). Alike but Not Alike: Welfare State and Unemployment Policies in Southern Europe. Italy and Portugal Compared. *International Journal of Social Welfare*, 22, 319–327.

Bettio, Francesca, Annamaria Simonazzi, and Paola Villa (2006). Change in Care Regimes and Female Migration: the 'Care Drain' in the Mediterranean. *Journal of European Social Policy,* 16:3, 271–285.

Bonoli, Giuliano (2005). The Politics of the New Social Policies. Providing Coverage Against New Social Risks in Mature Welfare States. *Policy & Politics, 33,* 431–450.

Bonoli, Giuliano (2007). Postindustrialization, New Social Risks and Welfare State Adaptation in Advanced Industrial Democracies. *Comparative Political Studies,* 40, 495–520.

Castel, Robert (1995). *Les métamorphoses de la question sociale. Une chronique du salariat.* Paris: Fayard.

Castel, Robert (2009). *La montée des incertitudes : Travail protections, statut de l'individu.* Paris: Le Seuil.

Castel, Robert, and Claude Martin (2012). *Changements et pensées du changement. Echanges avec Robert Castel.* Paris: La Découverte.

Castles, Francis G. (1993). *Families of Nations. Patterns of Public Policy in Western Democracies.* Aldershot: Hants.

Crouch, Colin (2015). *Governing Social Risks in Post-Crisis Europe.* Cheltenham: Edward Elgar.

Da Roit, Barbara, and Bernhard Weicht (2013). Migrant Care Work and Care, Migration and Employment Regimes: a Fuzzy-Set Analysis. *Journal of European Social Policy,* 23:5, 469–486.

Esping-Andersen, Gøsta (1990). *The Three Worlds of Welfare Capitalism.* Cambridge: Polity Press.

Esping-Andersen, Gøsta, Duncan Gallie, Anton Hemerijck, and John Myles (2002). *Why We Need a New Welfare State.* Oxford: Oxford University Press.

Ferrera, Maurizio (1996). The 'Southern Model' of Welfare in Social Europe. *Journal of European Social Policy,* 6:1, 17–37.

Ferrera, Maurizio (2000). Reconstructing the Welfare State in Southern Europe. In S. Kuhnle (ed.). *Survival of the European Welfare Systems,* 166–181. London: Routledge.

Ferrera, Maurizio (2005). Democratisation and Social Policy in Southern Europe: From Expansion to 'Recalibration'. Draft working document, United Nations Research Institute for Social Development.

Ferrera, Maurizio (2010). The South European Countries. In F. G. Castel, S. Leibfried, J. Lewis, and C. Pierson (eds.). *The Oxford Handbook of the Welfare State,* 616–629. Oxford: Oxford University Press.

Flaquer, Luis (2000). *Family Policy and Welfare State in Southern Europe. Working paper 185.* Barcelona: Institut de Ciencies Politiques I Socials. URL: http://www.recercat.net/bitstream/2072/1280/1/ICPS185.pdf

Flora, Peter, and Arnold J. Heidenheimer (1982). *The Development of Welfare States in Europe and America.* New Brunswick: Transaction Publishers.

Gal, John (2010). Is There an Extended Family of Mediterranean Welfare States? *Journal of European Social Policy,* 20, 283–300.

Hall, Peter (1993). Policy Paradigms, Social Learning and the State. The Case of Economic Policy-Marking in Britain. *Comparative Politics,* 25, 275–296.

Hall, Peter, and Michèle Lamont (eds.). (2009). *Successful Societies: How Institutions and Culture Affects Health.* Cambridge: Cambridge University Press.

Hall, Peter, and Michèle Lamont (eds.). (2013). *Social Resilience in the Neoliberal Era.* Cambridge: Cambridge University Press.

Jones, Catherine (1993). The Pacific Challenge: Confucian Welfare States. In Catherine Jones (ed.). *New Perspectives on the Welfare State in Europe*, 184–202. London: Routledge.

Karamessini, Maria (2008). Still a Distinctive Southern European Employment Model? *Industrial Relations Journal*, 39:6, 510–531.

Katrougalos, George S. (1996). The South European Welfare Model: the Greek Welfare State in Search of an Identity. *Journal of European Social Policy*, 6:1, 39–60.

Kersbergen Kees van, (1995). *Social Capitalism. A Study of Christian Democracy and the Welfare State.* London: Routledge.

Kersbergen Kees van, and Philip Manow (eds.). (2009). *Religion, Class Coalitions and Welfare States.* Cambridge: Cambridge University Press.

Le Bihan, Blanche, and Claude Martin (2010). Reforming Long-Term Care Policy in France: Public / Private Complementarities. *Social Policy and Administration*, 44:4, 392–410.

Le Bihan, Blanche, and Claude Martin (2012). Diversification of Policy Measures in the Elderly Care Sector: Towards Greater Flexibility for Care Users? *European Journal of Aging*, 9:2, 141–150.

Le Bihan, Blanche, Claude Martin, and Trudie Knijn (2014). *Work and Care under Pressure. Care Arrangements across Europe.* Amsterdam: Amsterdam University Press.

Leibfried, Stephan (1992). Towards a European Welfare State. In Zsuzsa Ferge and Jon E. Kolberg (eds.). *Social Policy in a Changing Europe*, 245–279. Boulder: Westview Press.

Lewis, Jane (1992). Gender and the Development of Welfare Regimes. *Journal of European Social Policy*, 2:3, 159–173.

Manow, Philip (2015). Workers, Farmers and Catholicism: A History of Political Class Coalitions and the South-European Welfare State Regime. *Journal of European Social Policy*, 25:1, 32–49.

Martin, Claude (1996). Social Welfare and the Family in Southern Europe. *South European Society & Politics*, Special Issue on Southern European Welfare States, 1:3, 23–41.

Martin, Claude (2000). Famille et précarité : la protection rapprochée. In Michel Joubert et al. (eds.). *Précarisation, risque et santé*, 29–45. Paris: éditions INSERM.

Martin, Claude (2003). The Rediscovery of Family Solidarity. In Trudie Knijn and Aafke Komter (eds.). *Solidarity Between the Sexes and the Generations. Transformations in Europe*, 3–17. Cheltenham: Edward Elgar.

Martin, David (1978). *A General Theory of Secularization.* Oxford: Basic Blackwell.

Moreno, Luis (1996). Southern Welfare State in Transition: Crisis, What Crisis? Issues for a Discussion, Unpublished paper presented at the Conference on Social Research and Social Policy in Southern Europe, National Centre for Social Research in Athens.

Moreno, Luis (2006). Le modèle de protection sociale des pays d'Europe du Sud: Permanence ou changement? *Revue française des affaires sociales,* n.1, 81–105.

Moreno, Luis (2008). The Nordic Path of Spain's Mediterranean Welfare. Center for European Studies Working paper series, n.163.

Moreno, Luis (2013). Spain's Catch Up with the EU Core: The Implausible Quest of a 'Flying Pig' ? *South European Society and Politics,* 18:2, 217–236.

Moreno, Luis, and Pan Marí-Klose (2014). Youth, Family Change and Welfare Arrangements. *European Societies,* 15:4, 493–513.

Naldini, Manuela (2003). *The Family in the Mediterranean Welfare State.* London: Frank Cass.

Naldini, Manuela, and Teresa Jurado (2012). The Institutional Context of Recent Family Changes. Welfare Reorientation in Spain and Inertia in Italy. Working paper for the 10th Annual ESPAnet Conference, University of Edinburgh, September 6–8.

Palier, Bruno (ed.). (2010). *A Long Goodby to Bismarck? The Politics of Welfare Reforms in Continental Europe.* Amsterdam: Amsterdam University Press.

Palier, Bruno, and Claude Martin (eds.). (2008). *Reforming the Bismarckian Welfare Systems.* Oxford: Blackwell.

Petmedisou, Maria (2013). Southern Europe. In Bent Greve (ed.). *The Routledge Handbook of the Welfare State,* 183–192. Oxon: Routledge.

Pierson, Paul (1994). *Dismantling the Welfare State? Reagan, Thatcher and the Politics of Retrenchment.* Cambridge: Cambridge University Press.

Polanyi, Karl (1957 [1944]). *The Great Transformation: The Political and Economic Origins of our Time.* Boston: Beacon Press.

Rimlinger, Gaston V. (1971). *Welfare Policy and Industrialisation in Europe, America and Russia.* New York: Wiley.

Rhodes, Martin (1996). Southern European Welfare States: Identity, Problems and Prospects for Reform. *South European Society and Politics,* 1:3, 1–22.

Rhodes, Martin (ed.). (1997). *Southern European Welfare States: Between Crisis and Reform.* London: Frank Cass.

Sapelli, Giulio (1995). *Southern Europe Since 1945. Tradition and Modernity in Portugal, Spain, Italy, Greece and Turkey.* London: Longman.

Saraceno, Chiara (2013). Family Policies. In B. Greve (ed.). *The Routledge Handbook of the Welfare State,* 381–390. Oxon: Routledge.

Saraceno, Chiara, and Wolfgang Keck (2010). Can We Identify Intergenerational Policy Regimes in Europe? *European Societies,* 12:5, 675–696.

Shalev, Michael (2007). Limits and Alternatives to Multiple Regression in Comparative Research. In Lars Mjøeset and Tommy H. Clausen (eds.). *Capitalism Compared,* 261–308. Amsterdam: Elsevier.

Svallfors, Stefan, and Peter Taylor-Gooby (1999). *The End of the Welfare State? Responses to State Retrenchment.* London: Routledge.

Taylor-Gooby, Peter (ed.). (2004). *New Risks, New Welfare. The Transformation of the European Welfare State.* Oxford : Oxford University Press.

Titmuss, Richard M. (1974). *Social Policy. An Introduction.* London: Allen & Unwin.
Trifiletti, Rossana (1999). Southern European Welfare Regimes and the Worsening Position of Women. *Journal of European Social Policy*, 9, 49–64.
Van de Velde, Cécile (2008). *Devenir adulte: Sociologie comparée de la jeunesse en Europe.* Paris: PUF.
Wilensky, Harold L. (1975). *The Welfare State and Equality: Structural and Ideological Roots of Public Expenditures.* Berkeley: University of California Press.

II. A European Periphery?

The Interruption of Industrialization in Southern Europe. A Center-Periphery Perspective

Annamaria Simonazzi and Andrea Ginzburg[1]

In 2012, Amartya Sen wrote in *The Guardian*: "The problems we are seeing in Europe today are mainly the result of policy mistakes: punishments for bad sequencing (currency unity first, political unity later); for bad economic reasoning (including ignoring Keynesian economic lessons as well as neglecting the importance of public services to European people); for authoritarian decision making; and for persistent intellectual confusion between reform and austerity". He concluded: "Nothing in Europe is important today as a clear-headed recognition of what has gone so badly wrong in implementing the grand vision of a united Europe" (Sen 2012). While there is now rather widespread consensus on the euro's structural design flaws, it is less common to find attempts to identify the distant origins of these flaws in the growth patterns, policy actions and narratives of Southern European countries *before*[2] implementation of the Monetary Union. With no claim to completeness, in what follows we shall try to provide an inevitably broad and rough picture of these developments.

The Embeddedness of Center-Periphery Relations in Time and Space

One of the side-effects of the economic crisis that began in 2007 is the rediscovery of the terms center and periphery to analyze the economic situations of the European countries. However, these terms are not free from ambiguity. For some authors who have developed dualistic European variants

1 We thank the editors for helpful comments and criticisms, without thereby implicating them for the final product.

2 For a contribution to an analysis of the relations between Germany and Southern Europe during the current crisis, see Simonazzi et al. (2013).

of the 'varieties of capitalism' approach initiated by Michel Albert (1991), center-periphery simply refers to two macro-groups of countries, Northern and Southern Europe, considered as *separate* units of analysis. Often with normative intent, these studies contrast German and Latin, or Mediterranean, models both in general and in specific areas (e.g. welfare). Analysis of the *relations* between the center and the periphery thus becomes secondary, while the focus is only on the characteristics common to the countries belonging to the two groups and on their separate evolution. On the other hand, the two terms obviously (at least within economics scholarship) refer to the dependency theory originally proposed in the fifties by Latin American economists. Whilst that theory had the merit of focusing on the aspects of dependence in international relations, it had the weakness of attributing underdevelopment, within a nationalist perspective, only to external circumstances, thereby exonerating national actors from any responsibility. Furthermore, the same dependency relations appeared to be eminently static, in the absence of analysis of the social configurations internal to the two groups of countries and of possible countertendencies[3] to the dependency relations.

With these caveats, it remains true that a center-periphery perspective, defined as the study of the evolution of the center-periphery relations, may be helpful to analyze the dynamics of the European integration processes of the second half of the 20th century. To avoid vagueness, the evolution of these relations should be based on both their chronology and the processes of geographical redistribution of international production: as the Italian philosopher Giambattista Vico observed (Vico 2011 [1725–28], 61), chronology and geography are the 'two eyes of history'. In regard to chronology, as the relations between center and periphery after the Second World War are reconstructed in what follows, it should be recalled that all the countries of the Southern European periphery can be defined as latecomers, but Italy embarked on a path of industrialization and integration into European trade earlier than all the other peripheral countries. As regards geography, "changing geographies of production" — wrote Hudson (2002, 2) — "are a product of the interplay of (*inter alia*) corporate, state and trade unions strategies, as companies pursue profitability, trade unions and workers seek new employment and/or protect existing jobs, and states attempt to balance the pursuit of accumulation in their territory with the claims of equity and socio-spatial justice". While it is questionable whether this formulation adequately

3 See Hirschman (1978) now in Hirschman (1981, 32).

describes the strategies pursued by the European states, it remains true that, again quoting Hudson, "these geographies are contingent outcomes of the co-evolution of the asymmetric power relationships between these individual and collective actors and institutions. Conceptually, this represents an attempt to recognize the variety of ways in which agency and action and the structural determinants of capitalist economies co-evolve in particular ways". It is important to remember the context[4] in which this co-evolution occurs, namely the European integration of peripheral countries and globalization, "for these are both a partial product of the strategies of companies, states and trade unions and in turn help set the parameters which shape the processes".

When one speaks of "structural determinants", it is customary to refer to price competitiveness, and thus to labor costs and productivity. Developments in relative unit labor costs are then used to explain differential GDP trends. But the experience of the past fifteen years has clearly shown the limitations of focusing only on this unit costs indicator and on this definition of competitiveness (see for example Simonazzi et al. 2013). Moreover, in the presence of bubbles or unsustainable increases in net public spending, the short-period GDP performance can hide the structural fragility of the underlying economic conditions. Furthermore, a policy implication of focusing only on price competitiveness is that the only necessary and sufficient measure to heal a distressed economy and restore growth is the reduction of relative costs, obtained mainly through an increase in 'labor flexibility'. This measure would be unnecessary and probably counter-productive if the underlying problem stemmed not from price competitiveness but from "product competitiveness, rooted in limited production capabilities." (Best 2013, 1; see also Ginzburg, 2012). In a regime where product-led competition and innovation prevail, the problem is the *rigidity* of the productive structure (associated with what may be called, to be brief, its insufficient 'quality'), not labor flexibility. We share with Michael Best the idea that "the evidence is abundant that peripheral economies suffer from a dearth of business enterprises that meet the performance standards required to compete and grow in the Single European Market" (ibid., 2).

In order to understand the divergent trajectories of the core and the peripheral European countries in terms of interdependent economies with different productive capabilities (see Graph 1 for the trend of GDP per capita

---

4 A more precise description of the context in which the transition from the Fordist to the post-Fordist regime (to use a synthetic current terminology that should be qualified) assumes prominent importance is presented below.

in the years 1960–2014), it is therefore necessary to start from two concepts. The first is the crucial distinction of countries between first-comer industrializers (the 'center') and latecomers (Italy) and late-latecomers (Spain, Portugal and Greece) in the periphery. The second concerns the concept of level of productive structure:[5] although differences in the production structure between center and periphery were very large at first, they were reduced until the beginning of the seventies, especially during the 'glorious thirties', but reopened again in the subsequent years, and especially after the crisis of 2008.

Graph 1: GDP per capita at constant prices

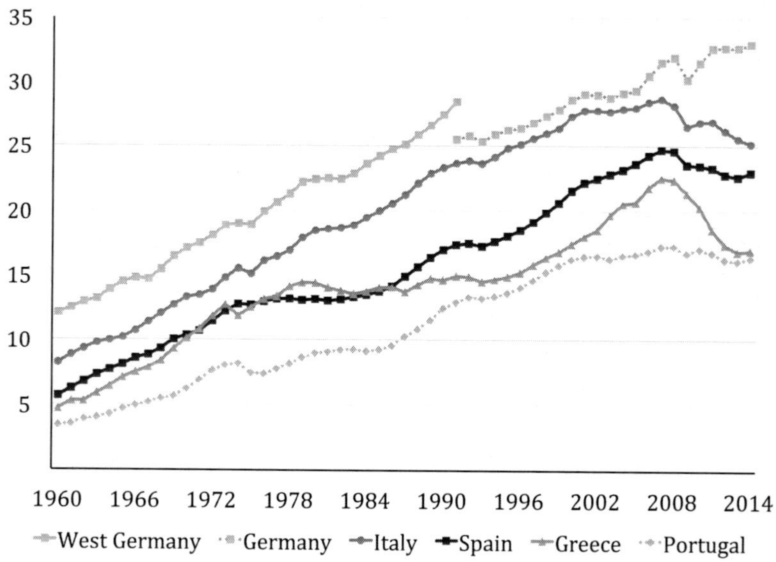

Source: Ameco

What is meant by 'productive structure'? As noted by Best (ibid., 2), "the absence of the concepts of productive structure and product-led competitive-

5 In some recent studies (Hidalgo et al. 2007; Hidalgo-Hausmann 2009), the productive structure of an economy is seen as a network that links specific products to specific capabilities. Economies that are more diversified and able to produce and export more exclusive products are defined as "more complex". For a study of the evolution of the production structures of the EU and its members based on the relationship between indicators of the complexity of the products exported and international trade patterns, see Reinstaller (2012).

ness from public discourse and academic economic analysis deflects 'growth' policy away from its proper focus". This absence — we might add — also hinders understanding of the determinants of the divergent development paths taken in Europe by the center and the periphery. We adopt a theoretical perspective that ideally combines the contributions of Albert Hirschman, Edith Penrose and Sebastiano Brusco. Here, the central role generally attributed to labor productivity in the development process is replaced by three circumstances, which, by mutually interacting, turn *ex post* into productivity performance: 1) Presence of innovative businesses whose organization is aimed "to compete on the basis of new products or processes and/or more effective use of new technologies and not primarily on the basis of price." (Best 2013, 3–4). 2) The activity of the firm is never isolated: its performance crucially depends on both the structured interrelationships (the linkages) that it can establish upstream and downstream, and the support received from the material and immaterial infrastructures, development agencies and financial institutions that sustain the process of innovation in the long term. 3) In product-led competition, a central role is played by industrial policy. It is the result of "triangular relations intersecting the three spheres of government, education and industry." From this it follows that a strategic policy of industrial development is incompatible with cuts in public budgets, and more generally in aggregate demand, which weaken or extinguish this triangular relationship. Industrial policy can encounter insurmountable obstacles if it is inconsistent with the main directions of macroeconomic policy. Finally, it should be emphasized that the notion of product-led competition is a relative concept. Indeed, it relates to the creation of new products and new markets *in a given productive system.* Thus, it does not concern only countries and markets at the frontier of knowledge, both technological and organizational; on the contrary, it takes on especial importance in peripheral countries. Obviously, apart from the advantages deriving from experience, the transfer/adaptation of technologies, organizations, business strategies originally designed in other socio-economic systems poses difficult, specific problems in both the supply and demand domains.

The three circumstances described above were asymmetrically distributed between the countries of the center and the Southern periphery of Europe at the beginning of the new stage of the Europeanization process of the early eighties, associated with the enlargement of EEC to Greece (1981) and Spain and Portugal (1986). In 1980, in a report on *Problems of Lagged Development in OECD Europe. A study of six countries,*[6] Fuà observed— implicitly recalling Gerschenkron's theses—that the structure and tendencies of latecomer European countries were different from those observed during the initial development phases of the older industrialized countries. The major differences concerned the technological gap, the demonstration effect on consumption, and the challenge of competition from more developed countries. These differences translated into strong internal productivity differentials across industries and regions ('dualism'), serious difficulties in providing regular employment to the potential labor supply, higher propensity to price instability and public deficits, and "a peculiar fragility of the balance of payments". Fuà concluded that the weaker competitive position originated persistent trade deficits: at the end of the seventies in all five countries, with the exception of Italy, that had succeeded in reaching a more balanced position, persistent trade deficits had to be permanently compensated by remittances and tourism. Subsequent developments led to the belief that this type of analysis had been overtaken by events: the per capita income grew also in the countries of the periphery, kindling hopes of a reduction also in relative income differentials. However, as shown by Graph 1, the undeniable, important *absolute* growth of per capita income in all the peripheral countries was accompanied by an increase in *relative* per capita income *gaps*, with respect to core countries (but also internal), heightened during the crisis that began in 2007. This suggests that an excessive focus on short-term, sometimes unsustainable, GDP increases may lead to ignoring too hastily long period considerations. Also for this reason, it is important to complement aggregate national account data with indicators of productive structure.

Over the thirty years of European integration since the early eighties, the Southern peripheral countries were exposed to macroeconomic and industrial policy measures that, though apparently neutral, generated increasing regional disparities, both between center and periphery and within countries. In what follows, we retrace the main phases of the process of the relative hollowing-out of the productive structures of the peripheral countries.

We make two assumptions. The first is that the crises of the center (which here, for simplicity, is Germany, West Germany until 1989), reflecting domestic and international circumstances, lead to internal reorganizations of its production structure that deeply affect the countries of the periphery. The

6 Cf. Fuà (1980, Italian translation 1985, 18–9). The six countries included Greece, Ireland, Italy, Portugal, Spain, Turkey.

center is enabled to strengthen its ability to stay in the market in the product-led competition by processes of 'creative destruction' and reconstruction undertaken with the support of industrial policies.[7] Conversely, the countries of the periphery fall behind and, also as a consequence of their policies, implement what might be called a 'plain destruction' of their capabilities to create new products, market niches and markets.

The second, related, hypothesis is that the crisis of the seventies, traditionally associated with the hike of oil prices, marked a profound break in the history of the relations between the center and the periphery of Europe: until then, even if at unequal speeds, the countries of the European periphery had taken significant steps along the path of industrialization. After the seventies, these processes were, again unevenly, disrupted. With reference to this pattern, Sapelli speaks of "weak industrialization", or "incomplete modernization" (see Table 1 for data on employment by sector as a percentage of total employment). According to this author (Sapelli 1995, 63–4), the Southern European countries belong to "socio-economic formations which cannot be defined simply as capitalist. They were of a new type. They had been determined by the character of the mixed economy and by the stratification of classes typical of societies where services had become predominant either after a very brief period of industrialization or by skipping industrialization completely". In these societies, "market forces were more evident than before, but in a social context dominated by reciprocity and patronage which did not allow the development of a complete contractual system". Obstacles to the completion of industrialization in the countries of Southern Europe therefore derived from the prevalence of cultural values and power systems based on status and clientelism, with respect to those based on contracts "typical of societies where the market economy has prevailed. The Weberian capitalistic society is the ideal example. However, this model has had little success in Southern Europe" (ibid., 16). A late and crony capitalism, brought in from outside, with a strong presence of the state in society, gave rise to what Sapelli, citing Huntington (1968), calls "a weak degree of institutionalization of the political-democratic system": that is, a poor ability to create "norms and democratic procedures of negotiation, compensation and regulation of interests." (ibid., 17). This interpretation of the industrialization processes (i.e. of the transitions to tertiarization) of the Southern

7 For the events associated with the mid-seventies crisis, see below, while for a reconstruction of the changes of the German development model in the early two-thousands, see Simonazzi et al. (2013).

European countries seems unconvincing. It is an 'essentialist' interpretation unable to explain either the first phase of industrialization or why the process halted precisely in the seventies. Moreover, the relations between center and periphery play no role in the 'early tertiarization' hypothesis.

Table 1: Employment by sector as percentage of total employment (average for period)

	1960-68			1968-73		
	Agriculture	Industry	Services	Agriculture	Industry	Services
Germany	11.9	47.7	40.4	8.5	47.9	43.6
Italy	27.7	36.4	39.5	20.4	39.1	40.4
Spain	33.4	32.7	33.9	26.7	35.6	37.7
Portugal	39.4	32.2	28.3	29.9	33.4	36.6
Greece	51.9	19.9	28.2	40.3	25.4	34.3

	1974-79			1980-91*		
	Agriculture	Industry	Services	Agriculture	Industry	Services
Germany	6.5	45.1	48.4	4.5	41.2	54.3
Italy	16.1	38.5	45.3	11.1	34.3	54.5
Spain	21.5	37.2	41.2	16.1	33.3	50.6
Portugal	32.9	34.0	33.1	23.3	35.4	41.3
Greece	33.6	28.9	37.5	27.6	28.2	44.2

	1992-1998			1999-2007		
	Agriculture	Industry	Services	Agriculture	Industry	Services
Germany	3.2	36.8	60.0	2.5	31.7	65.8
Italy	6.9	33.6	59.6	4.8	31.3	63.9
Spain	9.2	30.5	60.3	5.4	30.2	64.4
Portugal	12.3	32.9	54.8	12.0	32.6	55.4
Greece	20.3	23.8	55.9	14.3	22.3	63.4

	2008-2013		
	Agriculture	Industry	Services
Germany	1.6	28.5	69.9
Italy	3.7	28.6	67.7
Spain	4.2	22.9	72.9
Portugal	10.9	26.6	62.5
Greece	12.4	18.8	68.8

* West Germany 1980-1990; Portugal: 1980-89

Source: Sapelli (1995) and elaborations on OECD Data

Despite attempts to complicate the picture with many descriptive details, sometimes inconsistent with the basic thesis, the interpretative scheme appears to be a variant of the modernization theory, which reflects an idealized, atomistic development model of nineteenth-century England (or of the twentieth-century United States). This scheme refers to deviations from a unique optimal development model based on the choices of rational economic agents operating under perfect competition and favoured by an institutional framework consistent with it. Like all 'essentialist' models, also the optimal scheme tacitly assumes the end of history, as well as that of geography.

The Global Crisis of the Mid-Seventies in Southern Europe: Peripheral Tertiarization and Impoverishment of the Productive Structures

The global economic crisis of the mid-seventies, related to the synchronization of the recessive cycles of the major countries, was at the time the deepest since the end of the Second World War. Those events are well-known: the 1971 devaluation of the dollar; the huge increase in the price of oil[8] and other commodities in 1973; the 1974 drastic monetary and fiscal restriction aimed at addressing cost-push inflation (also associated with the strong wage increases in the previous years); and the deep balance of payment deficits of the commodity-importing countries. The economic and social effects of the crisis, in terms of employment reduction and productive capacity destruction, are also well known.

In a longer-term perspective, other aspects of a more enduring character emerge. The crisis can be analyzed from the perspective of the alternation of phases of homogeneization and heterogeneization of the major countries' productive structures, separated by moments of crisis and restructuring. According to the Japanese economist Akamatsu,[9] this alternation of phases characterizes the evolution of international economic relations. Between the

8 On the endogenous determination of the oil prices trend, namely its link with the dollar exchange rate and the domestic policy targets of the United States, see Schulmeister (2000).

9 See Akamatsu (1962) and Ginzburg and Simonazzi (2005).

late sixties and early seventies the competitive gap among the US, the major European countries and Japan was narrowing (as evidenced by the forces that led to abandonment of the Bretton Woods regime). Meanwhile, in the major central countries, given the prevailing income distribution, the long-term post-war development was leading to the saturation of the domestic demand for consumer goods–especially durable consumer goods, including cars, the greatest drivers of post-war growth.[10] The fact that the demand for consumer goods had become largely a question of replacement (rather than expansion in sales volumes) led to a strong differentiation of brands, to the multiplication of models (vertical differentiation), and to a dramatic shortening of products' lives.[11] In an environment of fierce oligopolistic competition, important consequences ensued: on the demand side, a boost to the search for still unexplored foreign market spaces; in terms of costs, a pressure to relocate production stages in lower wage areas, which, favoured by ITC technologies, eventually led to international fragmentation. In some areas there was a prevalence of manufacturing over distribution (producer-driven global value chains), in others a prevalence of distribution over manufacturing (buyer-driven global value chains). In the countries of the center, the shift in the forms of competition from quantitative expansion to qualitative product differentiation promoted a plurality of "services based" sales strategies. None of this could have happened without a strong expansion of financial services, first to finance direct investments in the peripheral countries, then to cover the time gap between sales and disposable income, and finally to finance mergers, acquisitions and alliances prompted by excess capacity and (organizational more than technological) economies of scale. For their part, financial institutions were only eager to find outlets for the petrodollars

10 Piore and Sabel (1984, 184), among the first authors to call attention to this crucial aspect, observe that "the saturation was especially true in the United States, where in 1979 there was one car for every two residents, compared with one for every four in the early fifties." Similarly, ninety-nine percent of American households had refrigerators and television sets and more than 90 percent washing machines. Evidence of the saturation of product markets has also been drawn from the constancy, in the seventies, of the ratio between goods and services growth at constant prices in the major industrial countries, despite the reduction in the relative prices of goods. Markets in which the elasticity of demand is price inelastic are generally termed 'saturated markets'. See on this Appelbaum and Schettkat (1999, 395–396).

11 According to Volpato and Stocchetti (2008), during the period 1984–2006 in Italy, in the car sector "the number of brands … remained almost constant while the number of models increased from 170 to 281 and the number of versions from 696 to 3440". For data on market saturation of 'white goods' in Italy, see Paris (2013).

recycled by the oil producers. Hence, one witnesses a general drive towards the hasty deregulation of capital movements, from which the receiving countries expected to finance imports of goods and technologies necessary for their growth. Logistics, transport and communications–not coincidentally areas where, as in finance, the impact of new technologies had been more disruptive of current practices–assumed strategic importance in accommodating the international reorganization of production.

The empowerment of finance in the areas of speculation in the flex-price segments (securities, bonds, commodities, real estate, etc.) is too well known to require summarizing here. Uncontrolled deregulation led to a series of financial crises that were particularly severe and long-lasting in the periphery (from Mexico in 1981 to Greece in 2010 and following years). Suffice it to recall that, in response to inflationary pressures and/or balance of payments crises due to monetary expansion and/or asset price bubbles of center-countries, recourse to drastically restrictive monetary policies had asymmetric effects: the fall in the prices of 'flex price' items hit countries in the periphery relatively harder, because of both their mono-specialization in commodities and the hasty return of capital to the safe-haven center countries.

To conclude, the seventies global crisis — as in different ways the next 2007–2015 global crisis — by raising the bar in the quality of performance standards required to compete, marked a turning point[12] in the diverging fortunes of center and periphery. In particular, when tracing the evolution of the economies of the European periphery, it is necessary to bear in mind that, from the early seventies onwards, they were operating in an international market regime increasingly dominated by the competition of differentiated products which led to the reorganization of a wide range of manufacturing and services operations. This new environment created highly selective opportunities for different countries and regions. Within the periphery, greater opportunities were opened for those firms provided with capabilities and inserted in productive structures better suited to filling the vacuum left by the core countries' shift in specialization and diversification, or better able to fit in the subcontracting chain of relatively sophisticated industrial components. Conversely, firms specialized in traditional products and unable to adapt, in a deflationary environment, to the new forms of competition encountered severe difficulties. The crisis also opened a gap in ag-

12 For an overview of the global implications of the mid-seventies crisis, although without reference to the center-periphery relation, see Cipolletta (2013).

gregate demand that political coalitions wanting to consolidate democratic institutions and/or reduce opposition eventually filled with welfare and construction expenditures. While, crisis after crisis, "free-trade imperialism" (to recall Gallagher and Robinson's famous expression) accentuated the impoverishment of the productive structure of Southern countries, the "peripheral tertiarization" based on construction and welfare found it increasingly difficult to reverse the hardships and inequities brought about by a limited and dependent capital accumulation.

Table 2: Rate of growth of real GDP and current accounts as a percentage of GDP (average values)

	Germany*		Italy		Spain		Portugal		Greece	
	GDP	C/C	GDP	C/C	GDP	C/C	GDP	C/C	GDP	C/C
1960–67**	3,8	0,5	5,6	1,4	7,7	-0,9	6,0	-3,6	8,3	-1,8
1968–73	5,0	1,2	5,1	1,3	6,7	0,4	7,0	-1,4	9,0	-1,5
1974–79	2,6	0,5	3,7	-0,2	2,3	-0,6	3,2	-7,4	3,4	0,9
1980–91	2,5	2,1	2,4	-1,1	2,8	-1,5	3,7	-7,9	0,9	-0,9
1992–98	1,4	-0,9	1,4	1,2	2,2	-1,5	2,7	-6,0	2,1	-2,1
1999–07	1,6	2,5	1,5	-0,6	3,9	-5,6	1,8	-9,5	4,0	-10,4
2008–14	0,7	6,4	-1,3	-1,3	-0,7	-2,7	-0,9	-6,0	-4,1	-8,8

* 1960–1991: West Germany
** Rate of growth of GDP: 1961–67
Source: Ameco

We have suggested that the different transitions to tertiarization may be better understood by analyzing the specific circumstances leading, in each country, to a halt in the industrialization process. We have also raised doubts about the thesis of 'premature tertiarization' attributable to some 'original' ('pre-modern') features of those countries' institutions. In our opinion, the focus should instead be on the 'premature liberalization' of these economies and on the political confrontation that eventually led to the choice of this development path. The following section will be devoted to analysis of the first halt, in 1963, in the Italian industrialization process. Like the other analogous successive industrialization interruptions of Southern countries, the Italian crisis was associated with a difficult phase of the European integration process. We shall argue that in all peripheral countries the 'solution' given to the specific crisis weakened, with the productive structure, also the country's resilience to the following, systemic crisis. In all peripheral countries, and with greater intensity in Greece and Portugal, even before the 2008 crisis, a reduced growth rate was associated with a higher current account deficit as a percentage of GDP (see Table 2), a tendency that we interpret as evidence of an increasing mismatch between aggregate demand and output composition (negative substitution of net imports).

The European Integration of a Latecomer Country, Italy

In 1948, per capita income in Italy was about three-quarters of that in Germany, two-thirds of that in France, and half of that in the USA (Barca 1997, 6); however, Italy's industrial base was more diversified than those of the other Southern European countries (Sapelli 1995, 76–7). Following the policy of import-substitution of investment goods implemented in the years before and after World War I, and during the twenty years of fascist dictatorship, Italy continued to develop a 'military-industrial' apparatus (mechanical engineering and steel industry, shipyards, automobiles, electricity and minerals). Industry, heavily protected by import barriers, was mainly concentrated in the North-West 'triangle' (Lombardy, Piedmont, Liguria). After the 1929 crisis, in 1933 the state created IRI, a public body[13] that brought together a group of bailed-out banks and firms in various sectors.[14]

Between 1948 and 1962, and in particular after 1953, the Italian economy underwent an intense phase of industrialization that in the space of a few years transformed the main features (and the landscape) of the Italian economy and society. Since 1951, gradual measures of foreign trade liberalization had favoured intra-European trade, resulting in 1957 in the Treaty of Rome. However, until 1956–57 Italian growth was driven mainly by domestic demand, and in particular by private investment (public investment would rise only in 1961–62): "At this stage, steel and energy investments of public bodies owe their importance to their strategic role in directing and enabling private investment, not to their size" (Barca 1997, 68). Moreover, these in-

13 With respect to classical nationalizations, in the 'IRI formula' listed companies were funded by both public and private capital, and public and private firms often coexisted in the same sector.

14 After having played a decisive role in the fifties and sixties Italian industrialization process, IRI, overloaded by debts, was liquidated in 2002 under the pressure of the European Economic Commission.

vestments, "aimed at substituting imports … [sought] to mitigate the old constraint of the limited availability of raw materials and energy" (Ciocca et al. 1973, 92).[15] Investment growth was stimulated by high profitability and strong consumption growth. Profit margins were high because of stagnant nominal industrial wages and stable prices, associated with high labor productivity growth. Total consumption growth was driven by the increase in average per capita income, brought about by huge, inter-sectoral, geographical and demographic shifts: between 1951 and 1963 more than three million people moved from agriculture to the industrial and the services sectors, and about 6–7 million from the countryside to the city (Barca 1997, 69). From the second half of the fifties onwards, also exports started to grow vigorously. In 1962, the current account was still in surplus: this was the culmination of the so-called 'economic miracle'.

Growth resulted in a rapid reduction in unemployment, which throughout the fifties had contributed, together with trade union repression, to dampening demands for wage rises. The resumption of trade union militancy was accompanied by a strong increase in wages, and thus of consumption, and, given important supply bottlenecks, huge consumer goods imports. The result was a strong price hike, a high current account deficit, and massive capital flights, caused also by fears of radical reforms by the new center-left government (for the first time since 1947, in 1962 the Socialist Party decided to support by an abstention vote the Government led by Christian Democrats, taking active part in the following year). On the eve of the April 1963 political elections, the new governor of the Bank of Italy, Guido Carli, implemented a monetary policy too expansionary; and also for this reason— he said later— he had to apply the monetary brakes "very vigorously".[16] The monetary squeeze produced a steep fall in private investments, which would recover only very slowly in the following years, despite a quick recovery in profit margins, amid high and persistent unemployment. A rapid increase in exports, with stagnant imports, led to almost a decade of highly positive current accounts, which were considered evidence of the success of the eco-

15 For data on import substitution of investment goods, possibly carried out to face the challenge of international competition, see Ciocca et al. (1973, 98).

16 In his memoirs (ibid., 1993, 268–9), Carli writes that the expansionary monetary policy responded not only to the desire not to interrupt the investment cycle underway, but also to the goal of "saving private property from the nationalizing fury of the socialists … I was on the side of capitalists. What I was never able to make people understand is that also unions should have been on the capitalists' side".

nomic policies adopted. The other side of these policies was the quantitative, and above all qualitative, destruction of productive capacity epitomised by the irreversible crisis of the Olivetti Electronic Division, which had just put an innovative portable computer model on the market (the Division would be sold to General Electric, which did not seize the opportunity to develop this new product line).

There was an obvious contradiction between the deflationary measures adopted by the coalition government to stabilize the economy and the longer-term policies needed to cope with the old and new imbalances in the Italian productive structure. In a longer-term perspective, inflation and external imbalances could be read as symptoms of the incompleteness of a 'viable' productive structure compatible with a more equitable income distribution. The experience of the Italian 'economic miracle' (before it abruptly came to a halt) — and the more lasting and administratively guided development model of the East Asian countries in the sixties and seventies — suggest that a broader internal market could have been obtained through import substitution *and* the creation of a sufficiently large (and territorially extensive) export base able to finance continuation of the industrialization process.

Could the 1963 crisis —with its important long-run repercussions— have had a different outcome? It is customary to answer this question in terms of choice between abstract principles, in this case between automatism (the market, possibly integrated by a legal framework[17] to achieve the competitive equilibrium described by the textbooks) or discretion (often assimilated to central planning). But an ill formulated question leads to misleadingly

17 According to Barca (1997), the 'original sin' of Italian capitalism was the absence of rules governing competition and procedures to monitor public actions. In this framework, rules and procedures are set exogenously by the state, since institutions and markets are considered separate entities whose interplay determines governance of the markets. Adopting the same dichotomic perspective, Bank of Italy officials placed high expectations in the 'modernizing' discipline enforced by external pressures (Monetary Union and the Single Market). However, in Italy the Authority for Guaranteeing Competition and Markets (CONSOB) was established in 1991 with no appreciable impact on the collusive and opaque functioning of the markets. From a different perspective that does not separate economics and politics, governance and rules are endogenous to the market system and depend on the specific configuration of economic activity: "the institutions of governance are influenced and often 'peopled' by the same producer constituencies with limited interest in market efficient outcomes" (Underhill 2007, 100). For a realistic account of the European process of establishing competition rules in the finance area, see Mügge (2010).

simple answers. There is a different way—between automatism and discretion—that requires reducing the level of abstraction from abstract principles down to deeper analysis of the insertion of the Italian productive structure in the international trade network, and careful assessment of the difficulties that the spontaneous forces of *this* market economy are able to solve. In an important document —the *Nota Aggiuntiva* (1962), presented to the Parliament in 1962 —the Minister of the Budget, Ugo La Malfa, argued that Italy's rapid post-war growth had been accompanied by sectoral, regional and social imbalances, and by distortions in the level and the composition of consumption and investment. This analysis prompted the proposal for a plan of coordinated actions targeted, not on the market, but on its extension and transformation, through state support for the creation of new activities. The two most dynamic components of effective demand—private consumption and exports—could slow down, the former because of saturation and the latter because of unpredictable external events, with serious consequences for the entire industry, and especially for the more backward sectors and areas. As regards investments, a program for development could reduce the persistent underestimation by private investors of the convenience of investing due to uncertainty, a limited horizon, private risk versus collective benefits. These policies today appear far-sighted and very distinct from a proposal of centralized planning. Compared with the views and actions of the protagonists of the economic policy of the time,[18] they reveal a wider breadth of vision, coupled with a more realistic consciousness of the latecomers' difficulties in expanding the productive basis through spontaneous market forces. Guido Carli, for instance, was less inclined than his predecessor to recognize the backwardness of the country and the need to broaden its industrial base. In 1959, while advocating an expansion of the tertiary employment, Carli remarked that a sustained effort to extend the industrial base was needed by economies "more backward" than Italy (Carli 1993, 162). After a political clash in which at a certain moment even the threat of a military coup was

18 In 1993, Carli argued that the *Nota aggiuntiva,* interpreted as a document advocating Stalinist-like coercive planning, was presented by the Minister of the Budget only to gain the benevolence of the socialists. In a recent testimony, the Treasury Minister, Emilio Colombo, said: "Tactically I supported programming, highlighting its progressive aspects; the socialists were passionate about programming … [Their] approach … to programming proved to be overambitious and unrealistic and diverted their attention from less ambitious but more concrete and therefore potentially more dangerous measures for the stabilization of the economy" (Carli 2014, 114).

envisaged,[19] the automatism of stabilization policies, which were presented as merely short-term measures, eventually prevailed.

By directing the economy away from indicative planning, the 1963 interruption of the Italian industrialization process had long-term effects that became evident at the time of the Treaty of Maastricht and the Stability Pact. It also affected the path of development in the Southern Italian regions—the so-called *Mezzogiorno*, which was severely hit by the stagnation of domestic demand in the sixties. This strengthened the pressure to use direct state intervention to promote the creation of basic industries (steel, chemicals, oil refineries). The declared intention was to provide cheaper inputs to the existing firms located in the North and to create new industrial initiatives in the South through forward linkages.[20] The vehicle of the public intervention was IRI, which in fact enormously expanded its activities in a variety of sectors. The per capita income gap between central-northern and southern Italy, which had increased in the early fifties, narrowed rapidly in the sixties largely as a result of state intervention. But it again widened drastically in the seventies in parallel with its crisis, and remained stable for almost forty years (to worsen again during the last crisis).

The failure of state intervention in the South was the result of a constellation of different circumstances that in the end proved to be cumulative: among them was the political conflict on whether government spending should be used for self-sustained industrial development or for the creation of an electoral consensus. The 1973–74 crisis shifted the balance between these two objectives in favour of the latter. The steep fall in demand, the ensuing collapse of basic commodities prices, due also to the entrance of new Asian competitors, led to huge IRI debts (Ravazzi 2013, 173ff). The crisis of the steel and shipbuilding industries accounted for more than 100% of the group's losses. The firms in the IRI group, having lost their financial and decision-making autonomy, had to ask the state to refinance even their current activities and to allow price adjustments.

The *Mezzogiorno* industrialization process was interrupted when a selective investment effort was needed to upgrade products and processes. In a situation of widespread distress, state intervention shifted towards creating dependent and assisted subjects through the nomination of incompetent but loyal managers, and increasing disability pensions and other transfers. Amid

19 See the *Piano Solo* prepared in 1964 by General De Lorenzo.

20 According to Hirschman (1958), the impact of forward linkages is in general weaker and more uncertain than that of backward linkages.

growing social unrest, new forms of rampant corruption and organized crime—both instrumental to social control and electoral support—also succeeded in seizing new opportunities for expansion. The increase in interest rates during the eighties led to an explosion of interest expenditures in the presence of a weaker productive structure. Also fiscal adjustment, long delayed but finally accelerated in the mid-nineties to meet the Maastricht criteria, penalized Southern Italy, since it was implemented through tax increases and spending cuts (and not through the reduction of tax evasion): fixed investment and transfer expenditures have a proportional higher weight in the Southern regions. After 1999, with the entry into force of the Treaty of Maastricht, the narrow export base of Southern Italy (nine percent of GDP, jumped to 13.1 per cent in 2013 due to the fall of the GDP; ICE 2015, 206) contributed to the reduction of the overall growth rate, thereby raising, together with Southern poverty, the debt parameters, given that exports are the only dynamic item in aggregate demand.

As regards private large firms, when in the eighties and nineties exchange rate devaluations became less frequent, rather than adopting the strategy of product innovation they preferred to delocalise their plants abroad. It was unexpectedly left to the industrial districts of the North-East and the Adriatic coast to take up the challenge of the new, post-Fordist competition based on small batches and differentiated products. In 1979, Wade (1979, 216), assessing the situation of the Italian *Mezzogiorno*, wrote words that today sound prophetic and not only restricted to North-South relations within Italy:

"Before 1950 the South was poor and in the large part self-sufficient. Now the development mechanism has transformed it into a place which is much less poor and much more dependent on the North. Whether one says that southerners are on the whole better or worse off depends on how much normative weight one gives to consumption on the one hand and 'autonomy' on the other. Some critics go so far as to say that the development program has failed because the South is now more dependent. I would wish to give more weight to the improvement in consumption, as a goal in itself, whether 'dependent' or 'independent'. However, the point is not only one of the values, but also whether the North will be able to continue underwriting the Southern living standards if the European economy expands more slowly or not at all over the next few decades. If not, the consequences for consumption standards of having become so dependent on northern transfers will be severe".

The Late-Latecomers' European Integration

After a brief spell of autarchy and import substitution, by the end of the fifties also the late-latecomer economies of Southern Europe moved, at different speeds and with diverse results, towards increasing commercial and economic integration with the core of the European Union.

The three countries started from different levels of industrial development: in the sixties employment in agriculture was 33.4 percent in Spain, 39.4 percent in Portugal, and 51.9 percent in Greece (Sapelli 1995 and Table 1)—but they all recorded high income growth (see Table 2 amd Graph 1) led first by investment and consumption, and then by exports. With the partial exception of Greece, where investment went mostly to construction, all countries placed especial emphasis on basic industry, which was deemed essential for the expansion of the industrial sectors of comparative advantage. The state supported accumulation either directly, through publicly-owned companies, or indirectly, through subsidies and other incentives to domestic and foreign capital. In Spain the state attempted to counter the excessive power of the private oligopolies—steel, electricity and coal—by direct public investment in heavy industry through the Instituto Nacional de Industria (INI, funded in 1941 along the lines of the Italian IRI) (Balbín 1999). In Portugal, national groups, with state support, invested in the machinery and chemicals industries (Mamede et al. 2014), while in Greece it was foreign companies that came to control the basic industry (steel and metallurgic industries, chemicals, plastics, electricity) producing inputs for the domestic market and for exports to their parent companies (Sapelli 1995). In the heyday of the Fordist regime of mass production, cost reduction was a strategic competitive factor in the core countries. Increasingly, the lower wages of peripheral countries attracted FDI[21] from the center to produce for export: cheap intermediate inputs for the capital and durable consumption goods sectors, and cheap final consumption goods. With the openness of their economies progressing, the commercial integration with the core deepened, and their economies grew increasingly attuned to the European cycle.

21 When comparing the evolution across countries of fixed investment as a percentage of GDP (Graph 2), an asymmetry between center and peripheral countries should be borne in mind. From the point of view of firms—as distinct from that of countries of belonging —FDI is much more important for the center countries, and should be ideally added to their fixed investment.

Graph 2: Gross Fixed Investment as a percentage of GDP, 1960–2014

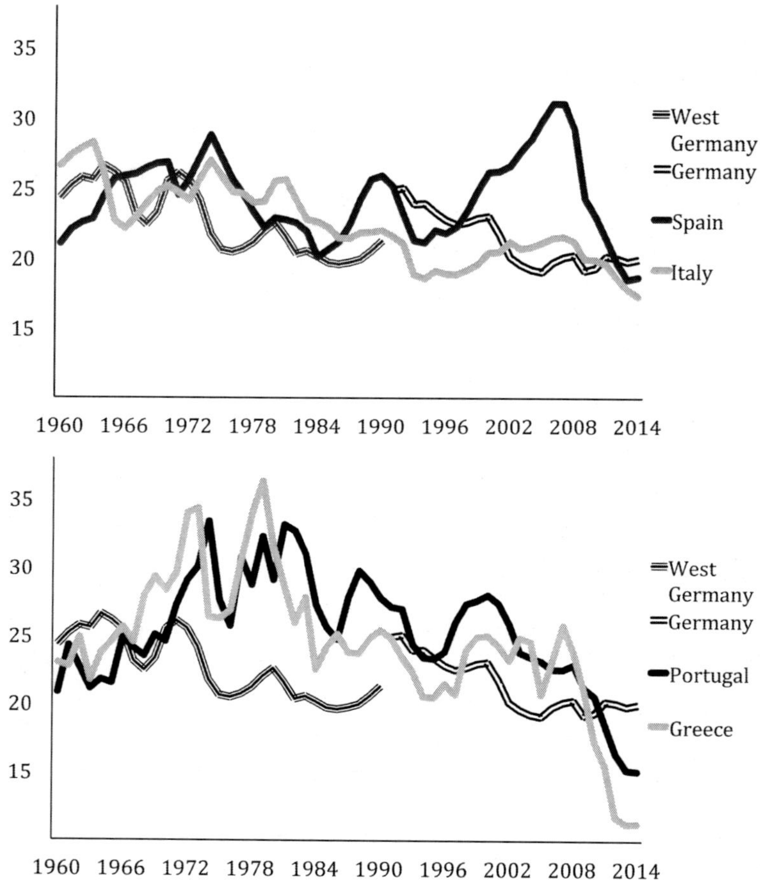

Source: Ameco

The process of growth changed the structure of the economy: the share of industry (measured at constant prices) increased in all countries; and it did so especially in Spain, the most advanced of the group. In that country, capital accumulation and consumption drove the expansion of the consumer goods industries and the transformation of the economic structure. The capital goods sectors were among the most dynamic: chemicals and petrochemicals, metallurgy and steel, transport equipment (Banyuls and Recio 2014). In spite of the suppression of free trade unions and the restriction of wage bargaining, under the Franco regime wages grew by and large in line with productivity (Toharia 1988, refers to it as 'pseudo-Fordism'). By ensuring the enlargement of the domestic market, the pattern of wages was an important factor supporting the economy's high rate of growth: between 1961 and 1972 private consumption increased by an average seven percent per annum. In the same period the share of industry increased by ten points at constant prices, while remaining practically constant at current prices. Productivity increases in industry, while allowing for comparable rate of growth of wages, translated into worsening terms of trade *vis-à-vis* services.

However, behind the apparent success in growth rates, the pattern of industrialization of the late-latecomers exhibited several weaknesses, similar to those evidenced for Italy, and, as anticipated by Fuà (1980), all linked to the narrow base of productive structure: unequal internal development, external disequilibria and an unsustainable demand pattern.

The rapidly increased liberalisation and openness to the world economy was not preceded or accompanied by the creation of a competitive productive base. Indicative planning remained largely on paper, while the process of industrialization responded to market incentives: it was left to the market to decide what to produce and where. Subsidies and incentives were poured into all sectors, but investment and industrial production remained strongly geographically concentrated (in the Basque countries, Catalonia and Madrid in Spain; in the Lisbon and Oporto area in Portugal; in Thessaloniki and Athens in Greece), leaving the largest part of the country behind. The industrial structure became even more polarized between big, domestic and foreign firms in key sectors (finance, basic industries, utilities, durable consumption in Spain; aluminium, oil refineries and chemicals in Greece) and a large number of small, non-competitive firms. This resulted in a dualistic pattern of industrialization divided between the 'modern' sectors—characterized by higher capital/labor ratio and productivity—and the traditional ones. Overall, the technical content of production remained low and FDI had the effect of increasing the specialisation of these countries' manufacturing industry in activities with low value added and low technological intensity (Mamede et al. 2014).

The process of accumulation and the build-up of a domestic industry of consumption goods were heavily dependent on a large and increasing flow of imports—of capital, intermediate and 'sophisticated' consumption goods—only partly matched by an increasing volume of exports based on competitively low labor costs (see Graph 3). The negative balance of trade was financed by remittances, tourism, FDI and financial flows (aid, subsidies and credits). The export of the growing surplus of labor, which the expansion of industry and services was insufficient to absorb, was made possible by the process of growth in the core European economies, and it responded to the double goal of defusing the time-bomb represented by a potential massive unemployment and financing the external deficit and the continuous expansion of domestic living standards (Fotopoulos 1992).[22]

Graph 3: Current accounts as a percentage of GDP, 1960–2014

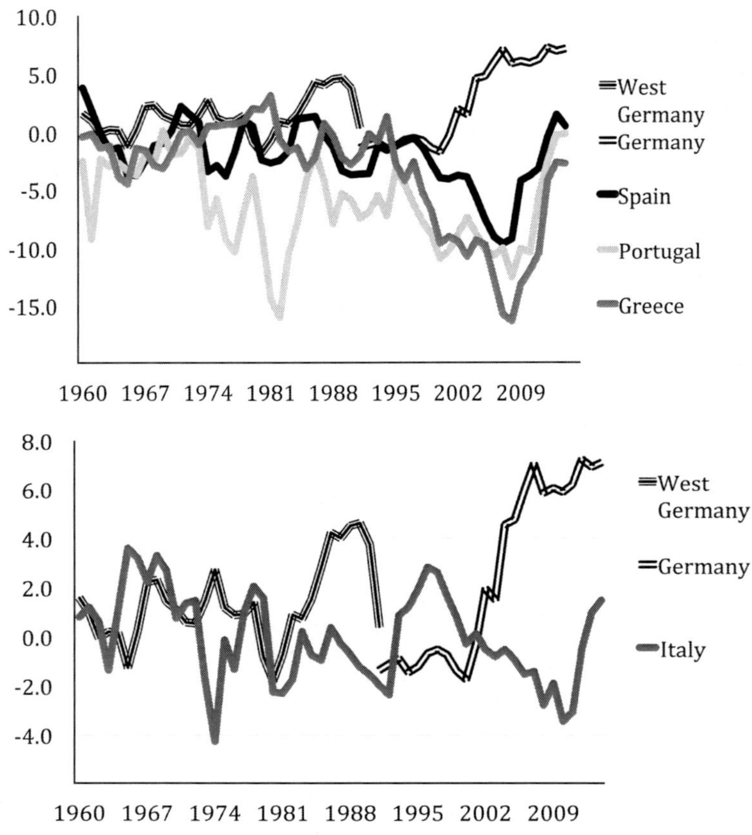

Source: Ameco

22 In Portugal in the eighties remittances reached more than 10 percent of GDP (Confraria 1999, 271).

The rapid expansion of incomes (Graph 1) and a high degree of inequality in their distribution, a huge black economy, significant capital inflows (remittances, aid, loans) and 'demonstration effects' skewed consumption away from basic goods and services towards a pattern of consumption in stark contrast with the level of development of these economies and with the quality of their production structures. In the poorest of the latecomer countries, Greece and Portugal, the volume and pattern of demand gave rise to the paradox of the emergence of a "consumer society without a production base" (Fotopoulos 1992).[23]

Democratic Transition and Restructuring without Reindustrialization, 1975–85

The transition of Spain, Portugal and Greece to democracy in 1975 coincided with international developments —change in the structure of demand and in the organization of production— that changed the context, the geography and the composition of industrial activity, transformed the factors of competitiveness, made a large part of the productive capacity obsolete or redundant, and ushered in a wave of restructuring and adjustment in core industries.[24]

The new governments had to face the consequences of this 'revolution': a difficult macroeconomic situation —high inflation rates and huge external deficits, swollen by the rise in the prices of oil and other raw materials, fall in domestic and foreign demand —and a hard process of adjusting the inherited industrial structure, at a time when the process of democratization had raised expectations of more widespread economic and social rights. The

23 Malthus (1974 [1834], 406) wrote: "if the master-producers, from the laudable desire they feel of bettering their condition, and providing for a family, do not consume their revenue sufficiently to give an adequate stimulus to the increase of wealth; if the working producers, by increasing their consumption, supposing them to have the means of so doing, would impede the growth of wealth more by diminishing the power of production, than they could encourage it by increasing the demand for produce; and if the expenditure of the landlords, in addition to the expenditure of the two preceding classes, be found insufficient to keep up and increasing the value of that which is produced, where are we to look for the consumption required but among the unproductive labourers of Adam Smith?"

24 See Balbín 1999, Banyuls and Recio 2014; Mamede et al 2014; Fotopoulos 1992.

weight of basic industries in total production called for drastic cuts in productive capacity (steel, coal, shipyards), which meant a massive destruction of employment. Entry into the global trade network of new low-cost producers significantly increased the exposure of the southern European industries to foreign competition due to the substantial overlap in industry structures, while the increase in wages and labor rights, entailed by the transition to democracy, eroded the price competitiveness of their exports, pushing the importing core countries to look for alternative cheaper sources.[25] The change in the patterns of consumption and the shift to product-led competition required an overhauling of their consumer goods industries that, left to market forces, they proved unable to perform. Domestic industry grew increasingly incapable of catering to domestic needs, let alone foreign ones. As the restructuring process gained momentum throughout Europe, unemployment soared,[26] drastically reducing emigration opportunities.

The socialist parties that came to government at the turn of the decade were committed to substantially transforming the structure of wealth, property and power, the purpose being to extend democracy from the political to the social and economic spheres (Tsakalotos 1998). In the original PASOK program, for instance, "an all-round modernization of the productive system was envisaged to take place through a significant expansion of the economic role of the state in the development process, with the aim to transform Greece from a dependent service economy, based on semi-skilled labor, to an independent industrial economy, based on skilled labor" (Fotopoulos 1992). Similarly, the electoral program of the Spanish Socialist Party "referred to a 'policy of expansion' within a strategy which focused on employment as the number one priority, to government investment as the 'motor' of the economy, and even to the idea of concerted planning, although it also contained orthodox references, such as to the prevalent role of the market and to anti-inflation policy" (Recio and Roca 1988, 140). However, none of

25 In 1987, gross hourly earnings of manual workers in Greece (expressed in purchasing power parities) were still about 56 percent of the EEC average (from 47 percent in 1977), but they were rapidly becoming uncompetitive with respect to wages in Eastern Europe, North Africa, and the developing world.

26 In Germany unemployment increased from less than 1 percent in the early seventies to a peak of 7.2 percent in 1985. In the same period, in Greece unemployment quadrupled (from about 2 to 7 percent); in Spain it soared from an average 3 to 18 percent; in Portugal from 2–3 to 10 percent; from about 5 to over 8 percent in Italy. It should be remembered that unemployment figures are very imperfect estimates of employment conditions, especially in peripheral countries.

these governments were prepared (or able, or willing) to risk a conflict with local interests and foreign capital in order to fulfil their election development promises. Faced with the challenge of "expanding the development role of the state, by adopting a radical restructuring program" (Fotopoulos 1992), they withdrew, attempting instead, at first, to expand the consumption function of the state, with the double objective of avoiding a massive rise in unemployment and reproducing the consumer society.

The public sector found itself under increasing pressure to absorb the rapidly rising surplus of labor and sustain demand in the face of a severe investment slump and the consequent fall in private consumption. The number of employees in the public sector increased, only partly in response to an increasing supply of social services (education, health and social security), which remained highly segmented and unequally accessed (Karamessini 2008). With the public share in the economy increasing, internal and external deficits soared (Graph 3). Under pressure from the EEC creditor partners,[27] the socialist governments turned to the new liberal agenda (Tsakalotos 1988, 118).

Thus, the crisis of the seventies marks a turning point in the economic development of the late-latecomer economies, which started to diverge again from the core. As argued by Mamede et al (2014), with reference to the Portuguese economy, these countries were 'stuck in the middle': "while insufficiently developed to compete in the most sophisticated markets, the price of [their] products in the international markets proved to be too high to compete with those of less advanced, emerging economies". This applies also to Spain, which has seen the development of a few big holdings with important internationalized activities (especially in Latin America) and advanced technology (transport infrastructure, telecommunications, renewable energies, finance): however, "they are far from being enough to drive the country behind them. The country does not have enough solidly grounded productive undertakings and general structure. The continuous surge of the real estate industry has hidden the weaknesses of the Spanish productive system but the crisis has exposed the poor base of Spanish economic dynamics" (Etxezarreta et al. 2011, 15).

27 The Greek government had to agree to macroeconomic stabilisation packages with the IMF in the late seventies and had to resort to emergency borrowing from its EEC partners in 1985 and in 1990. The two loans ($1.3 billion and $3 billion respectively) were made conditional on the implementation of increasingly stricter Stabilisation Programs. Portugal first received EC aid in 1974 and in the early eighties (Confraria 1999, 281).

The implementation of orthodox macroeconomic policies pre-empted the space for adoption of those industrial policies required to upgrade the industrial structure. At the same time, EU membership provided policy-making elites with a legitimation for shifting policies towards disinflation and the market approach to restructuring.

The German Internationalization Strategy: "Widen the Market and Narrow the Competition"[28]

According to conventional wisdom, the major force behind Germany's growth is its exports. The traditional 'neo-mercantilist'[29] model adopted by Germany in the sixties and seventies was (and still is) based on the accumulation of current account surpluses, which enable the financing of a huge flow of trade credits, direct investment, and aid in support of Germany's exports of investment goods. Until the establishment of the Monetary Union, "appreciation in the exchange rate allowed for reductions in the prices of imported raw materials, consumer goods and intermediate goods, thus help-

28 Adam Smith (1996 [1776], 278) wrote: "The intent of the dealers…in any particular brand of trade and manufacture is always in some respect different from, and even opposed to that of the public. To widen the market and to narrow the competition is always the interest of the dealers". We borrow the quotation from Mügge (2010).

29 The German neo-mercantilist policy has old roots. As Hirschman (1980, 146) recalls, since the beginning of the nineteenth century, "in the minds of the public and of many economists, the increasing importance of German foreign trade was coupled with an increasing precariousness of its economic basis". In 1903, Sombart had stated the so-called "law of the declining importance of export trade". His forecast was that the gradual industrialization of the agricultural countries, coupled with the increasing capacity to consume on the part of the home market, would lead to a reduction of the growth of foreign trade with respect to internal demand. This forecast raised in Germany the apprehension of being shut off from food and raw material supply, especially in wartime, and of depriving exports of their markets abroad. The collapse of foreign trade could be prevented either by obtaining "sufficient colonies, or, directly, by *preventing the industrialization of foreign nations*" (ibid., italics added, 148). An echo of this position may perhaps be detected, for instance, in the German fierce opposition to the exemption of investment expenditures from Maastricht parameters on public deficit. Or in an October 1974 statement by Helmut Schmidt (De Cecco 1976): "We must not save Italy, but give only as much help which enables it to be with his head out of the water, not on the beach. The Italian industry must be strengthened without chasing the mirage of product diversification, because in Europe we have to accomplish a precise division of labor".

ing curb the increase in domestic prices and safeguard the social pact upon which the system of industrial relations rested" (Simonazzi and Vianello 1999, 264). While the investment goods sector acquired increasing weight in the German industrial structure, the interests of the other sectors, more exposed to foreign competition, were taken care of by promoting an area of integrated trade within Europe to which they could delocalize the production of their inputs and export their final products. When the sharp appreciation of the D-Mark in the seventies risked putting also the powerful German industry (or at least its weakest, more price-elastic, products) in jeopardy, the German government fostered the institution first of the European Monetary System (EMS), and then of the Monetary Union, accepting—albeit reluctantly—a more flexible interpretation of the criteria for admission (ibid., 265). The creation of the EMS responded to German industry's need to restrain the pressure of foreign competition, and to create an area of relative stability within which to establish and consolidate stable networks of reliable suppliers in selected countries/regions (Northern Italy, Spain, center-northern Portugal). By securing an outlet for its mature sectors, the closer integration within the Single Market in the difficult times of the post mid-seventies downsizing and restructuring gained precious time for their restructuring.[30] Later, delocalization of stages of production beyond the European tariff wall via outward processing trade (OPT) represented the first step of a process of Eastern integration[31] with German industry; a process which reached full speed after the fall of the Berlin Wall and enlargement of the European Union. After establishment of the euro, the rapid increase of intermediate imports, especially from Eastern Europe, evidenced the transformation of the German economy into a 'Bazaar Economy'. On the cost side, it exploited, for instance in the case of Poland, the double advantage of

30 In the early eighties, 50 percent of West German foreign trade was directed to the EC (including Austria and Switzerland), the figure rising to 60 percent when Great Britain and Spain joined the EC.

31 The OPT of German "mature" industries was not confined to Eastern European countries; nor was Germany the only European country to resort to it. Italy, France, and the Netherlands all resorted to the delocalization of stages of production–to Turkey, the Northern African countries, and the Balkans—taking advantage of their lower labor costs to meet the increasing competition of the NICs (newly industrializing countries) in mature sectors (textiles and clothing, footwear, etc.). In the UK, where the market was dominated not by producers but by large retailers, the phenomenon took the form of delocalization of the entire production process, retaining only the two extreme stages—design and commercialization—within the country (Ginzburg and Simonazzi 1995).

lower labor costs and a stronger exchange rate. On the demand side, foreign loans and structural funds to the European periphery[32] financed its increasing gulf between imports and exports, allowing maintenance of a model that was no longer viable in the changed national and international context, but that continued to perform the task of providing a vent for the core country's increasing surpluses.

Given the much more fragile industrial structure of the peripheral economies, the successful restructuring of their industry would have required an overhauling of their policies of state intervention so that their enterprises would be able to compete on the basis of new products/technologies and not only on price. It was necessary to tackle the lack of business enterprise, create new competences, favour the establishment of backward and forward linkages to thicken the industrial fabric, and strengthen the formation of networks. That is, to implement the same policies that Germany, Japan and free-market economies such as the UK and the US had never relinquished.[33] It is true that the progressive tightening of macroeconomic conditions imposed by the Maastricht Treaty and the subsequent Stability Pacts reduced the room for implementation of selective industrial policies: the industrial retooling of the Southern European countries occurred in a context of economic stagnation and within a market philosophy of non-intervention. But tough external conditions do not reduce the responsibility of the peripheral countries' governments, which placed uncritical faith in the drive to efficiency that the tougher competition resulting from the creation of the single market would mean for European firms. "That the contemporaneous reduction of the possibility to intervene in support of national industries … would inevitably add to the pressure on the more exposed sectors was judged a price to be paid for progress along the road to efficiency" (Simonazzi and Vianello 1999, 271).

32 To which one should add the role played by KfW (*Kreditanstalt für Wiederaufbau*) in providing long-term subsidized financing to the importers of German capital goods.

33 See for instance Block (2008), Mazzucato (2013) and FINNOV Report (2012).

Concluding Remarks

We have argued that, by confusing the trigger for its underlying causes, the seventies crisis was mistaken as the 'oil crisis'. Only later was the major role played by other, more irreversible factors fully recognized: the collapse of the Fordist system and the overhauling and fragmentation of the international division of labor, with the disrupting entry of the newly industrializing countries (NICs) in heavy industry[34] and in the labor-intensive stages of production, to rapidly climb the technological ladder. Likewise, the current European crisis has been interpreted as the "financial and sovereign debts crisis", which is once again to miss its deeper-lying causes. The financial crisis has exposed the unsustainability of the old core-periphery model, which was required to tackle the broader context of change in technology and demand within a faulty institutional and macroeconomic framework.

The outbreak of the crisis coincided with the deployment of a new phase in the paradigm of international production and technology, with new emerging countries entering the scene. As in the seventies and eighties, this new phase calls for an overhaul of the production systems in the advanced countries: obsolete capacity will need to be scrapped, declining sectors will have to be abandoned. But the birth and growth of new sectors presupposes recognition of "the 'collective' character of innovation. Different types of firms (large and small), different types of finance and different types of State policies, institutions and departments interact sometimes in unpredictable ways" (Mazzucato 2013, 194). When the innovation process is visualized as occurring through "separate and isolated activities of the State and the firms", the innovation process fades and dies out. The lack of alternatives will mean greater demand for protection or soaring unemployment. No amount of labor flexibility can turn the industry-specific skills of laid-off workers into the new skills now in demand; and no amount of domestic deflation can stimulate the growth of innovative industries.

Once again the core country has found itself in a favorable position to tackle the crisis: it is true that the debt crisis in the countries of the periphery and the austerity imposed upon them has drained their demand for German products, but it has also crippled their economies, reduced their prices; meanwhile the low—even negative—interest rates accruing to Germany

34 On changes in the geographical distribution of world steel production, see Hudson et al. (1989, 18).

by virtue of its safe haven status have allowed its industry—and its government, directly or through its national investment banks[35]—to play the old game again. Restructuring at no cost, picking and choosing suppliers in the South, the East, and the Far East, and selling its quality products on credit to the world. However, if debts must be repaid, debtor countries must be enabled to produce income gainfully, or the core-periphery relation will be condemned to cyclical waves of financial crises.

As noted by Schulmeister (2012), systemic crises require systemic solutions. But they need also suitable spectacles to focus on those systemic links that, ignored by the prevailing theories, tend to emerge with dramatic emphasis in the course of the crises. At a higher level of generality, these links include the co-evolution, in the long term, of aggregate demand and supply (which in the crisis manifests itself as hysteresis, that is, permanent destruction of productive capacity), the relationship between the quantity of money and the level of activity of the real sector (which refutes the supposed neutrality of money on which the European Monetary Union was built), the interweaving of monetary and fiscal policy (with the associated link, under certain conditions, between bank risk and sovereign risk). At a lower level of generality, we find systemic links in the relations between the center and Southern European peripheries, that we have analyzed in the previous pages. These links concern also the relationships between productive sectors, for example between industry and the services. We found unconvincing the argument proposed by Sapelli, who attributes the slower growth of the peripheral economies to the prevalence of cultural values based on status and clientelism, instead of 'modern', contract-based 'weberian' relations. An incomplete liberalization would have given rise to a weak industrialization, and therefore (tautologically) to an 'early' tertiarization. We have argued instead that the arrest of industrialization processes, which began in the mid-sixties in Italy and in the mid-seventies in all the countries of Southern Europe, must be attributed to the raising of the bar in the quality of performance standards required to compete, associated with the market saturation for the main durable consumption goods. Just when the State should have taken up new tasks to strengthen the quality of the productive structure, 'early liberalization' policies prevented public investment guidance in the peripheries: in-

35 The German government has been very active in supporting change in the industrial composition and organization of production. Its actions have ranged from sustaining the network of local banks committed to financing the German Mittelstand to heavily subsidizing the growth of new sectors, as in the case of energy policy.

dustrial policies were redefined as policies for the guarantee of competition, thus hindering policies addressed to sustain diversification and upgrading. These policy decisions did not occur smoothly, but were associated with political and social conflicts (where also the cultural values highlighted by Sapelli played a role).

For the sake of brevity, we shared with Sapelli the restrictive assumption of an aggregate tertiary sector, without distinguishing between advanced and 'routine' services sectors and disregarding their linkages with the other sectors of the economy. The alleged economic miracles of Ireland (the 'Celtic Tiger') and Spain (flagship of the liberalization policy of the labor market), in the first half of the 2000s, have been interpreted as an exemplary model of 'highly skilled' tertiarization, as proved by the high percentage increase of employment in the financial intermediation and business services sectors. Only after the crisis was it realized that the other side of the miracle was the piling up of a high private debt, quickly turned during the crisis into a huge debt. Moreover, much of the employment in these sectors was less skilled than anticipated. In Ireland, for example, the expansion of the economy was based largely on the relocation of lower-end stages of the electronics value chain, attracted from very high tax benefits: a model that can hardly be generalized and, as it turned out, not sustainable.[36] As for Sapelli' thesis, also its opposite, that is, the thesis of "successful early 'service transition'" may be considered a variant of the theory of modernization. Ignoring altogether the difficulties inherent in any piecemeal socio-economic transplant given the specific embeddedness of economy and society in countries situated at different stage of development— a weakness shared by all 'exemplary models'— it suggests to extract from the country considered 'more advanced' the 'essential feature' that follower countries should acquire in order to achieve the performance of the leader. In this case, the key variable selected for interpretative or normative purposes is the one suggested by the supply side theory of human capital. Successful patterns of specialization would derive from the higher growth of sectors considered to be at higher educational and/or ICT

36 Wren (2013, 23), graphs 1 and 2, has highlighted the existence of a positive relationship between "the expansion of employment in low-end service sectors and the expansion of credit [indebtedness] to the private sector". "In contrast —she adds—there is no such link with manufacturing". The author does not connect this relationship with the lower wages paid in the tertiary sector, but with "the illusion of wealth" associated with the expansion of cheap credit. However, the author wonders whether in the economies that have adopted a service transition strategy "it is feasible to maintain the same levels of employment in the non-traded services sectors under more restrictive credit conditions".

intensity, such as Finance (a sector strongly linked with Real Estate Services). But, as noted in 1931 by an observer very attentive to systemic interactions, in a deep crisis, falling prices of assets such as houses and bonds impinge on banks' balance sheets, and "there is a degree of deflation that no bank can stand" (Keynes 1972, 157).

Works Cited

Akamatsu, Kaname (1962). Historical Pattern of Economic Growth in Developing Countries. *The Developing Economies*, 1: s 1, 3–25.

Albert, Michel (1991). *Capitalisme contre capitalisme*. Paris: Editions du Seuil (English translation 1993. London: Whurr).

Appelbaum, Eileen, and Ronald Schettkat (1999). Are Prices Unimportant? The changing Structure of the Industrialized Economies. *Journal of Post Keynesian Economics*, 21: 3, 387–398.

Balbín, Pedro Fraile (1999). Spain: Industrial Policy under Authoritarian Politics. In James Foreman-Peck and Giovanni Federico (eds.). *European Industrial Policy*, 233–267. Oxford: Oxford University Press.

Banyuls, Joseph, and Albert Recio (2014). *Industrial Policy in Spain* (mimeo).

Barca, Fabrizio (1997). Compromesso senza riforme. In Fabrizio Barca (ed.). (1997). *Storia del capitalismo italiano dal dopoguerra a oggi*, 3–115. Rome: Donzelli.

Best, Michael H. (2013). *Productive Structures and Industrial Policy in the EU*. URL: http://www2.euromemorandum.eu/uploads/best_productive_structures_and_industrial_policy_in_the_eu.pdf .

Block, Fred (2008). Swimming Against the Current: the Rise of a Hidden Developmental State in the United States. *Politics and Society*, 36: 2, 169–206.

Carli, Federico (ed.). (2014). *La figura e l'opera di Guido Carli. 2. Testimonianze*. Torino: Bollati Boringhieri.

Carli, Guido (1993). *Cinquant'anni di vita italiana*. Bari: Laterza.

Ciocca, Pierluigi, Renato Filosa, and Guido M. Rey. (1973). *Integrazione e sviluppo dell'economia italiana nell'ultimo ventennio: un riesame critico*. Contributi alla Ricerca Economica. Servizio Studi della Banca d'Italia, 3, 57–135.

Cipolletta, Innocenzo (2013). Gli anni Settanta: una frattura nel processo di crescita. In Francesco Silva (ed.). *Storia dell'IRI. I difficili anni '70 e i tentativi di rilancio*, 70–112. Bari: Laterza.

Confraria, João (1999). Portugal: Industrialization and Backwardness. In James Foreman-Peck and Giovanni Federico (eds.). *European Industrial Policy. The Twentieth-Century Experience*, 268–294. Oxford: Oxford University Press.

De Cecco, Marcello (1976). L'economia tedesca e il bastone americano. *La Repubblica*, 22 July.

Etxezarreta, Miren, Francisco Navarro, Ramòn Ribera, and Victòria Soldevila (2011). *Boom and (Deep) Crisis in the Spanish Economy: the Role of the EU in its Evolution.* 17th Workshop on Alternative Economic Policy in Europe, Vienna, September.

FINNOV Report (2012). European Commission. URL: http://www.finnov-fp7.eu/publications/finnov-policy-papers/finnov-final-policy-brief-reforming-a-dysfunctional-system .

Fotopoulos, Takis (1992). Economic Restructuring and the Debt Problem: the Greek Case. *International Review of Applied Economics*, 6: 1, 38–64.

Fuà, Giorgio (1980). *Problems of Lagged Development in OECD Europe. A study of Six Countries.*, Paris: OECD.

Ginzburg, Andrea (2012). Sviluppo trainato dalla produttività o dalle connessioni: due diverse prospettive di analisi e di intervento pubblico nella realtà economica italiana. *Economia & Lavoro*, 2, 67–93.

Ginzburg, Andrea, and Annamaria Simonazzi (1995). Patterns of Production and Distribution in Europe: the Case of the Textile and Clothing Sector. In Roberto Schiattarella (ed.). *New Challenges for European and International Business*, 259–283. Rome: Litografia Ranieri.

Ginzburg, Andrea, and Annamaria Simonazzi (2005). Patterns of Industrialization and the Flying Geese Model. *Journal of Asian Economics*, 15, 1051–1078.

Hidalgo, César and Bailey Klinger, Albert László Barabási, Ricardo Hausmann (2007). The Product Space Conditions the Development of Nations. *Science*, 317: 5837, 482–487.

Hidalgo, César and Ricardo Hausmann (2009). The Building Blocks of Economic Complexity. *PNAS*, 106: 26, 10570–10575.

Hirschman, Albert O. (1958). *The Strategy of Economic Development.* New Haven: Yale University Press.

Hirschman, Albert O. (1978). Beyond Asymmetry: Critical Notes on Myself as a Young Man and Some Other Old Friends. *International Organization*, 32: 1, 45–49.

Hirschman, Albert O. (1980 [1945]). *National Power and the Structure of Foreign Trade*. Berkeley: University of California Press.

Hirschman, Albert O. (1981). *Essays in Trespassing. Economics to Politics and Beyond.* Cambridge: Cambridge University Press.

Hudson, Ray, and David Sadler (1989). *The International Steel Industry. Restructuring, State Policies and Localities*. London: Routledge.

Hudson, Ray (2002). Changing Industrial Production Systems and Regional Development in the New Europe. *Transactions of the Institute of British Geographers*, 27: 3, 262–281..

Huntington, Samuel P. (1968). *Political Order in a Changing Society*. New Haven: Yale University Press.

ICE (2015). *L'Italia nell'economia internazionale*. Rome.

Karamessini, Maria (2012). Continuity and Change in the Southern European Social Model. *International Labor Review*, 147: 1, 43–70.

Keynes, John M. (1972 [1931]). The Collapse of Monetary Values and its Consequences on the Banking System. In *The Collected Writings of John Maynard Keynes, volume IX, Essays in Persuasion*. London: Macmillan.

Malthus, Thomas R. (1974 [1834]). *Principles of Political Economy: Considered with a View of Their Practical Applications*. Clifton: Kelly.

Mamede, Ricardo P., Victor C. Simões, and Manuel M. Godinho (2014). Assessment and Challenges of Industrial Policies in Portugal. In Teixeira et al. (eds.)., 258–277.

Mazzucato, Mariana (2013). *The Entrepreneurial State. Debunking Public vs. Private Sector Myths*. London: Anthem Press.

Mügge, Daniel (2010). *Widen the Market, Narrow the Competition: the Emergence of Supranational Governance in EU Capital Markets*. Amsterdam: Universiteit van Amsterdam.

Nota Aggiuntiva alla Relazione generale sulla situazione economica del paese 1961 (1962). Camera dei Deputati, May. URL: http://www.fulm.org/doc/2974/nota-aggiuntiva-20140326125800.pdf.

Paris, Ivan (2013). White Goods in Italy during a Golden Age (1948–1973). *Journal of Interdisciplinary History*, 44: 1, 83–110.

Piore, Michael J., and Charles F. Sabel (1984). *The Second Industrial Divide: Possibilities for Prosperity*. New York: Basic Books.

Ravazzi, Piercarlo (2013). L'IRI negli anni Settanta: accelerata espansione, «ipertrofia» e crisi. In Francesco Silva (ed.). (2013). *Storia dell'IRI. I difficili anni '70 e i tentativi di rilancio*, 165–266. Bari: Laterza.

Recio, Albert, and Jordi Roca (1998). The Spanish Socialists in Power: Thirteen Years of Economic Policy. *Oxford Review of Economic Policy*, 14: 1, 139–158.

Reinstaller, Andreas (2012). *The Development of Productive Structures of EU Member States and Their International Competitiveness. Final Report for the European Commission*, Vienna: WIFO.

Sapelli, Giulio (1995). *Southern Europe Since 1945. Tradition and Modernity in Portugal, Spain, Italy, Greece and Turkey*. London: Longman.

Schulmeister, Stephan (2000). Globalization without Global Money: the Double Role of the Dollar as National Currency and World Currency. *Journal of Post Keynesian Economics*, 22: 3, 365–393.

Schulmeister, Stephan (2012). The European Monetary Fund. A Systemic Problem Needs a Systemic Solution. *WIFO Working Papers*, 414. URL: http://stephan.schulmeister.wifo.ac.at/fileadmin/homepage_schulmeister/files/EMF_Concept_07_11.pdf.

Seers, Dudley and Bernard Schaffer, Maria-Liisa Kiljunen (eds.). (1979). *Underdeveloped Europe: Studies in Core-Periphery Relations*. Hassocks: The Harvester Press.

Sen, Amartya K. (2012). Austerity is Undermining Europe's Grand Vision. *The Guardian*, July 3.

Simonazzi, Annamaria, Andrea Ginzburg, and Gianluigi Nocella (2013). Economic Relations between Germany and Southern Europe. *Cambridge Journal of Economics*, 37: 3, 653–675.

Simonazzi, Annamaria, and Fernando Vianello (1999). Financial Liberalization, the European Single Currency and the Problem of Unemployment. In Maurizio Franzini and Felice R. Pizzuti (eds.). *Globalization, Institutions and Social Cohesion*, 257–282. Berlin: Springer.

Smith, Adam (1996 [1776]). *An Inquiry into the Nature and Causes of the Wealth of Nations*. Chicago: University of Chicago Press.

Teixeira, Aurora A.C., Ester Silva, and Ricardo P. Mamede (eds.). (2014). *Structural Change, Competitiveness and Industrial Policy: Painful Lessons from the European Periphery*. London: Routledge.

Toharia, Luis (1988). Partial Fordism: Spain between Political Transition and Economic Crisis. In Robert Boyer (ed.). *The Search for Labour Market Flexibility, The European Economies in Transition*. Oxford: Clarendon, 119–139.

Tsakalotos, Euclid (1998). The Political Economy of Social Democratic Economic Policies: The PASOK Experiment in Greece. *Oxfort Review of Economic Policy*, 14: 1, 114–138.

Underhill, Geoffrey R.D. (2007). When Will Politics End and the Market Begin? Whither 'Free' Trade after Doha. *Journal of International Trade and Diplomacy*, 1: 1, 91–126.

Vico, Giambattista (2011 [1725–28]). *Principi di scienza nuova*. Milan: Mondadori.

Volpato, Giuseppe, and Andrea Stocchetti (2008). *Managing Product Life-cycle in the Auto Industry: Evaluating Carmakers Effectiveness*. URL: http://mpra.ub.uni-muenchen.de/29381/1/MPRA_paper_29381.pdf.

Wade, Robert (1979). Fast Growth and Slow Development in Southern Italy. In Dudley Seers et al. (eds.), 197–221.

Wren, Anne (2013). Introduction. In Anne Wren (ed.). *The Political Economy of the Service Transition*. Oxford: Oxford University Press, 1–70.

Migration and Southern Europe. A Center-Periphery Dynamic?

Russell King

Migration has played a central role in the social and economic history of Spain, Portugal, Italy and Greece. Few families in the four countries under consideration, it seems, do not have some relative who was abroad in the past, or is abroad today. In the past, it was older kinsfolk or ancestors in the United States, South America, or North-West Europe; today it might be sons and daughters seeking employment in the UK, France or Germany as an escape from the economic crisis. This chapter examines the shifting role and nature of migration—chiefly international migration—over the seven decades since 1945. Its guiding concept is that migration from and to those countries can be interpreted as part of the condition of *peripherality* with respect to other parts of Europe.

Postwar migration in Southern Europe, as Italy, Spain, Portugal and Greece are commonly referred to, runs through four main phases, marked by *migration transitions* from one phase to the next (Skeldon 2012). These phases are sequenced as follows, with their approximate dates.

- Emigration, mainly low-skilled labor migration, to North-West Europe and other parts of the world (North and South America, Australia), 1945 to the early-mid seventies.
- Return migration, seventies and eighties; but some forms of return are still ongoing such as 'retirement return' and the 'pseudo-return' of the second generation, born abroad of migrant parentage.
- Immigration from a wide variety of countries worldwide, in North and Sub-Saharan Africa, South and East Asia, Latin America and Eastern Europe, eighties to today, but slackening off since 2008.
- 'New emigration' of young, well-educated people seeking employment and new lifestyle experiences in Northern Europe since the nineties, accelerating after 2008.

These four phases also correspond to specific 'types' of migration, defined by motivation, migrants' socio-economic status, directionality, and the intensity of the flow—its concentration in space and time. Other migration types should also be recognised, running alongside or in the interstices between the four main types sketched out above. These include internal migration; the migration of Northern Europeans to settle in Southern Europe, often in retirement; the migration or mobility of students, notably under the Erasmus scheme; and the post-crisis return migration of some of the immigrants who arrived in Southern Europe during the nineties and two thousands.

Center-periphery is not the only organizing principle around which this chapter is based. Also highly relevant in conditioning the geographical evolution of flows both out, in terms of destination countries, and in, in terms of origin countries, has been the progressive expansion of the European Union, especially its Southern enlargement in the eighties, and the Eastern enlargement in 2004 and 2007. Indeed, in some respects these expansions can be seen as attempts to incorporate peripheral countries within the EU space; yet at the same time their very peripheral position is confirmed by their second-tier economic status. Meanwhile, alongside the center-periphery model which I favor in this account are two opposing theoretical stances which compete for dominance in the field of migration theory. These are the rational-choice optic of neoclassical economics, which sees migrants as utility-maximizing individuals moving freely in response to spatially uneven economic stimuli, above all the availability of jobs and higher wages; and the neo-Marxist historical-structural school, which sees migration not as a response to, but as part and parcel of the production and reproduction of spatially uneven development and of the desire of the owners of capital (governments and employers) to constantly seek out exploitable 'reserve armies' of cheap labor (King 2012, 11–23; Castles et. al. 2014, 28–33).

The chapter now unfolds as follows. The next section expands on the relevance and attractiveness of center-periphery thinking for the study of migration, especially as regards Southern Europe. This discussion provides a theoretical platform for the subsequent four sections, devoted to the four chronological stages of the 'migration story' of Southern Europe indicated above. From the point of view of the *raison d'être* of this book, what is interesting, even remarkable, is the similarity between the four countries under consideration in terms of their evolving migration dynamics since 1945, such that one can argue for a specific *South European model* of migration (King

2000).[1] The conclusion re-evaluates the significance of the center-periphery framework in the light of the recent experience of the region.

Centers, Peripheries, and Migration

It is the fundamental tenet of this chapter that international migration is one of the 'ties that bind' the periphery to the core of Europe. These population flows have been ever-present throughout the past several decades, varying only in intensity from one period to the next, and from one Southern European country to another. What is more controversial is how to interpret the parallel statistical series on migrant flows and on spatial economic trends. This is where ideology steps in. The battle is between the push-pull functionalists and neoclassical economists on one side, who see migration as a beneficial spatial reallocation of labor for the good of all (sending countries, receiving countries, the migrants themselves) and destined ultimately to attain a no-migration equilibrium as wages are equalized; and the neo-Marxists on the other, who view migration as the very essence of the continued dependency of the migrant-sending periphery on the migrant-receiving center.

Let me illustrate this interpretive dilemma by referencing a nearby country which hardly features in this book yet which has had the most dramatic exposure to the effects of migration in recent years—Albania. Here the mass emigration of around one third of the country's population since the end of the communist era in 1991 has had two countervailing effects. On the one hand, emigration has helped significantly to eradicate household poverty and boost gross national income via remittances and some inward foreign investment. On the other hand, the scale and persistence of migration have consolidated Albania's status as a labor-exporting periphery lacking endogenous stimuli for development (King 2005).

The center-periphery (or core-periphery) framework has multiple roots in history, political economy, development studies and economic geography. Its tap-root lies in the writings of Latin American dependency-school theorists, notably André Gunder Frank (1967); other important influences come

1 The model applies, to a greater or lesser extent, to Cyprus, Malta and Slovenia (King and Thomson 2008). Ireland has also followed a similar four-stage evolution of migration types.

from Wallerstein's world systems theory (1974, 1979), and, in a European context, books by Seers et. al. (1979), Arrighi (1985) and Hudson and Lewis (1985). Other chapters in this book have explored this heritage of writings on centers and peripheries more thoroughly. By the eighties the dependency relations of core-periphery structures were routinely embedded in geographers' analyses of the European, especially Southern European, space economy,[2] although, rather curiously to my way of thinking, migration failed to receive the attention it deserved as a crucial element of center-periphery structures and dynamics. This chapter is a contribution to rectifying that oversight.

My starting point for the rest of this discussion is the pioneering but surprisingly little-cited volume edited by Seers et. al. (1979) on core-periphery relations in Europe, in which the *dependency* of the four Southern European countries on the European and global core economies is the central spine of the analysis. According to Selwyn's essay in that volume, the periphery of Europe has several distinctive features, the chief of which is lack of effective control over its own resources. Hence, "the major economic decisions—what to produce, where and how to produce it, the origin of inputs, the marketing of outputs, what to consume, what and where to invest—all these will either be taken in the core or will be profoundly influenced by discussions in the core" (1979, 37). King (1982) and Williams (1984) reinforce these points and add others: the lack of endogenous innovation and the consequent reliance on imported ideas and technology; poor linkages *within* the periphery despite geographical proximity, especially between Spain and Portugal, and between Italy and Greece; and above all the dominant directional flows of people—of migrants from South to North, and reverse flows of tourists. Schneider et. al. (1972) diagnosed the early postwar decades of socio-economic change in Southern Europe—a period when economic growth indicators were consistently positive—as a case of modernization rather than true development, which ultimately failed to correct the structural pressures behind migration or to curb the coercive power of national and regional elites.

Seers et. al. (1979, xiii-xiv) point out that, whilst the center-periphery metaphor for the world economy is non-geographical, for Europe the spatial pattern is clear: there is a Southern periphery (Portugal across to Greece), a Western periphery (Ireland and Scotland), and a Northern one (Finland, which they class semi-periphery). The Eastern periphery was, at the time of

2 See, amongst others, Gottmann (1980), King (1982), Ilbery (1984), Williams (1984), Hudson and Lewis (1985), Hadjimichalis (1987), Keeble (1989), Hebbert and Jansen (1990), Hadjimichalis and Sadler (1995).

their writing, cordoned off by the Iron Curtain, remaining a functionally separate, but still a spatially coherent, political and economic bloc. Moving to the subnational level enhances the peripheral ring effect even more: those regions which are furthest from the European core (Andalusia, the Italian *Mezzogiorno*, the West of Ireland, the Scottish Highlands and Islands, Northern Scandinavia) are, on most counts, the most disadvantaged. Seers' map of the European core takes the form of an oval with its longest axis aligned from Barcelona to Helsinki, and its shortest axis stretching from Manchester to Vienna (Seers 1979, 21).

Migration is one of the most fundamental features of center-periphery systems in general, and in Europe in particular. The empirical characteristics of Western Europe's postwar labor migration system will be described in the next section. Usually, peripheral countries and regions are poorer, have labor surpluses and high unemployment, and hence act as reservoirs of labor which, under certain circumstances, can be 'exported' to the countries of the core. This migration may be temporary, followed by return migration; circular, with a back-and-forth regime; or permanent, with no return, except for visits. These different temporalities of migration have differential effects on the periphery. According to neoclassical migration theory, if the migration is permanent and on a sufficiently large scale, the effect will be to rebalance the spatial allocation of supply and demand for labor, and therefore wages should equalize. As surplus labor is siphoned out of peripheral areas by emigration, wages should rise in response. Likewise, the supply of extra labor through migration to the core countries will alleviate labor shortages, and this buoyant influx of migrant labor will hold wages down. Temporary and circular migration has different effects on the sending area: remittances are sent back to remaining family/household members,[3] and these may be used to sustain living costs, improve the quality of life of those remaining behind (better food, housing, consumer products etc.), and perhaps be invested in agriculture or a business venture. Migrants who return may bring back with them skills, training and experience acquired through working abroad, but that depends on the kinds of work performed, which are often low-status manual-labor jobs with little or no human-capital endowment. Even so, the general experience of living and working abroad for several years will inevitably involve exposure to a different way of life and set of cultural values, and

3 Remittances may also be sent by permanent migrants, but are likely to fall off as the migrant settles long-term with their family members abroad.

therefore the migrant may return home having internalized new behavioural norms and values, for instance regarding work, gender relations, child-rearing, political transparency etc.

By the sixties all four Southern European countries were generating substantial invisible export revenues from migration (remittances and repatriated savings) and tourism (tourists' spending in situ), although the greater industrial strength of the Italian economy meant that the relative weight of remittances and tourism receipts was less in this country. Table 1 sets out the figures for 1970, at the height of the postwar labor migration era for Southern Europe. The data in Table 1 only capture the statistical-financial picture for one moment, and these data-series exhibit trends which can be both steady and volatile. On the whole, for Southern Europe, remittances have been on a downward trend, in terms of their relationship to visible merchandise exports, since the seventies, and tourism receipts have increased as mass tourism has taken hold. But Seers et. al. (1979, xvi-xvii) argue that this is a potentially fragile dependency, since the control over both migration and tourism lies external to the countries involved. Governments of the destination countries of migrants can suddenly decide to block immigration (as happened in North-West Europe in 1973), either due to an economic downturn or in response to anti-immigration political pressure from the electorate. When this happens, the potentially beneficial economic effects of migration—mainly remittances—may be lessened, and migrants may be encouraged or even forced to return home. Tourism, likewise, is highly sensitive to economic fluctuations as well as to international competition from alternative tourist destinations.

Table 1: Receipts from migration and tourism as a percentage of total exports of merchandise, 1970

	Migrant labor	Tourist receipts	Both together
Portugal	55	25	80
Spain	20	68	88
Italy	8	12	20
Greece	54	32	86
Yugoslavia	46	9	55
Turkey	30	16	46

Source: Seers et al. (1979, 312–315)

Over time, theoretical reasoning behind the effectiveness of labor migration in contributing to the development of the migrants' countries of origin has fluctuated like a pendulum between accounts of optimism and pessimism: optimism during the early postwar decades of mass migration, i.e. the fifties and sixties; pessimistic during the recession-bound seventies and eighties; renewed optimism during the neoliberal era of the nineties and two thousands; and perhaps the beginnings of a swing back to neo-pessimism in the last few years (de Haas 2010, 2012; Gamlen 2014). Combined with center-periphery theory, these pendulum swings help us to interpret the chronology of migration in postwar Southern Europe over the past seven decades.

The "Golden Age" of Labor Migration from Southern Europe?

The question mark in the heading above refers to the interpretation of the phrase "golden age". For the development of Western Europe as a whole, the extra supply of migrant workers moving from the peripheral countries to the reconstructing and industrializing economies of the core was a fundamental driving force for the sustained growth—the "long boom"—that lasted until the economic shut-down caused by the 1973 oil crisis. Economists therefore see this as indeed a golden age, when factors of production—particularly for the production of industrial goods—were able to be brought together in a harmonious growth-oriented combination, sustained by a buoyant consumer demand for these mass-manufactured products. In Fielding's words, this migration of "mass collective workers" was essentially Fordist in nature, geared to staffing those Fordist factories producing standardized goods for a mass consumer market that was riding the wave of postwar prosperity (1993, 13).

For the migrant workers themselves, however, life was tough: steady and reasonably well-paid jobs, yes, and certainly by comparison to the standards of living in the countries they came from, but work which was often characterized by the "3Ds"—dirty, dangerous and demeaning. Typical jobs consisted of manual labor in coal mines, quarries and brickfields, in heavy-industry steel and auto manufacturing plants, and in consumer-market "brown" and "white" goods factories. Others worked on construction sites, or in low-grade service jobs collecting refuse, cleaning offices and hospitals, or working in the transport sector. Poor-quality and overcrowded accommodation—in hostel dormitories or in cramped flats with shared facilities—added to the low quality of life endured by the migrant workers at this time.

There are many detailed studies of this period, some of which have become classics of critical scholarship. Not all of them explicitly employ a center-periphery framework of analysis, but this optic can easily be reinscribed into their theorization and interpretation. Piore's was the fundamental thesis on the crucial role of migrant labor in fuelling growth in the postwar industrial economies of Western Europe and North America; the labor migration system was demand-driven and controlled by the governments, industrial employers and capitalists of the economies of the core (Piore 1979). Kindleberger's (1967) analysis was built on dual-sector theory: in his view surplus labor from the rural sector in Southern Europe was not only instrumental in undergirding industrial growth in North-West Europe, but only when such surplus labor had been removed from the South could the economies of Italy, Greece, Spain and Portugal be expected to develop themselves. Castles and Kosack (1973) were much less sanguine about the growth potential of the Southern periphery. They wrote (1973, 8) that whilst labor migration was highly profitable for West European capitalism, "it did nothing to alleviate the backwardness of the regions from which the migrants came"; indeed they saw it as more of a hindrance to development because of its excessive scale, selectivity (taking away physically-fit young adults), and minimal returns in the form of remittances (often "wasted" on unproductive spending). Likewise, returning migrants were not innovative entrepreneurs with enriched human capital, as they were constructed by the "optimistic" scenario, but were more often the sick, the exhausted and the retired (Castles and Kosack 1973, 408–420).

Much of the irony, tragedy and poignancy of South European labor migration at this time was brilliantly captured in the photographs and terse text of Berger and Mohr's *A Seventh Man* (1975). They wrote: "The migrant comes to sell his labour… he has no rights, claims or reality outside his filling… a certain kind of job… It is not men who migrate but machine-minders, sweepers, diggers, cleaners… To become a man (a husband, father, citizen, patriot) a migrant has to return home—the home he left because it held no future for him" (1975, 58).[4] Others drew attention to the impact of

4 Their use of masculinist language is deliberate, and related to the title—one in seven male workers in Europe is a migrant. Whilst it is true that many migration flows from Southern Europe in the early postwar decades were made up largely of men, this was not always the case, and the role of women migrants, either as independent actors or as part

labor migrants on class structure. Employing orthodox Marxist and dependency analysis, they argued that migration benefited only the ruling elites of both sending and receiving countries by acting as a factor of stability. Both at home and abroad, it fragments the working class and derevolutionizes it (Castles and Kosack 1973; Castells 1975; Nikolinakos 1975). Carney (1976) summed up the effects of labor migration as tantamount to a permanent drain of value and surplus from Southern Europe; an ongoing process of the reproduction of underdevelopment for the region.

Cutting across the conflicting ideological interpretations of the neoclassical optimists and the pessimistic neo-Marxists were the more neutral accounts of geographers and demographers who recorded and mapped the statistical parameters of the South-North migration flows of this era (Livi Bacci 1972; Salt and Clout 1976; King 1993, 1998). Flow-maps give a clear indication of the periphery-to-core spatial pattern. It is as if North-West Europe acted as a giant magnet drawing in migrants from all parts of the European periphery; except, at this time, the East. The symmetry is almost perfect. Moving anti-clockwise round the continent: Finland to Sweden; Ireland to Britain; Portugal and Spain to France; Italy to France, Germany and Switzerland; Greece, Yugoslavia and Turkey to Germany. The Southern flank of Europe is the dominant labor-supply periphery, which also extends to the Maghreb: Moroccans, Algerians and Tunisians to France; Moroccans also to Belgium and the Netherlands.[5]

Statistics provide a more fine-grained evolutionary picture, but are subject to the usual caveats about migration statistics: their failure to record clandestine and irregular migration (which was substantial especially from Portugal and Spain to France); and the danger of repeat-counting when back-and-forth migration occurs—for example with the "guest worker" migration to Germany and Switzerland where workers were "rotated" on short-term contracts.

A first chronological point to note is that Spain, Portugal, Italy and Greece all have a migration history that long pre-dates 1945, mainly cross-Atlantic but also within Europe (there were, for example, 900,000 Italians in France in 1931—King 1993, 20). These earlier migrations, like those of

of family migration and reunion, was for long overlooked. In a well-phrased riposte to the title of Piore's similarly masculinist analysis, Mirjana Morokvasic wrote a landmark paper entitled "Birds of passage are also women" (1984).

5 For examples, see the several maps I have created in earlier publications (King 1993, 21, 24–25; 1994, 224; 1998, 265).

the postwar decades, were born largely out of poverty and unemployment; for the Spanish and Portuguese, there was also a strong element of colonial settlement and involvement in farming, business development and administration in South America. Italians and Greeks were more oriented to the United States, although Italian migration was also significant to Argentina and Brazil. According to Sapelli (1995, 31–32) this earlier history of emigration created a "culture of emigration", legitimizing and normalizing the practice, and creating myths about emigration as the route from "rags to riches". Some of these overseas migrations continued into the early postwar decades, notably Italians, Greeks and Portuguese to the USA and Canada, and Italians and Greeks to the new destination of Australia. But, overall, the fifties and sixties saw the redirecting of Southern European emigration to Northern Europe.

Amongst the earliest postwar migrations, starting as soon as the war was over, were Italians recruited to work in French and Belgian mines and in the steel plants and brickfields of England and Wales. Spanish and Portuguese migration also got off to an early start, attracted by the working opportunities in France and facilitated by the setting up of the Office National d'Immigration in 1945. Germany, which took over as the main pole of attraction for Southern European migrants only after 1961, drew its labor supplies mainly from Italy, Greece, Yugoslavia and Turkey. Smaller numbers of Spaniards and Portuguese also went to Germany in the sixties and early seventies, and also to Switzerland where, however, Italians had always been the numerically largest migrant nationality.

The German *Gastarbeiter* model can be considered paradigmatic of this period, not least because it mirrors the center-periphery framework of how labor migration is structured and managed. As a leading economy of the "core", West Germany instituted the economic policy of *Konjunkturpuffer*, using migrant labor as a buffer against economic cycles, managed via a series of bilateral recruitment agreements with several Southern European and Mediterranean countries. When the economy entered a boom period, migrant labor was imported from the periphery on short-term contracts; then, when a cyclical downturn occurred, migrant workers were laid off and the unemployment was exported back to the periphery via return migration. The guest worker model also accorded with the German exclusivist stance towards citizenship, available only to those of German "blood". This ethnic dogma allowed the anachronistic declaration "Germany is not a country of immigration" to be maintained until the late nineties, in defiance of the reality of having the largest immigrant population in Europe.

In practice the guest worker model, in its purest form, was doomed to become extinct because of the European Community's increasing promotion of the social rights of migrants, and in particular their right to a family life. The EU institutional context is the final piece in the jigsaw of interlocking factors which, in combination, explain the scale and significance of mass labor migration up to the threshold year of 1973–74. Inscribed within the Treaty of Rome (Articles 48 and 49) were rules facilitating the free movement of labor, which were progressively implemented during the sixties; by the latter part of that decade regulations permitting family reunion were also in place, enabling guest workers to turn themselves into permanently settled migrant communities (King 1998).

The initial beneficiary of free movement of labor was Italy, founder-member of the Common Market, and the main repository of underemployed rural labor in the fifties and sixties within the fledging Community. Once Italian workers could no longer satisfy the labor demands of the other five Community members, the latter started recruiting from outside the European Community via a multitude of bilateral agreements (see Salt 1976, 98–100). Meanwhile, Italian workers were increasingly absorbed by the country's expanding industrial economy, which saw large-scale internal migrations from the rural South to industrial centers like Milan and Turin in the North. Free movement was subsequently accorded to Greeks, Spaniards and Portuguese following the accession of these countries to the European Community in the eighties, by which time the main stimuli driving South-North migration had waned.

Quantifying the aggregate scale of South-North labor migration during the alleged golden age is circumscribed by the manifold problems of measuring migration: stocks vs flows, gross vs net migration, migrant workers versus total population movement. Added to which are the already-noted problems of double-counting with repeat migration and under-enumeration of irregular movers, as well as the issue of classification by citizenship/nationality.[6] Tables of comparative statistics often fail to spell out these caveats.[7] My aggregation of annual gross emigration data for 1960–73, culled from the OECD's SOPEMI database (Continuous Reporting System on Migration), show the following results (King 1984, 148). Italy sent 3.5 million emigrants, with annual peaks of around 380,000 in the early sixties, declining to 150,000 in the early seventies. Portugal sent 1.4 million; here the annual peak came much later, in 1969–71 (over 150,000 per year). Greece sent 1 million with the main peaks of around 100,000 annually coming in 1963–65 and again in 1969–70. Finally for Spain, for which the available figures refer only to workers, the total is 1.1million, with peaks of above 100,000 in 1964 and 1969–72. *Stocks* of Southern European *workers* living abroad in Europe in 1973 were 858,000 Italians, 527,000 Spaniards, 469,000 Portuguese and 332,000 Greeks. Also to be noted were 582,000 Turks and 535,000 Yugoslavs (King 1994, 226).

Return Migration to the Periphery

Late 1973 witnessed the event which precipitated an economic crisis in the industrialized countries of Europe and elsewhere—the quadrupling of oil prices by the OPEC bloc. The impact on European migration trends was immediate: most labor-importing countries simply stopped the inflow of migrant workers, and encouraged those already there, especially the unemployed, to return to their countries of origin. This was *Konjunkturpuffer* in

6 There is no space here to spell out all these complications, but one example can illustrate the inherent complexity of migration data. The net flow of migrants between Italy and France over, say, a five-year period is made up of at least four separate movements: Italians emigrating to France, their return migration, French people migrating to Italy, and their return migration to France. Additionally there may be non-Italian and non-French "transit migrants", for example Tunisians migrating first to Italy and then onward-migrating to France. If migration is measured by the citizenship of the migrant, then complications arise with Italian migrants (and their descendants) who have acquired French nationality and who return-migrate to Italy: are they recorded as Italian return-migrants or French in-migrants?

7 For instance the table of net migration statistics for European countries in Seers et. al. (1979, 318) makes no such comments and contains some scarcely believable figures—net emigration loss for Greece of 3.5 million during 1950–60 and another 3.8 million during 1960–70, compared to equivalent figures for Spain (total population more than three times that of Greece) of 826,000 and 551,000.

action. But it would be a mistake to put all the emphasis on the oil-price hike to explain the *Gastarbeiter-Stop*. At least three other factors were less dramatically in operation too. First, there were signs that the Fordist model of industrial growth was already exhibiting signs of crisis before 1973, due to its inherent structural rigidities in the systems of mass industrial production, and to the saturation of consumer demand for these standardized goods. Second, the Southern European migrant-supply countries were already seeing their reserves of available migrants run dry, none more so than Italy, where emigration had already peaked as early as 1961, but also Spain and Greece. This was less the case for Portugal, whose emigration potential revived after joining the EU in 1986. For Greece, an early paper by Nikolinakos (1973) traced the beginnings of structural shortages in the Greek labor market to the sixties when foreign labor from countries like Egypt and Pakistan started to appear in Athens and Piraeus, for instance working in the port industries. And third, the halting of migrant labor by countries like West Germany, the Netherlands and Switzerland could also be related to growing social and political tension surrounding what were perceived as excessive concentrations of immigrants in certain cities and regions.

Hence, the mid-late seventies and much of the eighties were a period of net return migration to the four countries in question.[8] Once again, it would be a mistake to attribute this return wholly to loss of employment in the host countries. Empirical surveys of returned migrants revealed the complexity of their decision-making (King 1979; King et. al. 1986). Whilst some survey respondents articulated their decision mainly in economic terms (loss of job in the destination country, or availability of jobs in the improving economies of Southern Europe), it was more common to frame the return mainly in terms of culture, nostalgia, or family-related factors such as the need to care for aged parents or the wish to have children educated in the country of origin.

How does return migration impact the development of the periphery? According to the optimistic scenario, return brings back individuals and families with new skills learnt abroad, savings to invest, and new ideas about how society should be improved. In Cerase's four-type model of return migration, based on his study of return from the United States to Italy, this is the "return of innovation" (Cerase 1974; his other types are the returns of failure, conservatism and retirement). Cerase notes that, unfortunately for

8 But not so for Turkey, where the still-backward state of the Turkish economy, and political instability there, encouraged most Turkish families in Europe to stay put and ride out the recession.

the country and place of origin of the migrant, the return of innovation is not common, since the more innovative and development-minded migrants are precisely those who are likely to stay put and make successful lives for themselves in the destination country. Most returnees, according to Cerase, have either minimal impact on home-country development (because they return as destitute failures, or as retirees looking for a leisured life), or they act in a "conservative" way (eg. by buying land and building a new house) and therefore merely reinforce existing social structures.

Numerous other studies of return migration to Southern Europe generally reinforce the pessimistic scenario (see the review by King 1979). The more successful returnees aspire to a *nouveau-riche* class-status, but rarely create investments that are of long-term benefit to the local or regional economy. The building of migration-financed new houses stimulates the construction industry and contributes a kind of cosmetic makeover to the local built environment, but the result is "modernization without development" (Schneider et. al. 1972). There is, above all, an aversion to going back to working the land, since this represents merely scraping a living, and was what migrants were escaping from in the first place. There are, of course, some individual cases of successful return in terms of regional and local development—for instance returnees who invest in viable businesses in the tourist sector (Manganara 1977; King et. al. 1984), or in fishing (Mendonsa 1982)—but the general picture is one of unfulfilled expectations. Two reasons can be suggested for this disappointing outcome. First, most returning labor migrants have low levels of education and training, and so can hardly be expected to be entrepreneurial upon return. Second, the places that they left from—mostly rural areas, often in hilly and mountainous environments—hold few possibilities for migrant-financed, or any other, development, having been abandoned and depopulated by previous out-migration. Only by moving to coastal and urban areas can returnees hope to build a better future for themselves and their families after return (King et. al. 1986).

Return migration is still an ongoing process, but the demography of the returnees has changed. For the past twenty years or so, those coming back to their Southern European home countries are mainly retired labor migrants—Cerase's "return of retirement"—who go back to their towns and villages of origin for the final stage of their lives. Like most return decisions, this one is finely balanced between the pull of nostalgia and lifestyle on the one hand, and distancing from other family members abroad and better health services on the other hand. Those with children and grandchildren in Northern Europe may move back and forth in a transnational lifestyle, as long as their health and finances permit (Bolzman et. al. 2006; Rodriguez and Egea 2006).

Another form of relocation is that of the second generation, born abroad to immigrant parents, who decide for reasons of ethnic belonging, climate, lifestyle, family connections or (rarely) job opportunities, to move to their parental homeland, which they will have kept in touch with by regular holiday visits throughout their earlier lives. According to a growing literature on the phenomenon of "second-generation return", their reactions are mixed. Some feel instantly at home and decide that this is where they truly "belong", whilst others are disillusioned by the difficulties of getting a job and by the higher levels of gossip, social control and corruption in the "South" (for examples see Wessendorf 2007; King and Christou 2010; Sardinha 2011).

Immigration to Southern Europe: from Periphery to Semi-Periphery

If return migration was the first counter-flow that helped to tip the balance in the Southern European countries from net out-migration to net in-migration in the seventies, far more important in later decades was immigration from other countries (King and Black 1997).[9] These large-scale inflows, a new experience in the migration history of Southern Europe, implied a repositioning of the region within the global arrangement of centers and peripheries. From a position which was unequivocally on the periphery of Europe, Southern Europe shifted to a situation where it was, obviously, still located on the Southern margin of the European core, but where it now acted as a receiving context for millions of migrants arriving from Africa, Latin America, the Middle East, Asia and, after 1990, Eastern Europe. The opening up of Eastern Europe as the new, migrant-sending periphery of Europe gave Southern Europe an enhanced status as "semi-periphery" (or, perhaps, "semi-core"). Meanwhile, the true, "outer periphery" was made up of those much poorer, underdeveloped countries of what used to be called the Third World, now more commonly referred to as the Global South. Now, South-

9 The net migration balance turned positive in Italy in 1972, in Spain and Greece in 1975, and in Portugal in 1981 (Montanari and Cortese 1993, 218–221).

ern Europe finds itself on the front line of the Global North. The Mediterranean has become Europe's Rio Grande. Our news media and screens are daily filled with the human tragedies that unfold as migrants from the Global South, driven by poverty, violence and the hunger for a better life, try desperately to gain a foothold in Europe, often landing on the continent's insular outposts of Lampedusa, Malta or the Canary Islands.

The rather rapid transition of Southern Europe from a region of mass emigration to one of mass immigration is one of the most remarkable episodes of recent global migration history. Several factors combine to explain this migration turnaround, such that the region now occupies a strategic position within the international division of labor and the resultant global systems of migration (King and Rybaczuk 1993; King et. al. 1997; King 2000).

As with most migrations, the key underpinning factors are economic and demographic. There is no doubt that, between the seventies and nineties, the economies of the four Southern European countries were transformed. The gap between Southern Europe on the one hand, and Northern Europe on the other, was significantly narrowed on the basis of standard economic indicators such as per capita GDP, activity rates and the distribution of employment amongst agriculture, industry and services. As noted before, remittances and return migration probably played a rather minor role in this economic catching-up: more important was membership of the European Union and the availability of regional development and structural funds, the growth of the tourist industry, and of the tertiary sector in general. Agriculture saw its share of total employment decline rapidly: from 20 to 9 percent in Italy between 1970 and 1990, from 27 to 12 percent in Spain, 30 to 18 percent in Portugal, and 41 to 25 percent in Greece (OECD data quoted in King and Konjhodzic 1996, 30). With industry holding on to its employment share of around 30–38 percent (lower in Greece), the slack was taken up by a dynamic tertiary sector.

Perhaps more important than this shift in sectoral employment is the specific character of the economy and labor market in the Southern European countries, and especially the buoyant informal sector—what is often referred to as the *secondary labor market* of casual, insecure, poorly paid and unprotected jobs where few or no taxes are paid, as opposed to the *primary labor market* of secure, better-paid regular jobs protected by social insurance and other employee benefits. In all four countries, the expansion of the informal sector coincided with, but was not directly caused by, the influx of migrant workers who found it easier, especially if they lacked documents and legal status, to get employment in the secondary labor market. The weight of the informal economy was estimated at around 20–30 percent of GDP in all four countries in the eighties and it was present in most areas of employment, from farming and fishing, through industrial workshops and construction, to tourism, carework, transport and other service activities (King and Konjhodzic 1996, 47).

The demographic factors have to do with the complex interrelations between labor-market needs, past migration processes, both internal and international, and the spatial contrasts in fertility-rate trends between Southern Europe and adjacent migrant-supply regions to the south and beyond. The labor needs created by the development of intensive specialized agriculture, industry, tourism and services in the Southern European countries since the sixties were initially satisfied by utilizing surplus rural-sector labor from within each country. This needed labor was delivered by rural-urban commuting or longer-distance inter-regional migration—for instance from the rural South of Italy to Piedmont and Lombardy in the North, or from Andalusia to Barcelona and Catalonia. Contemporaneously, these same regions of rural out-migration were also losing workers to international migration, as we have seen. To take once again the example of the Italian *Mezzogiorno*, this region witnessed an out-migration of 4 million people between 1951 and 1971: half migrated abroad, and half internally within Italy—to Rome and the North (Sapelli 1995, 45). But by the early seventies, these rural supply sources had run out, due to prior waves of out-migration and the knock-on effect of falling birthrates choking off the supply of new labor market entrants. At this point the Southern European countries turned to immigrants to take up the slack. Each of the four countries evolved its own geography of migrant origins, based on a combination of geographical proximity, cultural, linguistic and colonial links—although for some origin countries none of these factors applied (eg. Chinese and South Asian migrants). The push-factor pressures of poverty and high demographic growth meant that migrants from many parts of the less developed world were keen to come, either aiming for Southern Europe as an end-destination or aspiring to use the region as a gateway to Northern Europe. Portugal drew in migrants from its former African colonies (Cape Verde, Angola and Guinea-Bissau mainly), from Brazil and, after 1990, from Eastern Europe (especially Romania and Ukraine). Spain allowed in migrants from Morocco and Algeria, from South America (particularly the Andean countries of Peru, Ecuador and Colombia), and, again more recently, from Eastern Europe (Poland, Romania, Bulgaria). Greece hosted migrants from one dominant country, neighbouring Albania, which accounts for around 60 per cent of the country's immigrants. Italy exhibits the greatest diversity of migrant origins. By 2010 the three largest groups were from Romania, Albania and Morocco, but there were also very substantial numbers from China, Ukraine, Moldova, Ecuador, Ghana, Senegal, Bangladesh, Tunisia, and many other countries.

As stated in the introduction, I have argued that there is a shared and specific model of immigration in Southern Europe (King 2000), and its key features are as follows. First, there is the unavoidable imperative of *geography*. Southern Europe constitutes the *porous frontier* to the "European fortress", with long coasts which are difficult to patrol and block access to. The efforts of the EU border control agency Frontex often only result in migrants taking greater risks in their desire to land somewhere on the European shore.

Secondly, and related to the geographical openness of the entire Mediterranean Basin to criss-crossing maritime, island and land routes, the nature of the migrants' entry has often been *clandestine*, channelled along routes of least resistance which can rapidly switch in response to control strategies. Even so, the picture of desperate "boat people" which dominates the news media about migrants and refugees in Southern Europe should not distract from the main method of arrival, which is legal entry on a tourist or visitor visa, and then overstaying. The main policy instrument, observable across all four Southern European countries, has been to *regularize* large numbers of irregular migrants every few years. This process started in the eighties in Spain and Italy, was then followed by Portugal and Greece (the latter only starting in 1998), and lasted until the early two thousands. It has faded as a policy instrument since it is thought to encourage more clandestine arrivals in anticipation of a future regularization.

Third, the specific *economic history* and *current economic structure* of the Southern European countries sets the scene for the very different role that migrants play in the labor markets of these four countries, compared to the highly regulated way that Southern European emigrants were functional to the Fordist model of Northern Europe during the migration boom years of the fifties to mid-seventies. The "late-developer" nature of the Southern European economies saw them evolve into a structure of mostly *small enterprises* surrounded by a large and dynamic *informal economy*. Only in Northern Italy, typified by the huge Fiat plant in Turin, did a Fordist industrial structure emerge. Elsewhere, what the Southern European labor market demanded was a flexible, low-cost labor reserve available for casual, short-term and seasonal work in agriculture, fishing, tourism and construction—all sectors which are either inherently seasonal or governed by fluctuations in demand and location.

Fourth, there is a demand for *domestic and care labor*, reflecting two trends in the region. The first is the rising levels of labor force participation by local women, creating demands for domestic cleaners, baby-sitters, and carers for elderly or sick family members. Entrenched gender behaviour means that, in general, husbands and male family members do not make themselves available for these household and family tasks. The second problem is the weak welfare state, which relies on a family model of care for elderly relatives and sick family members. Residential homes for the elderly and frail are not well developed, and there is a stigma of shame suffered by families who put their older members in care homes. The solution is to bring carers into the family domain by hiring female foreign carers and helpers, often on a live-in basis. Preferred nationalities for this kind of work are those from South America, the Philippines and Eastern Europe.

Given the variegated, but nearly always low-status nature of the jobs done, many of the employment niches mentioned above are characterized by specialization according to nationality and gender, as well as by extreme diversity of national and social origins, although this is less the case in Greece where Albanians are by far the dominant immigrant group. At the other end of the social and wealth spectrum, not to be forgotten are the Northern Europeans—British, Germans, Dutch, Scandinavians etc.—who have settled along the coasts and islands of Mediterranean Europe, or in rural landscapes such as Tuscany and Umbria in Italy. The most typical group are the elderly retired foreigners, who see themselves as "expats" rather than "immigrants". Although, for some, there are undoubted problems of failing health and social isolation, not to mention lack of integration into the host society, most of them live leisured lifestyles and try to imagine themselves as enjoying a permanent holiday in retirement (King et. al. 2000).

New Emigration and the Return of the Center-Periphery Dynamic

This is the fourth and final stage of Southern Europe's postwar migration history, and continues up to the present day. The year 2008, the onset of the current financial crisis, which has impacted Southern Europe more severely than countries to the North, is often seen as the trigger-date of this latest wave of emigration; in fact, 2008 did not mark the beginning of the new emigration from the South, but accentuated what was already in motion since the nineties, if not before. It became clear that, to follow Sapelli's (1995) diagnosis, Southern Europe had achieved only a kind of "incomplete" development with respect to the core. This lack of economic maturity rested on two enduring features of the region's history: its weak industrialization and shaky productive system; and its clientelistic and often corrupt political structure, both at the national level and in the *caciquismo* of local and regional elites. Hence there emerged a gap between the aspirations of particularly the younger, more educated cohorts of the population, who had become accustomed to "European" levels of material consumption and quality-of-life, and the countries' economic systems which did not have the productive capacity to sustain these expected standards without resort to borrowing, credit, and ultimately, catastrophic indebtedness.

One of the long-standing results of the South European trajectory of economic history, and in particular the direct transition from a rural, agricultural economy to one based on urbanization and services, is the accompanying interaction between the labor market, class formation and the education system. The "missing" (except in North-West Italy) phase of industrialization has resulted in a lack of vocational education, including at degree level, directed to industrial, technical and product-marketing courses. Instead there is an over-production of humanities, social sciences and law graduates, which the labor market is not able to absorb. This situation is exacerbated by the way that, in many graduate employment sectors, the older generations cling on to their positions, power and resources. Nowhere is this more true than in the university sector!

Thus, the recent increase in highly qualified emigrants from Southern Europe is not just a result of the 2008 financial crisis, but reflects a much deeper structural crisis in graduate unemployment which goes back two or more decades. Nearly twenty years ago, Antonio Negri (1997, 43) wrote the following striking words about Italy: "exile is the usual condition for intelligent Italians, and always has been. Exile is the condition for reproducing creative thinking in Italy. Aside from that, all that's left are the academy, the bureaucracy, and the church".[10] In Italy, as in the other Southern European countries, these three sectors are male-dominated, gerontocratic, hierarchical, and inimical to change via what is too often perceived as the threatening infusion of young blood. Hence the frustration of unemployed or underemployed, poorly paid young people (some of them not-so-young) who can only find a logical escape through emigration. This situation had already existed before 2008, but has become significantly worsened by the recession. Table 2 shows the rise in unemployment rates during five years spanning the financial crisis.[11]

Table 2: Unemployment rates, 2007–08 and 2012–13 (All figures are percentages of those available to work)

	total		youth (under 25)	
	2007–08	2012–13	2007–08	2012–13
Portugal	8.7	15.7	16.5	37.0
Spain	9.8	25.4	21.9	53.7
Italy	6.4	11.7	20.8	38.0
Greece	8.0	25.8	22.5	56.8

Source: Eurostat. Note: the figures are two-year averages to iron out fluctuations

What is different about this recent periphery-to-center migration compared to that of the Fordist era of mass labor migration? Just about everything, except the reproduction of the geographical flows. The earlier migrations were mainly of rural-origin, poorly-educated workers destined for jobs in factories or on construction sites. Hiring was highly regulated by bilateral recruitment quotas in which workers, mainly men initially, were screened for their good health and suitability for these types of work. Although their contracts were originally short-term, the migration as a whole morphed into a family-based settlement which led to the formation of established ethnic communities which remain today as a key component of the social geography of Northern European cities.

10 Negri, radical activist, Marxist sociologist and political philosopher, went into exile in Paris in 1984, when he was condemned in absentia to 30 years in prison for alleged leadership of the Red Brigades and associated murders, including that of Prime Minister Aldo Moro.

11 The vulnerability of small peripheral countries at this time is also revealed by the large increases in percentage of unemployed posted by the following EU countries: Cyprus, Slovenia, Bulgaria, Ireland, Latvia and Lithuania.

The recent wave of emigration out of Southern Europe is unregulated, since they are "free movers" within the EU, their mobility lubricated by the largely borderless Schengen-space and by the low fares of budget airlines.[12] Such migrants are part of a growing trend in intra-European cross-border mobility which had been growing well before the 2008 crisis (Recchi and Favell 2009). To a much greater extent than before, South-North migrants are well-educated young men and women drawn from urban, middle-class social backgrounds. Whilst the economic motive remains paramount in many cases, this is not the whole story: many are also driven to migrate by adventure, love, a desire for a different lifestyle, and the opportunity to improve or learn English or other languages. Family migration and family formation are not uppermost in their minds: this is generally postponed until later.

The work performed by these more recent migrants varies but generally does not include jobs in factories or on building sites; these jobs are nowadays left for migrants from Eastern Europe or elsewhere. The jobs they access depend very much on their language skills and qualifications, and how they can deploy these in a competitive and hierarchically segmented labor market. Some, with good language skills, well-regarded and relevant degrees, and good CVs, get top jobs in finance, management, marketing, international organizations, research and teaching, the media and arts, or a specialized industry (IT, pharmaceuticals etc.). They are what Adrian Favell (2008) calls "Eurostars" and they are a significant if not always very visible presence in cities like London, Paris, Brussels, Amsterdam and Berlin. These high-flyers are the pioneers of the idea and reality of European integration (Recchi and Favell 2009). But others do not fare so well. Lack of language competence and inability to market their qualifications restrict them to low-grade jobs in the service sector, working for instance in hotels and restaurants, or as nannies and au-pairs. Depending on their ability to improve their language and communication skills, and their ongoing work experience, they may be able to escape these low-paid jobs and move to better employment; or they may be stuck in such jobs until they return-migrate.

Whilst the broad South-to-North geography of the more recent flows repeats the patterns of earlier outward flows to Northern Europe, there are differences. The first is the scale of the movement: not as great as the mass-migration of the Fordist era. The second regards the precise destinations: no

12 Mainly Ryan Air and EasyJet, which tap into the dual mass markets of Northward-flying migrants and Southward flying tourists. The UK and Ireland are extra-Schengen and so operate border controls, a minor inconvenience for EU citizens.

longer the industrial cities and regions, but now aimed at the major capital cities and centers of employment in the activities mentioned above. The third is the rise to prominence of the UK, and particularly London, as the favoured destination. This was already true for the pre-crisis movement of Southern European graduates, dating back to the nineties (Favell 2008, 30–45), but has been reinforced since the crisis, partly because of the relative buoyancy and open nature of the UK economy, and partly because London offers such a wide range of employment opportunities (King et. al. 2014). Table 3 illustrates the strong growth of Southern European workers coming into the UK as measured by national insurance registrations.

Table 3: National Insurance registrations of Southern European workers entering the UK, 2006–07 and 2012–13

	2006–07	2012–13
Portugal	10,810	24,531
Spain	10,690	45,442
Italy	12,800	32,743
Greece	3,530	8,655

Source: Department for Work and Pensions. Note: figures refer to tax year

A further difference between "then" and "now" is more about the temporalities of mobility. Early labor migrants travelled by train across Europe, returning home for holiday visits by train or, later, by car. Nowadays the "Ryan Air" and "EasyJet" generations fly back and forth, often with great frequency, for a few tens of euros. Moreover, they are building on a multitude of previous experiences of mobility—on holiday with their parents, or summer language schools in places like Brighton or Dublin, or an Erasmus year in a university in Northern Europe.

Despite the publicity attracted to this new European migration in the government and media, in-depth studies of the post-crisis migration from Southern Europe are rather rare. Here I pick up two examples where some published research exists—the cases of graduate Italians in the UK (Conti 2012; King et. al. 2014, 16–23) and of highly educated Greek labor emigrants to Europe and North America (Labrianidis and Vogiatzis 2013).

Table 3 shows that in the fiscal year 2006–07, just before the crisis, Italians were the leading Southern European nationality for new National Insurance Number (NINo) registrations in the UK—12,800. By 2012–13 they had been overtaken by Spanish nationals—probably reflecting the depth and suddenness of the Spanish economic crisis—but nevertheless, the number of Italians registering had grown substantially, to nearly 33,000. Conti (2012, 5) confirms that the bulk of recent Italian entrants to the UK labor market are graduates. This has given rise to widespread concerns in Italy about the possibility of a brain drain. Both Becker et. al. (2004) and Conti (2012) find that the percentage of graduates amongst the total flow of emigrants from Italy has been increasing, and that it occurs from all parts of Italy, not just the unemployment-ridden South where the region's labor market cannot absorb more than a fraction of the graduates produced by the Southern universities. Interestingly, graduates emigrating from the North of Italy are likely to already have jobs and to see their departure for the UK as part of a project of income advancement, career progress, and self-development in a more open labor market, where people are valued for their CVs and not for their "connections". They are particularly attracted to the meritocratic system in the UK, compared to the closed and nepotistic character of the Italian professional employment sectors—none more so than the university sector, still run on almost feudal lines. The quotes from interviews carried out by Conti (2012) reveal that Italian graduates in the UK can be compared to refugees fleeing a corrupt and anachronistic political and social system. They are pessimistic of the ability of the Italian government to resolve the many problems that beset the country and to offer young people a better chance.

The Greek case represents the most widely-known drama of the 'euro-crisis' and has yet to run its course, with tense ongoing negotiations and stand-offs between the new left-wing government and the European and international financial bosses. Hadjimichalis (2011) sees the Eurozone crisis as a reassertion of the center-periphery dynamic within Europe, the peripheral indebted countries (Spain, Portugal, Italy, Greece, Ireland) becoming powerless against the financial control exerted by the "core" led by Germany. But there are important internal factors too. Labrianidis and Vogiatzis (2013, 538) summarize the causes of the Greek debt crisis as a combination of dysfunctional financial mechanisms at global, European and national levels, the historic uneven development of the Greek economy, and the dangerous structural reliance on informal economic activities. The youth unemployment figures (Table 2) are the highest of any EU country. This is not matched by a comparably high rate of recent emigration to the UK (Table 3), largely because recent Greek emigration has spread to other destination countries in Europe such as Germany and the Netherlands, as well as to North America (Labrianidis and Vogiatzis 2013).

Like the rest of Southern Europe, but to an extreme degree, Greek society has an obsession with higher education. At one level, close to 90 per cent of young adults are or have been enrolled in higher education, but there are caveats to this. Most tuition is free, lecture attendance is not closely monitored, and there are lax time limits on completing a degree. Many students prolong their registration in order to avoid military service and to continue to enjoy travel and health subsidies. As a result it is estimated that about half of all enrolled students are "non-active" students, which explains the low rates of actual graduation (Labrianidis and Vogiatzis 2013, 530).

The online survey conducted by Labrianidis and Vogiatzis in 2009–10 (1821 valid responses) revealed some interesting insights into the nature of Greek graduate emigration at that time, just after the onset of the crisis but before its most severe impact was felt in this country. The following refer to the percentage of total respondents rating various motives for emigration as "very important": "better career prospects" 75, "interesting job in my field" 71, "chance to upgrade knowledge in my chosen field" 60, "better income" 52, "unable to find suitable job in Greece" 51, "desire for work experience abroad" 46, "studied abroad and stayed on to work" 38, "corruption and lack of meritocracy in Greece" 34. These findings indicate that income maximization is not the most important motivating factor for emigration, ranking some way below factors relating to career development and knowledge acquisition (Labrianidis and Vogiatzis 2013, 542).

Another interesting question in the same survey related to motives that could lead graduates to return to Greece. Taking again those factors rated as "very important", and listing only those motives scoring at least 30 percent of respondents, the authors record the following data: "finding a job in Greece relevant to my qualifications" 64, "if both my partner and I could find satisfactory jobs" 59, "if salaries in Greece were commensurate to those abroad" 59, "if the Greek state acknowledged the contribution of Greek scientists working abroad" 50, "if there was significant social progress in Greece" 39, "if there was a campaign to fight corruption and bureaucracy and reward merit" 37 (Labrianidis and Vogiatzis 2013, 543).

Conclusion

The figures quoted above are very revealing of the continued relevance of center-periphery structures, and also mentalities, in the unfolding patterns of Southern European migration and possible return migration. The Italian findings show that many of the new emigrants are so disenchanted with the state of affairs in Italy, both with regard to their own chances of getting a decent job there and with the inability of the government to tackle the endemic corruption in politics and society, that they cannot foresee a likely return. The Greek data, too, indicate that the conditions for return are unlikely to be fulfilled in the very near future, despite the demands for reform being made both from outside and within the country.

Both studies reveal that, underlying the center-periphery contrast, at least in the eyes of the interviewees and respondents, is a clash of mentalities. One of the most widely-used words in the interviews with Italian graduates in the UK was *mentalità,* which can be interpreted at multiple levels (King et. al. 2014, 21–23). First, the "national character" of Italy is seen as one dominated by patriarchy, gerontocracy, clientelism and suffocating bureaucracy, producing a society which is stagnant and inimical to change, especially for young people, who must go abroad to progress in their lives. Second, at a local or regional scale, Italians exhibit a "provincial mentality" whereby they are strongly linked to their city or local region, and suspicious of "outsiders", even from other parts of Italy. And third, there is the "family mentality" which expects loyalty to the family above all else—what Edward Banfield famously but controversially called "amoral familism" (1958).

What does this construction of the European South as riven by corruption, clientelism and other "backward" mentalities mean for migration types and center-periphery relations? In the past, European center-periphery structures and mechanisms were conceived largely within the economics of regional inequalities and the consequent labor-migrant flows of the *Gastarbeiter* era (Seers et. al. 1979). The guest workers were less concerned about the type of jobs on offer, and more preoccupied with acquiring what was for them a decent income. Recent emigration is still strongly shaped by economic factors, above all those linked to the crisis of graduate and youth unemployment, but cultural factors are stressed too—a reflection perhaps of a more critical perspective on society nurtured through the experience of higher education.

On the macro-geographical scale, the spatialities of uneven development across Europe have reasserted themselves with the latest crisis. Seers et. al.'s (1979) and King's (1982) core-periphery maps, and Dunford's (1994) map of "winners" and "losers" have shown themselves to be enduring (Williams 2009; Hadjimichalis 2011). Nothing has changed with regard to Southern Europe's peripheral situation within Europe and semi-peripheral position within the world economy and global migration flows. This latest economic downturn—a conjuncture of epic proportions for Southern Europe, and for other parts of the global economy—has revealed once again the ironic combination of fragility and stability of the South European model of economic, political and social organization: vulnerable to exogenous forces beyond its control, but at the same time too stable and inbred to effect radical change.

Works Cited

Arrighi, Giovanni (1985). *Semiperipheral Development: The Politics of Southern Europe in the Twentieth Century*. Beverly Hills: Sage.

Banfield, Edward C. (1958). *The Moral Basis of a Backward Society*. Glencoe: The Free Press.

Becker, Sascha O., Andrea Ichino, and Giovanni Peri (2004). How Large is the 'Brain Drain' from Italy? *Giornale degli Economisti e Annali di Economia*, 63:1, 1–32.

Berger, John, and Jean Mohr (1975). *A Seventh Man: The Story of a Migrant Worker in Europe*. Harmondsworth: Penguin.

Bolzman, Claudio, Rosita Fibbi, and Marie Vial (2006). What to Do after Retirement? Elderly Migrants and the Question of Return. *Journal of Ethnic and Migration Studies*, 32:8, 1359–1375.

Carney, John (1976). Capital Accumulation and Uneven Development in Europe: Notes on Migrant Labour. *Antipode: A Radical Journal of Geography*, 8:1, 30–38.

Castells, Manuel (1975). Immigrant Workers and Class Struggles in Advanced Capitalism: the West European Experience. *Politics and Society*, 5:1, 33–66.

Castles, Stephen, and Godula Kosack (1973). *Immigrant Workers and Class Structure in Western Europe*. London: Oxford University Press.

Castles, Stephen, Hein de Haas, and Mark J. Miller (2014). *The Age of Migration: International Population Movements in the Modern World*. Basingstoke: Palgrave Macmillan.

Cerase, Francesco P. (1974). Migration and Social Change: Expectations and Reality. A Case Study of Return Migration from the United States to Italy. *International Migration Review*, 8:2, 245–262.

Conti, Francesca (2012). The Present Significance of National Identity Issues: the Case of Italian Graduates in the UK. *Bulletin of Italian Politics*, 4:1, 5–22.

de Haas, Hein (2010). Migration and Development: a Theoretical Perspective. *International Migration Review*, 44:1, 227–264.

de Haas, Hein (2012). The Migration and Development Pendulum: a Critical Review of Research and Policy. *International Migration*, 50:3, 8–25.

Dunford, Mick (1994). Winners and Losers: the New Map of Economic Inequality in the European Union. *European Urban and Regional Studies*, 1:2, 95–114.

Favell, Adrian (2008). *Eurostars and Eurocities: Free Movement and Mobility in an Integrating Europe*. Oxford: Blackwell.

Fielding, Anthony (1993). Mass Migration and Economic Restructuring. In Russell King (ed.). *Mass Migration in Europe: The Legacy and the Future*, 7–18. London: Belhaven Press.

Frank, André Gunder (1967). *Capitalism and Underdevelopment in Latin America*. New York: Monthly Review Press.

Gamlen, Alan (2014). The New Migration-and-Development Pessimism. *Progress in Human Geography*, 38:4, 581–597.

Gottmann, Jean (ed.). (1980) *Centre and Periphery: Spatial Variation in Politics*. Beverly Hills: Sage.

Hadjimichalis, Costis (1987). *Uneven Development and Regionalism: State, Territory and Class in Southern Europe*. London: Croom Helm.

Hadjimichalis, Costis (2011). Uneven Geographical Development and Socio-Spatial Justice and Solidarity. *European Urban and Regional Studies*, 18:3, 254–274.

Hadjimichalis, Costis, and David Sadler (eds.). (1995). *Europe at the Margins: New Mosaics of Inequality*. Chichester: Wiley.

Hebbert, Michael, and Jens Christian Hansen (eds.). (1990). *Unfamiliar Territory: The Reshaping of European Geography*. Aldershot: Avebury.

Hudson, Ray, and Jim Lewis (eds.). (1985). *Uneven Development in Southern Europe*. London: Methuen.

Ilbery, Brian W. (1984). Core-Periphery Contrasts in European Social Well-Being. *Geography*, 69:4, 289–302.

Keeble, David (1989). Core-Periphery Disparities, Recession and New Regional Dynamisms in the European Community. *Geography*, 74:1, 1–11.

Kindleberger, Charles P. (1967). *Europe's Post-War Growth: The Role of Labour Supply*. London: Oxford University Press.

King, Russell (1979). Return Migration: a Review of Some Case Studies from Southern Europe. *Mediterranean Studies*, 1:2, 3–30.

King, Russell (1982). Southern Europe: Dependency or Development? *Geography*, 67:3, 221–234.

King, Russell (1984). Population Mobility: Emigration, Return Migration and Internal Migration. In Allan Williams (ed.). *Southern Europe Transformed: Political and Economic Change in Greece, Italy, Portugal and Spain*, 145–178. London: Harper and Row.

King, Russell (1993). European International Migration 1945–90: a Statistical and Geographical Overview. In Russell King (ed.). *Mass Migration in Europe: The Legacy and the Future*, 19–39. London: Belhaven Press.

King, Russell (1994). Migration and the Single Market for Labour: an Issue in Regional Development. In Mark Blacksell and Allan M. Williams (eds.). *The European Challenge: Geography and Development in the European Community*, 218–241. Oxford: Oxford University Press.

King, Russell (1998). From Guestworkers to Immigrants: Labour Migration from the Mediterranean Periphery. In David Pinder (ed.). *The New Europe: Economy, Society and Environment*, 263–279. Chichester: Wiley.

King, Russell (2000). Southern Europe in the Changing Global Map of Migration. In Russell King, Gabriella Lazaridis and Charalambos Tsardanidis (eds.). *Eldorado or Fortress? Migration in Southern Europe*, 1–26. Basingstoke: Macmillan.

King, Russell (2005). Albania as a Laboratory for the Study of Migration and Development. *Journal of Southern Europe and the Balkans*, 7:2, 133–155.

King, Russell (2012). *Theories and Typologies of Migration: an Overview and a Primer.* Malmo: Malmo University, Willy Brandt Working Papers in International Migration and Ethnic Relations 3/12.

King, Russell and Richard Black (eds.). (1997). *Southern Europe and the New Immigrations.* Brighton: Sussex Academic Press.

King, Russell, and Anastasia Christou (2010). Cultural Geographies of Counter-Diasporic Migration: Perspectives from the Study of Second-Generation 'Returnees' to Greece. *Population, Space and Place*, 15:2, 103–119.

King, Russell and Indira Konjhodzic (1996). Labour, Employment and Migration in Southern Europe. In John Van Oudenaren (ed.). *Employment, Economic Development and Migration in Southern Europe and the Maghreb*, 7–106. Santa Monica: Rand.

King, Russell and Krysia Rybaczuk (1993). Southern Europe and the International Division of Labour: from Emigration to Immigration. In Russell King (ed.). *The New Geography of European Migrations*, 175–206. London: Belhaven Press.

King, Russell, and Mark Thomson (2008). The Southern European Model of Immigration: Do the Cases of Malta, Cyprus and Slovenia Fit? *Journal of Southern Europe and the Balkans*, 10:3, 265–291.

King, Russell, Anthony Fielding, and Richard Black (1997). The International Migration Turnaround in Southern Europe. In Russell King and Richard Black (eds.). *Southern Europe and the New Immigrations*, 1–25. Brighton: Sussex Academic Press.

King, Russell, Alan Strachan, and Jill Mortimer (1984). Return Migration and Tertiary Development: a Calabrian Case-Study. *Anthropological Quarterly*, 57:3, 112–124.

King, Russell, Alan Strachan, and Jill Mortimer (1986). Gastarbeiter Go Home: Return Migration and Economic Change in the Italian Mezzogiorno. In Russell

King (ed.). *Return Migration and Regional Economic Problems*, 38–68. London: Croom Helm.

King, Russell, Tony Warnes, and Allan Williams (2000). *Sunset Lives: British Retirement Migration to the Mediterranean*. Oxford: Berg.

Labrianidis, Lois, and Nikos Vogiatzis (2013). The Mutually Reinforcing Relation between International Migration of Highly Educated Labour Force and Economic Crisis: the Case of Greece. *Southeast European and Black Sea Studies*, 13:4, 525–551.

Livi Bacci, Massimo (ed.). (1972). *The Demographic and Social Pattern of Emigration from the Southern European Countries*. Florence: Dipartimento Statistico Matematico dell'Università di Firenze, Serie Ricerche Empiriche, vol. 7.

Mendonsa, Eduardo L. (1982). Benefits of Migration as a Personal Strategy in Nazaré, Portugal. *International Migration Review*, 16:3, 635–645.

Montanari, Armando, and Antonio Cortese (1993). South to North Migration in a Mediterranean Perspective. In Russell King (ed.). *Mass Migration in Europe: the Legacy and the Future*, 212–233. London: Belhaven Press.

Morokvasic, Mirjana (1984). Birds of Passage are also Women. *International Migration Review*, 18:4, 886–907.

Negri, Antonio (1997). Italy, Exile Country. In Beverly Allen and Mary Russo (eds.). *Revisioning Italy: National Identity and Global Culture*, 43–51. Minneapolis: University of Minnesota Press.

Nikolinakos, Marios (1973). The Contradictions of Capitalist Development in Greece: Labour Shortages and Emigration. *Studi Emigrazione*, 10:30, 222–235.

Nikolinakos, Marios (1975). Notes Towards a Theory of Migration in Late Capitalism. *Race and Class*, 17:1, 5–17.

Piore, Michael J. (1979). *Birds of Passage: Migrant Labor and Industrial Societies*. New York: Cambridge University Press.

Recchi, Ettore, and Adrian Favell (eds.). (2009). *Pioneers of European Integration: Citizenship and Mobility in the European Union*. Cheltenham: Edward Elgar.

Rhodes, Robert E. (1978). Intra-European Return Migration and Rural Development: Lessons from the Spanish Case. *Human Organization*, 37:2, 136–147.

Rodriguez, Vicente, and Carmen Egea (2006). Return and the Social Environment of Andalusian Emigrants in Europe. *Journal of Ethnic and Migration Studies*, 33:7, 1083–1102.

Salt, John (1976). International Labour Migration: the Geographical Pattern of Demand. In John Salt and Hugh Clout (eds.). *Migration in Post-War Europe: Geographical Essays*, 80–125. London: Oxford University Press.

Salt, John, and Hugh Clout (1976). International Labour Migration: the Sources of Supply. In John Salt and Hugh Clout (eds.). *Migration in Post-war Europe: Geographical Essays*, 126–167. London: Oxford University Press.

Sapelli, Giulio (1995). *Southern Europe Since 1945. Tradition and Modernity in Portugal, Spain, Italy, Greece and Turkey*. London: Longman.

Sardinha, João (2011). Returning Second-Generation Portuguese-Canadians and Portuguese French: Motivations and Sense of Belonging. *Journal of Mediterranean Studies,* 20:2, 231–254.

Schneider, Peter, Jane Schneider, and Edward Hansen (1972). Modernization and Development: the Role of Regional Elites and Noncorporate Groups in the European Mediterranean. *Comparative Studies in Society and History*, 14:3, 328–349.

Seers, Dudley (1979). The Periphery of Europe. In Dudley Seers, Bernard Schaffer and Marja-Liisa Kiljunen (eds.). *Underdeveloped Europe: Studies in Core-Periphery Relations*, 3–34. Hassocks: Harvester Press.

Seers, Dudley, Bernard Schaffer, and Marja-Liisa Kiljunen (eds.). (1979). *Underdeveloped Europe: Studies in Core-Periphery Relations.* Hassocks: Harvester Press.

Selwyn, Percy (1979). Some Thoughts on Cores and Peripheries. In Dudley Seers, Bernard Schaffer and Marja-Liisa Kiljunen (eds.). *Underdeveloped Europe: Studies in Core-Periphery Relations*, 35–43. Hassocks: Harvester Press.

Skeldon, Ronald (2012). Migration Transitions Revisited: Their Continued Relevance for the Development of Migration Theory. *Population, Space and Place*, 18:2, 154–166.

Wallerstein, Immanuel (1974). *The Modern World-System.* New York: Academic Press.

Wallerstein, Immanuel (1979). *The Capitalist World-Economy.* London: Cambridge University Press.

Wessendorf, Susanne (2007). 'Roots migrants': Transnationalism and 'Return' among Second-Generation Italians in Switzerland. *Journal of Ethnic and Migration Studies*, 33:7, 1083–1102.

Williams, Allan (ed.). (1984). *Southern Europe Transformed: Political and Economic Change in Greece, Italy, Portugal and Spain.* London: Harper and Row.

Williams, Allan M. (2009). International Migration, Uneven Regional Development and Polarization. *European Urban and Regional Studies*, 16:3, 309–322.

III. Modernity and Other Master Narratives

Southern Europe and the Master Narratives of 'Modernization' and 'Modernity'

Wolfgang Knöbl

Giulio Sapelli's book *Southern Europe Since 1945. Tradition and Modernity in Portugal, Spain, Italy, Greece and Turkey,* published exactly 20 years ago, was a brilliant and, above all, daring comparative study. As an economic historian Sapelli not only looked into the economic, social and political history of rather different societies in order to find their commonalities; he also took it for granted that Turkey has to be included in such a comparative endeavour, i.e. that Turkey is indeed an essential part of Europe. At that time such a stand was as unusual as it is still today. But it was this surprising methodological move which made the book so interesting for a broad readership. Sapelli's resumé and diagnosis after his tour de force through the history of these five societies since the end of World War II, however, was anything but positive or optimistic, something which he already had indicated in the introductory chapters of the book: "Southern Europe [still] is a land of clientship and patronage and is characterized by the presence of status systems not by contractual ones. Late industrialization, insufficient penetration of market mechanisms and the overwhelming presence of the state in social and economic life are all factors which have been decisive in forming the economic and social life of these countries." (Sapelli 1995, 10) As Sapelli explained, the processes of fast social change, of industrialization and bureaucratization, did not really touch and transform old social relationships which still resemble the ones of traditional rural societies: Social change in the South of Europe was either too fast or—until then—did not last long enough in order to result in a "Weberian capitalistic society" (ibid., 13) and to bring about truly modern structures: "We are talking about changes over a few generations while in Continental Europe the same changes evolved over centuries." (ibid., 13) The diagnosed problems in the economic and social sphere—so Sapelli argued—had their repercussions in the political one as well, which also means that the status of democracy in these countries was and still is more precarious than further north. Using the language of Modernization Theory, Sapelli argued that "modernization" indeed happened in Southern Europe, but it was a somewhat deviant and incomplete form which makes the five countries under investigation different from "the rest of the other Europes" (ibid., 13).

It will not be the task of this chapter to argue with Sapelli's diagnosis; there is no need for that anyway because important phenomena highlighted by Sapelli at least partly explain why, for example, Portugal, Spain, Italy, and Greece have been hit harder than other European countries by the economic and financial crisis of 2008 and after. Nevertheless, it might be helpful—and this will be done in the following pages—to reflect on the terminology used by Sapelli, i.e. to historicize Sapelli's admittedly sophisticated and revised modernization approach. Such an approach has been criticized since the sixties from a whole variety of different theoretical camps, to be sure. And yet, it still might be illuminating to point to the peculiarities of this paradigm because at least bits and parts of it are used even today in social scientific analyses of the current situation in Southern Europe, something which is even true with respect to the debate on "globalization" and on the position of these five countries in a presumably globalized world. With this aim in mind, it is certainly not necessary to go into details of Sapelli's impressive study. I will focus instead on some studies published in the fifties, sixties and seventies which used the modernization approach (and which also influenced Sapelli's much later work) in order to analyse Spanish and Italian history and society because looking into these early attempts most distinctly brings to the fore the conceptual difficulties and problems just mentioned and thus might help to better see the path ahead of all those who are going to study the current situation in the South of Europe; this seems a particularly necessary step because some of the problematic concepts discussed are most likely to reappear again and again and not necessarily to the benefit of the historical and social sciences. The very short conclusion tries to make this point clearer by looking back at Sapelli's book.

The Structure of Modernization Theory: Claims and Assumptions

Modernization Theory emerged in the fifties in the political context of the Cold War.[1] It was basically a reaction to President Truman's Inaugural Address in 1949 which had promised US-help to the less-developed world in order to contain communism.

> "For the first time in history, humanity possesses the knowledge and skill to relieve suffering of these people. The United States is pre-eminent among nations in the development of industrial and scientific techniques. The material resources which we can afford to use for assistance of other peoples are limited. But our imponderable resources in technical knowledge are constantly growing and are inexhaustible. I believe that we should make available to peace-loving peoples the benefits of our store of technical knowledge in order to help them realize their aspirations for a better life."[2]

As it turned out, however, this US-help did not always work properly; from the very beginning problems came to the fore and resistance could be detected so that the need for theoretical orientation was articulated in order to explain the successes and above all the problems in developing non-western countries or even whole world-regions. American social scientists began to react to this need but had to acknowledge at the same time that they were not really well trained and equipped in order to formulate rather general theories of social change. This is so because up until the late forties, American political science, for instance, had much expertise in analyzing voting behaviour and governmental structures. But it was not really ready to dissect the relationship between social and political macro-processes. The same was true with respect to sociology in the US: This discipline was well versed in analyzing communities and patterns of urban migration, but it did not have much thought about other macro-phenomena—not the least because the works of European social scientists such as Marx, Durkheim, Tönnies and Max Weber were not really well known outside of rather narrow intellectual circles in Chicago, Boston, or New York City. It has to be remembered that it was not before the publication of Talcott Parsons's major book *The Structure of Social Action* in 1937 that Durkheim's and particularly Weber's works were

1 In the following paragraphs I will use arguments presented in Knöbl 2001, 25ff.

2 Truman, Public Papers (http://www.trumanlibrary.org/publicpapers/index.php?pid=1030&st=Inaugural&st1=)

really introduced into the US-American context.[3] But getting to know the works of Durkheim and Weber was one thing, having a viable macro-theory on social change suitable for the situation after 1945 was quite another. And such a theory was simply missing when Truman's developmental vision had to be implemented.

American scholars, however, reacted rather quickly, and in the early fifties a couple of conferences at the University of Chicago, at MIT and at Harvard University were organized which brought together anthropologists, economists, geographers, political scientist, psychologists, and sociologists whose task it was to reflect on this very topic. As it turned out, some theoretical tools, especially those coming from sociology, were regarded as helpful so that a kind of a consensus began to emerge which only after some years, namely in the late fifties and early sixties, came to be known as Modernization Theory. Thus, this theory was created already *before* the terms "modernization" and Modernization Theory were coined and it relied on seven more or less interrelated assumptions which I am going to phrase in our current language:

1. Modernization is a global and irreversible process that began with the Industrial Revolution in the mid-18th century (or maybe even earlier) in Europe and now affects all societies.
2. Despite the global character of modernization processes, the focus of studies on modernization should be on individual (and isolated) societies—conceived of as coherent and structured entities preferably to be analyzed within the theoretical framework of structural-functionalism.
3. The trajectory of historical development, that is the process of modernization, is from traditional to modern societies.
4. Traditional societies and less-developed countries are dominated by personal beliefs, values, and normative patterns which can be described by terms such as "ascription," "particularism," and "functional diffuseness" and which have proven to be barriers to economic and political progress.
5. In contrast, modern societies in Europe and North America are characterized by secular, individualist, universalistic, achievement-oriented, and scientific values and exhibit concurring normative patterns.
6. The motor for modernization processes is more or less endogenous, so that external barriers to development such as imperialism or the condi-

3 The reception of European thought was then further pushed by the arrival of many émigré-scholars who had fled fascism and war in Europe.

tions of global markets are of only secondary or even minor importance (see point 2 again).
7. Modernization is a relatively uniform and linear process to be detected in all countries, no matter how different.[4]

These assumptions were often framed in a functionalist language—something quite important in order to understand the further development of the theory. Functionalist reasoning assumed that different parts of a society—being interdependent—will move in the same direction with basically the same pace. This kind of reasoning, by the way, was highly attractive to policy makers who could argue that, for example, if one makes a traditional national economy more dynamic and thus modern, then other parts of this nation, for instance its culture, its polity etc. will also modernize rather soon: Economic growth will lead to a somewhat individualistic culture, an individualistic and tolerant culture will create democracy, democracy will guarantee the flourishing of the sciences which in itself will help to make the economy more dynamic. A functionalist framework in this context meant that theorists (and politicians) tended to believe in a kind of self-propelling dynamic which—once started—was about to go on and on until a truly and full-blown modern society would be established.

With this theory at hand, modernization theorists self-confidently believed that they worked with a macro-approach at the same or even higher level of generalizability than Marxism (see the sub-title of Walt Rostow's famous book *The Stages of Economic Growth. A Non-Communist Manifesto*); they claimed to have a truly universalistic theory, one to be used in *all* contexts. "Marx was a City Boy" (Rostow 1955)—this was the title of one of Rostow's famous essays suggesting that Marx (and Marxists) never understood transformation processes in the countryside. This is quite in contrast to Modernization Theory, at least according to Rostow's opinion, because this theory has integrated *all* valuable arguments of the sociological classics,

4 Needless to say, these seven points are somewhat artificially created by myself since no single publication explicitly denoted these seven assumptions. However, if one reads the most prominent and influential works of Modernization Theory at that time one would realize that they are not far off the mark. Classical works of Modernization Theory include Daniel Lerner's "The Passing of Traditional Society" (1958), Seymour Martin Lipset's (1959) *Political Man*, Neil J. Smelser's (1959) *Social Change in the Industrial Revolution*, Walt Rostow's (1960) *The Stages of Economic Growth*, David McClelland's (1961) *The Achieving Society*, or Gabriel Almond and Sidney Verba's (1963) *The Civic Culture. Political Attitudes and Democracy in Five Nations.*

valid points made by Durkheim as well as by Tönnies and by Max Weber, so that the explanatory power of the theory simply *must be higher* than the one of Marxism which—at least according to Rostow—always had remained a rather one-dimensional and thus somewhat parochial theory which at best was applicable to urban and highly industrialized structures. Modernization Theory should and could claim to be able to explain social change all over the world, both *most recent* developments such as those in the fifties and sixties in Asia, Latin America and Africa and those *long since past* such as the rise of Europe and the West which had started during the European Reformation.

At least one more theoretically relevant aspect should be mentioned here, one which was already implied by some of the arguments referred to above: "Modernization", indeed, was a process-term at the *highest level of abstraction*—its meaning was almost identical to "social change". Using such an abstract term and at the same time using a functionalist theoretical framework meant that *sub*-processes of modernization such as individualization, secularization, mass mobilization and communication, democratization, capitalization, urbanization etc. were seen as closely interrelated, i.e. in harmony with and tied to each other so that it was not necessary to look into details; it seemed superfluous to ask whether, for instance, some of these sub-processes might block each other and whether modelling the interaction of five, six or even more sub-processes in a convincing way is possible at all. Thus, the use of a term at the most abstract level such as "modernization" almost automatically led to a kind of deductive reasoning, something that was acknowledged only after a while when the original optimism of modernization theorists was beginning to fade away. But this is another and rather big question and should not concern us here. The next paragraph has the much more modest aim to focus on social scientific analyses of Southern Europe and of the Mediterranean region published during the high times of Modernization Theory, i.e. in the fifties and sixties.

Theorizing Modernization in the South of Europe: The "Difficult" Cases of Spain and Italy

Since the late fifties Modernization Theory, as characterized above, was intensely used especially in comparative studies. And this use undoubtedly had enormous results because it was due to its impact that *comparative* sociology, *comparative* political science, *comparative* anthropology experienced a huge upswing at that time—"huge" because comparative research which at the turn of the century had made up the core of Durkheim's and Weber's work had been neglected after their death—and not only within sociology. It was not before the fifties and thanks to Modernization Theory that comparative ambitions returned within the social sciences. Interestingly, however, not the whole world seemed to be equally suitable for being studied from a modernization perspective. When one looks into the journal *Economic Development and Cultural Change*, the interdisciplinary flagship of Modernization Theory founded in 1952, one quickly realizes that in the fifties virtually no single article on the countries analysed in Sapelli's book can be found. The journal, of course, is full of papers on theoretical questions concerning modernization and economic growth. But it is wrong to assume that the editors were mainly publishing articles on abstract theory. On the contrary: Dozens of case studies on particular aspects of Indian society, of Latin American and African countries and even some on Japan and regions in the US can be found as well. The South (and the rest) of Europe, however, is neglected, at least if one does not count one article on *Ancient* Greece and one on emigration from Italy in the decade *before* World War I. The situation slightly changes in the sixties, but even then papers on Turkey, Greece, Spain, Portugal and Italy are not easy to detect, and, above all, only the ones published *at the end* of this decade do have at least some theoretical ambitions, especially when the focus is on Italy's dual regional economy and the problem of the *Mezzogiorno* (Singh 1967; Schachter 1968).

Basically the same claims can be made with respect to another highly influential, prestigious and (although often somewhat *critical* of Modernization Theory) theoretically ambitious journal such as *Comparative Studies in Society and History*, founded in 1958. Here, again, one will find many studies on India, on China, on Latin America. Europe and the U.S. were not so much in the minds of the authors writing in this journal. To be sure, there is probably an easy explanation at hand for this very fact: The editors wanted to make *Comparative Studies in Society and History* less euro-centric, less focussed on western affairs than many main stream journals of that time so that they simply preferred articles on the non-western world. But there are reasons to doubt whether this explanation is the only plausible one. *Another and possibly better explanation* would almost certainly point out that applying Modernization Theory (or any other theoretical approach available at that time) to *Europe's* most recent past (the 19th and above all the 20th century) was a hard thing to do because in many parts of Europe historical processes were not as smooth as they were claimed to be, at least by the true believers of Modernization Theory. Functionalist logic—see assumption 2 above on page 176—rarely met the empirical evidence—particularly not in Continental Europe![5] The rise of Fascism in an economically and culturally highly developed country such as Germany was above all an anomaly, not a proof of the validity of functionalist reasoning which believed in the co-evolution of economic, cultural and political processes, which claimed a kind of *Wahlverwandtschaft* of capitalism and democracy. And these very anomalies could also be seen in Southern Europe because the authoritarian dictatorships there seemed to create the same theoretical problems as the ones encountered in interpretations of German history. Even more, sectional and regional conflicts and cleavages such as the question of the South in Italy or the relationship between Catalonia and the 'rest' of Spain were not only phenomena outside of the focus of modernization theorists who believed—see again assumption 2—in the quasi-natural unity of countries and nations but were difficult to grasp from *any* theoretical perspective. Thus, Southern Europe was a problematic case and so it is no wonder that in *Comparative Studies in Society and History* too one could find articles on Renaissance Florence but almost nothing about modernization processes in contemporary Southern Europe.[6]

But maybe one could even also find one more explanation for the neglect of studies on contemporary Southern Europe, a more *cultural* or *ideological* (and not so much theoretical) one, an explanation to be framed by the following question: Would the emphasis of grave political, economic and cultural differences between countries in Western Europe not have undermined the assumption that there is a "West", that there is a "western hemisphere" which not only includes parts of Europe but also and above anything else the United States, a hemisphere characterized by clearly defined common features such as a prospering market economy, a democratic political culture etc. etc.? Focusing too much on the "problems" and "anomalies" of Southern Europe would have undermined such Cold War premises of many North American and West European social scientists who, therefore, preferred to

5 Only time would tell that the assumed functionalist logic failed in other regional contexts as well—but that is a different question.

6 Here one should stress again that *Comparative Studies in Society and History* was certainly not a flagship of Modernization Theory but a rather pluralist journal in which strong criticisms of this theory also appeared very soon.

believe that these very "problems" and "anomalies" in Southern Europe are to be regarded as negligible, as exceptions, or as only temporary deviant cases which, therefore, do not deserve the same degree of attention as countries such as India or China do.

Be it as it may, it is undoubtedly true that during the fifties and sixties countries in Southern Europe were very rarely studied in a systematic way in the context of international social sciences discourse. And yet, at least a few texts were published, even some clearly written from the perspective of Modernization Theory. But the authors of these works usually framed their arguments in a peculiar way. I will first discuss the case of Spain.

First of all, it was not really difficult to use Modernization Theory in a *local* context, i.e. to use it in order to make sense of empirical data coming from community-studies. A well-known anthropological study of this type done in the late sixties and published in the early seventies was Richard A. Barrett's *Benabarre: The Modernization of a Spanish Village*. Situated in Huesca Province in the sub-Pyrenean zone, this small village of less than 1.200 inhabitants went through typical stages of modernization. As the American author argues: The villagers acknowledge and welcome the increasing living standard and the reduction of poverty, the levelling of social hierarchies and their future integration into national life:

> "The change which is occurring in the countryside is therefore bound to affect the Spanish political equation. The integration of villagers into the orbit of urban culture has enabled them to participate in national life as never before. Moreover, the education they are providing their children will equip the latter with skills and opportunities unavailable to their parents. And whether the peasant is transformed by becoming an entrepreneurial farmer, or by becoming a factory worker, in either case he will be more capable of recognizing and defending his political interests than any previous generation." (Barrett 1974, 106).

Such a smooth picture of modernization could only be upheld, however, when the wider context, the *national* and *macro* framework, was disregarded (as is sometimes the case in anthropological or sociological community studies such as the one done by Barrett) or believed to be insignificant—at least in the long run: When one assumed, as was quite reasonable to do if one believed in the premises of Modernization Theory, that the Franco-régime was bound to doom anyway, that figures such as Franco in Spain or Salazar in Portugal were somewhat archaic remnants in an increasingly industrialized and then democratized Western and Southern Europe, then the neglect of the wider political context made sense. If, however, one regarded such a functionalist assumption with some suspicion, if one took the existence of Franco's dictatorship seriously, took it seriously *in theoretical terms*, and thus saw a kind of a undeniable cleavage between dictatorial political structures on the one side and economic and social processes on the other, such a stand was not acceptable because it undoubtedly contradicted the functionalist logic of Modernization Theory.

This was the starting point of "heterodox" theories of modernization. Heterodox theorists of this kind dissolved the functional logic of Modernization Theory and admitted that different spheres of a society might develop along different paths: mass communication might lead to democracy, but it also might be otherwise; individualism might create the conditions for scientific progress, but sometimes it might not, and so on and so forth. Dissolving the functionalist logic, however, made Modernization Theory less attractive—at least if one believes in the task of theories to make predictions. Heterodox theorists were well aware of that and prepared to lower their ambitions. But that alone did not put them in *one* camp because starting from this point at least two different choices could be made: A) One could talk of "*partial* modernization" (as suggested by Dietrich Rueschemeyer 1970) assuming that only some subsystems of a society might modernize rather quickly whereas the rest might fail to develop a modern form. This solution, however, simply took for granted that all those social phenomena and institutions looking similar to equivalent ones in the US or in the UK were to be called "modern", the rest, however, only—and somewhat pejoratively—'partially modern' or non-modern. Thus, in the background of this solution there was a clear normative yardstick for how to categorize social structures—and not everyone could be convinced that this somehow Anglo-centric way of theorizing social change is the right way to proceed. B) If one saw the problem of solution A as too big to be accepted, then one could decide to denote basically all institutions in the age of modernity (whatever that is) as "modern". The problem with this solution, of course, was that it became increasingly unclear why one should call social phenomena and institutions "modern" at all if all the phenomena in a peculiar period are modern anyway. What was the use of the term "modern" if there was nothing left outside of this category? That was a problem, indeed, but this solution at least had the advantage that it might open a new perspective on certain elements within modern societies which so far have always been categorized as "traditional", "reactionary", "archaic" or "non-modern". And it allowed the elimination of that irksome normative yardstick that was so important for those preferring solution A.

It was Stanley Payne, historian of Spain and prominent analyst of European Fascism, who in 1972 grappled with these problems in a review essay entitled "Political Ideology and Economic Modernization in Spain"—and in the end decided to choose solution A! Payne's basic argument was that the form politics had taken in Spain was always rather strange since clearly structured economic interests had never been formed and articulated: After the Napoleonic period a kind of status-politics had emerged which has been shaping the political system in a different way compared to Western Europe. As Payne claimed, in the 19th century the politically dominant provincial middle classes in this more or less liberal political system had no developmental vision for their country (Payne 1972, 156). It was not so much the class structure, the existence of large masses of poor peasants (a picture that according to Payne is too simple anyway) which blocked modernization, but the non-existence of modernizing elites that led to an imbalance between economic modernization processes on the one side and a political system that reacted rather helplessly towards social change on the other. No wonder, therefore, that in the twenties and thirties political debates rarely dealt with problems of technological modernization, but instead focussed on property relations and division of land. Paradoxically, it was only with the rise of dictatorships in this period that at least a kind of development vision was about to be implemented: Thus in the times of Primo de Rivera's rule and in the first years of Franco's régime a modernizing move occurred and actually met some economic success. But this kind of progress brought about another imbalance, one almost the opposite of the one of the 19th and early 20th century:

> "During the nineteenth and early twentieth centuries, Spain had a political system too advanced for its society and economy. After three decades of development dictatorship, a new industrialized Spain has an economy and a society that, measured by most normal Western political indices, are more advanced than the formal articulation of its political system." (Payne 1972, 181)

Thus, in contrast to "most normal" European countries Spain seemed to be out of balance all the time, this country had never experienced more than partial modernization—not the least due to its political structure![7] Thus

7 It should be mentioned here that Payne published another relevant essay almost 15 years later comparing Italy, Greece, Spain, and Portugal. As he argued, all four "southernmost countries of Europe" had suffered societal imbalances in their histories but it was Spain

Payne had to face the fact that Spain seemingly never came close to the "standard" model of Western political systems, i.e. English or French or US-democracy, a model which was never seriously questioned by him with respect to its analytical fruitfulness so that he simply characterized the processes happening in Spain as *partial* modernization.

Whereas Payne in a heterodox manner tried to modify Modernization Theory by getting rid of its functionalist reasoning—for him imbalances and *Ungleichzeitigkeiten* (non-synchronicities) were not just temporary conditions but the very essence of Spanish history and society—other critical analysts of Spanish history began to ask more fundamental questions. In a 1972 article on modernization in Catalonia and western Sicily anthropologists Peter Schneider, Jane Schneider and Edward Hansen doubted whether it makes sense at all to use "modernization" and "development" as synonyms. Clearly influenced by Latin American Dependencia Theory they focused not so much on *imbalances* between the political and the economic system as has been suggested by Payne. They were more interested in *different types* of industrialization and argued that the way industries in Catalonia emerged was a rather strange form of development; in fact, it was not development at all because since the 19th century the local bourgeoisie had always been dependent on foreign capital and had suffered all the disadvantages of such a subaltern position. Yes, they argued, Catalonia was and is in a process of modernization, but modernization will probably not lead to "development" proper (Schneider et al. 1972).

Thus, an interesting dialogue was about to emerge around that time between classical modernization theorists, somewhat heterodox proponents of this theory such as Payne and strong critics of Modernization Theory such as Schneider, Schneider and Hansen—and all this might have led to fruitful results if historical contingencies had not intervened, i.e. Franco's death in 1975! This event changed the political situation in Spain, democratized politics and thus 'synchronized' the political and economic system. Payne's (and Schneider, Schneider and Hansen's) diagnoses of imbalances and fractures could be declared invalid—*at least for the current situation*. And, indeed, the demise of Franquismo seemed to prove Modernization Theory correct—this was the conviction of many sociologists. Modernization Theory became triumphant in the works of sociology dealing with Spain—a narrowly circum-

that had to face the consequences of a really extraordinarily long early liberal period of political instability (Payne 1986, 102f.).

scribed theoretical sea-change that predated the much broader one when the theory joyfully returned on a more global scale after 1989 and the collapse of the USSR. Already in the eighties, but even more so in the nineties, Spanish main-stream sociologists could therefore self confidently declare:

"It was a good thing that we had been introduced to sociology when functionalism and theories of economic growth have been the foremost theoretical orientations of the social sciences because a Marxist sociology could not have been an intellectual alternative in a society experiencing annual growth-rates of about 6 percent."[8]

Spain, so it was assumed in 1992 when this sentence was written down, was on her way into the future, she would catch up with the other West-European countries, she would indeed "develop" in the proper meaning of the word (and in contrast to the sceptical diagnosis of Schneider, Schneider and Hansen), and if this is so then the Franco period had to be interpreted in a specific way: Franco and his regime had only *delayed* the development of a normal political life and culture, his regime had to be regarded as an aberration that prevented the normal articulation of interests in politics.[9] Spain has had to pay the price, but only temporarily, because now everything seems to be on the right track again.

Interestingly, in this essay by José Félix Tezanos just referred to, the historical picture of Spain's past turned out to be a rather smooth one again; gone are, for example, the ambivalences emphasized by Payne when this author pointed to the developmental visions of Primo de Rivera's and Franco's (early) regimes. Now, in this new optimistic mood of the post-transition-period, Franco was simply seen as someone who had delayed and blocked political processes that almost by definition—by functionalist logic!—would have come anyway (see Garcia-Petit and Schäfers 1979); Franco became the anti-thesis of modernity, his regime was solely interpreted as a somewhat

---

8 My translation, W.K. The original German version reads: "Es mag sehr gut gewesen sein, daß wir in eine Soziologie eingeführt wurden, als der Funktionalismus und die Wachstumstheorie die vorwiegenden wissenschaftlichen Orientierungen in den Sozialwissenschaften waren, denn die marxistische Soziologie hatte in einer Gesellschaft mit jährlichen Wachstumsraten von etwa sechs Prozent keine intellektuellen Alternativen zu bieten." (del Campo 1992, 189)

9 "Así, por una parte, el franquismo supuso un poderoso freno al cambio político, que a su vez acabó dificultando y conflictualizando determinados aspectos del campio socioeconómico. De igual manera el franquismo, al impeder una vida política normal, creando un largo paréntesis de vacío politico durante casi cuarenta años, dificultó la racional organization social de la defensa de los intereses sociales y politicos, así como el ajuste de los intereses económicos." (Tezanos 1984, 21)

traditional obstacle to modernization. In this perspective it was never asked whether Franco's authoritarianism, whether even Fascism could be seen as a modern phenomenon.

To save the reputation of sociology as a discipline, however, it is fair to say that not all sociologists shared the assumption of a close interrelationship between democratization and modernization. At least some other voices could be heard in the early eighties. José Casanova, nowadays based at Georgetown University in Washington D.C. and one of the most influential sociologists of religion, published important historical-sociological pieces on Spain and had taken up Payne's insight that the modernization of Spain should not be seen through the lens of "Franco the obstacle". As Casanova recalled in the early eighties: Franco's régime in the late fifties became a kind of developmental dictatorship quite successfully organized by technocrats (Casanova 1983, 957). No wonder, therefore, that in the sixties this régime was widely perceived—despite its ugly and brutal aspects—as a model of Keynesian export-orientation (Casanova 1982, 29). Thus, Casanova pointed to the seemingly self-evident, but often forgotten argument (Casanova 1983, 930f.) that *any* process of social differentiation almost *by definition* creates the possibility of imbalanced relationships between sub-systems and thus permanent (and not just temporary) *Ungleichzeitigkeiten*.

If Casanova's argument is correct, then the division between *the* "traditional" and *the* "modern" is much more difficult to make than is usually assumed: at least one should not exclude the possibility that even politically reactionary and fascist régimes might have tried in the past and might try in the future to steer and direct processes of economic development, i.e. might foster "modernization". It follows that "modernization", encompassing so many sub-processes (see above), is always a kind of queer concept: To call something "modern" or "traditional" is a rather arbitrary judgment, depending as much on normative standards as on the evaluative standpoint from where the evaluation is made. We will have to wait and see whether the interpretative schemes being used in analyzing Spain will have changed when the first theoretically ambitious articles and books after the beginning of the Spanish crisis in 2008 are published, whether Spain's booming period of the eighties and nineties will still be regarded as phases of successful modernization. How "modern" was Spain in the last two decades of the 20th century? One should be curious and—above all—attentive with respect to the way social scientists and historians will answer this question!

*

For modernization theorists, Italy seemed to be an easier case to analyse—and if it was only for the simple reason that its Post-World War II political history was not characterized by major changes and transitions, that Mussolini's dictatorship was already gone and thus real political obstacles for political modernization were seemingly missing. In addition, because Italian scholars (in contrast to those of Spain) after the end of World War II had almost immediately become part of a transnational social science community, the analysis of the case of Italy shouldn't meet too many obstacles. And yet, particularly two problems existed which were rather difficult to solve and thus have been in the focus of modernization theorists from the very beginning: 1) The problem of the South's backwardness, and 2) the evaluation of the Italian democracy's stability and prospects after its rather long period of fascist rule.

Edward C. Banfield's famous *The Moral Basis of a Backward Society* published in 1958 tackled the first problem by making the following argument: Economic development is dependent on an ethos that allows to establish co-operative forms of actions. It will only happen and endure if in the political and societal sphere actors work together because there is no way of dealing successfully with problems of economic development if political parties with a broad constituency are not focussing their programs on building infrastructures to be used by everyone, on organizing political coalitions between different groups in order to get things done. But such a form of political co-operation can not be taken for granted—not in many parts of the non-western world and not in Southern Italy! Why? By studying the small town of "Montegrano" (in reality Chiaromonte) in the mountainous region of Basilicata, Banfield, a rather conservative political scientists based at that time at the University of Chicago, found a seemingly strange kind of culture that blocked this very co-operation between different actors. Citizens of "Montegrano" did not co-operate, but not—as one might expect—because of poverty, because of a lack of knowledge, or because of a kind of suspicious attitude towards the political sphere (Banfield 1963, 35f.). The real reason for this non-co-operative behaviour and *la misèria* in Southern Italy—so Banfield argued—had to do with peculiar family structures. In "Montegrano" the nuclear family was at the centre of this culture, it was the basis of all actions—even those in the public sphere: "Maximize the material, short-run advantage of the nuclear family; assume that all others will do likewise"

(Banfield 1963, 85). This attitude, Banfield called it "amoral familism", had enormous consequences for the wider context because it made long lasting co-operation between and outside families almost impossible and even prevented the emergence of the idea of a common good, a real political community such as a functioning city. Reform associations, voluntary organizations etc., i.e. a viable civil society, would and could not emerge because everyone was so focused on the advantages of his or her own family; stable political organizations could not develop (only fragile political parties) because everyone was selling his/her votes to the highest bidder—an ideal breeding ground for clientelism.

Banfield was convinced that this culture of the Italian South was a highly stable one so that impulses for change could only come from the outside. What he was waiting or hoping for was the influence of the political left, the Catholic Church, or the industry of Northern Italy because only such *external* forces could somehow undermine this "amoral familism" (Banfield 1963, 164). The rise of living standards and the influence of the media could bring to the fore further changes but—as Banfield made clear—it will certainly take some generations until a new political culture could and would come into being (Banfield 1963, 175).[10]

Within international social science discourse, Banfield's thesis was interpreted as a *general* statement to be taken into consideration in all attempts to study cultural and political change[11]—a model that is still influential today as the debate on "social capital" in response to Robert Putnam's book *Mak-*

10 It should be mentioned here that both Banfield's empirical findings and his theoretical conclusions have not gone unchallenged. As Paolo Macry has argued, it is simply wrong to separate cultural and material-territorial factors in order to explain differences between northern and southern Italy; the family structure in southern Italy had much to do with territorial and market conditions and is therefore not to be regarded as an independent variable that explains economic failure or success (Macry 1997; Dunnage 2002).—A more theoretical argument against the Banfield-thesis was brought forward by David Moss: As he pointed out, it is simply not more than a guess when one claims that clientelism will necessarily prevent mass-mobilization. One could also make the reverse point, namely that it is the *weakness* of patronage relationships and clientelistic structures that makes collective action difficult because patronage can also lower information costs and thus facilitate the emergence of social movements. As Moss claims it is the *quality* of patronage and clientelism that makes all the difference which means that the North and the South of Italy are not divided by the absence or presence of clientelistic networks but by the different structures of these networks (Moss 1995).

11 See Lepsius (1990 [1965]) where the author very much builds upon material and arguments to be found in Banfield (1963).

ing Democracy Work. Civic Traditions in Modern Italy (1993) clearly shows. And, what is more relevant for our topic, Banfield had also set the agenda for a research tradition within Modernization Theory that, in order to analyse Italy, basically looked into her political *culture*. This can be seen in Gabriel Almond and Sidney Verba's famous *The Civic Culture* (originally published in 1963) which compared the political attitudes of people in five countries—in the US, Great Britain, West-Germany, Mexico, and Italy. The reason why the authors included Italy in their study is easy to explain: they were interested in the prospects of a democratic régime in a country which had experienced a rather *long* period of authoritarian rule. And Italy seemed to meet the point even better than West-Germany did. Whatever the peculiarities of the comparative designs of this study, with respect to the early sixties Almond and Verba claimed to have found out that—and this certainly did not come as a surprise—Italians felt a kind of alienation[12] towards their national political system and that in contrast to American, British and German citizens they had a "parochial" attitude towards politics which means that they neither monitored the actions of their governments very closely nor took actively part in the political process on the national level (Almond and Verba 1989 [1963], 49). This "parochial political culture" of Italy—so Almond and Verba argued—is certainly not as supportive to a true and lively and, above all, stable democracy as a "civic political culture" (to be found in Britain and the US), but like Banfield the authors nevertheless hoped that change would come—most likely by external impulses affecting family structures because only in this case and with the help of political education, new voluntary associations and new structures of work and thus a stable social and political system will emerge (Almond and Verba 1989 [1963], 370ff.).

Here is not the right place to comment on Almond and Verba's study and their use of the rather vague concept of "political culture" (Elkins and Simeon 1979). Suffice to say that, *firstly*, this so incredibly successful concept was above all coined in order to get around the empirical problems classical modernization theorists already had to face in the fifties: As Almond later claimed, this very concept *was created in response to the demise of the optimistic belief* in smooth processes of modernization (Almond 1980, 6). Using the normative yardstick of the more or less linear developmental path of

12 "Alienation in Italy involves the withdrawal of attention as well as the absence of political pride. In Germany we have the interesting combination of high exposure and attentiveness to the political system, along with an absence of pride in it." (Almond and Verba 1989 [1963], 68)

the US and Great Britain, the "political culture"-concept should be able to make sense of the complex history of especially those countries where imbalances between sub-processes of modernization could be detected, where the functionalist logic obviously failed—and this was particularly the case in Southern Europe of the post-World War II period where in the midst of economic progress, regional cleavages or fragile democratic structures had to be explained. However, was it really about *explanation* in the proper meaning of the word? When, according to classical Modernization Theory, all societies will move from a traditional form to a modern one (see again assumptions 3 to 5 on page 176) and when, at the same time, some societies make this move much faster than others, then an explanation is needed. "(Political) culture" promised to be such a causal variable that could explain why different societies behave so differently. But in such an explanatory scheme the variable "political culture" is only meaningful *if* it is really something different from features of tradition/traditional forms of society or the modern/modern forms of society.

But is a "parochial political culture" (Almond and Verba 1989 [1963]) really different from traditional patterns, from important features of a traditional society? Is a "participant political culture" (ibid.) really different from features of a modern society? When one reads assumption 4 on page 176 again, one will immediately realize that there is talk of "particularism" and "ascription" in order to define "tradition"—indeed of cultural phenomena that are not far away from this "parochial political culture". And when one reads assumption 5 one will realize again that in order to define 'the modern' there is talk of "universalism" and "achievement"—indeed of cultural phenomena not far away from this "participant political culture". If this is the case, however, then the whole argument becomes somewhat tautological because in the end it is argued that countries are still traditional because they still have a traditional political culture, that countries have become modern because they already had a modern political culture. Almond himself, at least partially, seemed to have admitted this by saying that the concept was used *both* as a dependent *and* independent variable.[13]—I am not arguing here that the concept of political culture is completely useless, but at least one should

13 "It is quite clear that political culture is treated as both an independent and a dependent variable, as causing structure and as being caused by it." (Almond 1980, 29). One has to admit that this sentence in itself and Almond's contextualization of this sentence is not automatically nonsensical. But it is also true that Almond and Verba, in the original book, never made a big effort to explain how political culture came into being by struc-

acknowledge that it is difficult to use and that the danger of tautological reasoning is never far away.

Secondly, one should also mention that Almond and Verba's concept was an *a-historical* one as well because they did not bother too much in asking why and how a peculiar political culture came into being at all (Pateman 1980, 62).[14] This was a problem especially for those who—like historically minded political scientists and sociologists—were used to working with a wider time frame and were more interested than Almond and Verba in historical developments.

Difficult Cases Indeed! "Corporatism", the Desperate Search for Historical Answers and the Current Resurgence of Essentialist Concepts?

It was exactly this problem that incited the debate on *corporatism* (and leads us back to Spain again) since from the very beginning this concept had a truly historical twist—at least according to the opinion of its proponents! Here I would like to focus on the work of Howard Wiarda, an eminent political scientist who had pioneered the work on corporatism in Latin America in the sixties and seventies and who would later start to use the concept also in European contexts. Wiarda's work is relevant because his publications are quite close to questions of political culture and they are most clearly related to Southern Europe, especially to Spain and Portugal. Looking back at his own career in 2009, Wiarda had pointed out that the development of the concept of corporatism was a kind of reaction against studies written within the paradigms of System and Modernization Theory so dominant in the sixties (Wiarda 2009, 87). However, as Wiarda himself states, he also was not too far away from the modernization approach. No wonder, therefore, that he wanted to keep the concept of corporatism "vague because, with corporatism, I sought to capture a mood, a style, a whole way of thinking and operating—a *political culture*—rather than any precise institutional arrangement." (Wiarda 2009, 93; my emphasis). And he adds that, when working

ture and thus have made the readers believe that political culture is above all the explanans in their book.

14 For an overview of the debate on political culture see Somers (1995).

on this phenomenon he was not fixed on a particular term; true, in the end he called it "corporatism", but he also could have called it "*Mediterranean Politics*" (Wiarda 2009, 93f.; my emphasis). And here we are in the midst of our topic. When he published his famous essay "Toward a Framework for the Study of Political Change in the Iberic-Latin Tradition: The Corporative Model" in 1973, Wiarda was a specialist in Latin American politics. Criticizing *some* of the assumptions of early Modernization Theory he was not convinced that modernization would lead to identical results everywhere. As he argued, there are different types of development and worlds, and Latin America could be regarded as a "fourth world of development". (Wiarda 1973, 209) Why is that the case? The reason is that Latin America in the 15th and 16th century had imported Spain's and Portugal's political traditions;[15] the colonies in Latin America were shaped by the traditions of absolutist Spain and Portugal, political and social life in the colonies became deeply influenced by "a political culture and a socio-political order that at its core was essentially two-class, authoritarian, traditional, elitist, patrimonial, Catholic, stratified, hierarchical, and corporate." (Wiarda 1973, 209) The political discourse of these countries was based on an organic and certainly not individualistic understanding of social life which stressed the authority of the state and its task to organize society. This is so because Spain and Portugal and the Latin American colonies and countries were always bypassed by "the great revolutions associated with the making of the modern world. The Protestant Reformation, the rise of capitalism, the scientific revolution, the rise of socially more pluralistic and politically more democratic societies, the Industrial Revolution and its many-faceted ramifications—all of these had little effect on the nations of the Iberic-Latin culture area." (ibid.) And Wiarda continues: Political thought in Spain and Portugal was based on "Roman law (one can still profitably read Seneca for an understanding of the Iberic-Latin tradition), Catholic thought (Augustine, Aquinas), and traditional, le-

15 One should add here that within classical Modernization Theory there was always the attempt to explicitly interpret Spain as a somewhat exotic, not European case. As has been argued by Eric N. Baklanoff (1968, 589; my emphasis): "Within the Atlantic community of nations, Spain occupies the extreme southwest extension of the European continent, politically separated from the rest of Europe by the Pyrenees Mountains. In their historical-cultural orientation and in their economic life, *the Spaniards more closely resemble the peoples of Latin America than their neighbors in Northwest Europe.*" It is interesting to see that geographical myths (see the first part of the quotation) could be used not only to characterize Non-European regions but also parts of Europe itself (cf. Lewis and Wigen 1997).

gal precepts (the *fueros* or group charters of medieval times, the law of the *Siete Partidas* of Alfonso the Wise). In comprehending the Iberic-Latin systems, one must think in terms of a hierarchically and vertically segmented structure of class and caste stratifications, of social rank orders, functional corporations, estates, juridical groupings and *intereses*—all fairly well defined in law and in terms of their respective stations in life—a rigid yet adaptable scheme whose component parts are tied to and derive legitimacy from the authority of the central state or its leader." (Wiarda 1973, 210–11) As Wiarda made clear, in 1973 he was looking for the Latin American equivalent to Louis Hartz's "Liberal Tradition" in the US—and as it turns out, it was "corporatism"! But luckily "corporatism" does not only fit Latin-America: Even Spain and Portugal in the 20th century can fruitfully be regarded as "offshoots of a Catholic, Iberic, patrimonialist, semi-feudal Europe *circa* 1500" (Wiarda 1973, 233) so that according to Wiarda "corporatism" also fits the then current situation in at least parts of Southern Europe and thus its odd and backward structures.

Wiarda was not the only one who had argued that way. Quite well-known specialists on Latin America such as Charles W. Anderson (1992 [1964]), Richard Morse (1964), Claudio Véliz (1980), and Charles Wagley (1992 [1968]) had been heading in the same direction and by doing so—although not all of them had much expertise in Spanish and Portuguese history and society—had confirmed the stereotypical picture of these two South-European countries, had confirmed the old protestant equation between Catholicism and backwardness.[16] Again, here is not the place to discuss whether this kind of "intellectual history" makes sense at all.[17] More important is a general point: It might be worthwhile to know this particular debate on political culture and corporatism since Giorgio Agamben's (2013)

16 See the "beautiful" argument made by Richard Morse: "A Protestant civilization can develop its energies endlessly in a wilderness, as did the United States. A Catholic civilization stagnates when it is not in vital contact with the diverse tribes and cultures of mankind." (Morse 1964, 177)—For the complexity of a protestant and anti-catholic bias within the intellectual circles of Italy and Germany see Borutta (2010); for the anti-Catholic attitudes of Max Weber, one of the founding fathers of the modern social sciences, see Käsler (2004).

17 Quite a few corporatist and authoritarian regimes in Latin America like the one of Péron in Argentina did not have much to do with traditional Catholicism, political elites in important periods of Latin American history were anything but traditional supporters of the Catholic Church and important currents of Catholicism were not always conservative and traditional—something which must be true for the "mother-countries", Portugal and Spain, as well (cf. Waisman 1987, 96ff).

recent and—as I think—rather odd attempt to revive Alexandre Kojève's old concept of *l'Empire latin* seems to indicate that culturalist and essentialist explanations (whatever they intend to achieve) are never far away when political and social crises are in sight.

Whether historians and social scientists in the very near future will be impressed by such attempts remains to be seen. If we return to the past, to the debate of the sixties and seventies on the then recent past, i.e. fascist period in Italy, one clearly sees that somewhat heterodox modernization theorists were the most convincing. These heterodox theorists rarely used concepts such as "tradition" or "political culture", no wonder, therefore, that they were also not very impressed by corporatist reasoning à la Howard Wiarda! Much more common have been studies such as the one published in 1970 by Roland Sarti who had favoured solution B to the problem of how to proceed after the dissolution of Modernization Theory's functionalist logic (see page 182). As he made quite clear, it does not make much sense to label Italian fascists "traditional". Fascists also wanted a kind of modernization of Italy even if—due to their need to make coalitions with more conservative and traditional forces—their policy at the beginning of Mussolini's regime was quite muddled and diffuse (Sarti 1970). Sarti's argument on Italian fascism went parallel with and radicalized a position already taken by Ralf Dahrendorf in his *Gesellschaft und Demokratie in Deutschland* some years earlier (1968 [1966]) when this prominent German sociologist had claimed that Nazism had at least unintentionally modernized Germany's social structure by pushing aside the aristocracy of the Kaiserreich and by breaking down the pillarization (*Versäulung*) of the Weimar Republic (Dahrendorf 1968 [1966], 431ff.).[18] Modernization—so the basic argument was—should not be seen from a normative point of view because if this is the case, then one loses the ambivalences of processes of social change, then one cannot understand why reactionary and even fascist forces acted in many ways like those who had completely different projects, or why their actions often led to consequences they never had anticipated etc. Equating only *positively* evaluated processes with "modernization" overlooks that modernization is a "queer" concept that encompasses many different sub-processes (see above!)! That should be kept in mind because otherwise one gets the complexity of historical processes wrong.

18 For the parallel discourse in Germany and Italy cf. Levy 1996, 182.

Is that really true? At least Tim Mason in an important article published in 1988 did not believe so.[19] His central argument was directed against the aforementioned solution B: According to him, when using concepts such as "modernization" and "modernity", one should not forget that these are undoubtedly normative concepts—and this has to be acknowledged because otherwise they are in danger of getting trivialized. If everything is somehow modern, then the talk of "modernization" and "modernity" loses its meaning (Mason 1988, 136f.). Fascism—according to Mason—was certainly not a truly modern phenomenon: As he argued, mass murder and killing was not the negative side of modernity, "it was not the negative side of anything, rather the central realities of fascism." (Mason 1988, 140) But can historians and social scientists really stick to such a strong normatively loaded concept, does Mason's position make much sense? Whatever the answer, the debate on the interpretation of Italian fascism has already proceeded into the difficult terrain of debates on the true meaning of modernity, something which seems to be almost unavoidable if one cannot and does not believe any longer in the functional interdependence of economic and political processes. It remains to be seen whether the current economic and financial crisis, especially in Southern Europe, will lead to a resurgence of modernity- and modernization debates. If this indeed takes place, then the author of this chapter hopes that the discussants in this debate will look closely at very similar debates of the past so that they will realize how difficult and even aporetic this modernization discourse has always been. And this brings me to my very short conclusion and back to Sapelli's book.

Conclusion

Should we really speak of a Southern European modernity—as Giulio Sapelli seemed to have suggested in 1995 when he published his *Southern Europe Since 1945. Tradition and modernity in Portugal, Spain, Italy, Greece and Turkey* discussed at the beginning of this chapter? The answer is difficult—not the least due to the fact that the readers of Sapelli's work might not really

19 See also more recently Mark Roseman (2011), who argues that the concept of "modernity" is not really helpful in analyzing Nazi-Germany due to the notorious vague character of the term and its normative connotations.

be sure which type of modernity concept this author was really proposing or defending: On the one hand Sapelli (1995, 13) characterized the processes happening in these five countries since 1945 as "modernization without development"—thus explicitly using the *dependencia*-argument by Schneider, Schneider and Hansen mentioned above. On the other hand, Sapelli also makes the argument (used by Payne and others who have favoured solution A [see page 182]) that it is basically "partial modernization" which took place in that region, that late modernization only insufficiently affected social life in the South of Europe, and that it allowed the precarious co-existence of 'tradition *and* modernity', as the subtitle of the book suggests; here Sapelli points to the somewhat odd mixture of institutional and cultural phenomena in order to characterize these five southern countries. Thus, Sapelli clearly speaks of modernization (without development). But does he speak of "modernity", a *South European* modernity? Maybe he was deliberately vague because he knew the difficulties of *any* attempt to give a clear meaning to the terms "modernization" and "modernity". Probably he knew Tim Mason's position referred to above: Mason was quite right to argue that "modernity" and "modernization" were—and he explicitly used a term coined by Scottish philosopher W. B. Gallie—'essentially contested concepts' (Mason 1988, 129)[20] which, despite their problems and difficulties, will have the chance to survive for a very long time because these concepts do have many normative implications which almost guarantee a lively and ongoing debate between supporters and opponents of these very norms. Whether these debates in the end will help to develop a better empirical picture of Southern Europe's past and future remains to be seen, however. Doubts remain especially because an intense debate on "modernity" and "modernization" has already been going on since the seventies and it could and should be asked whether their application to the South of Europe will really bring fruitful results in the historical interpretation of this region. But that is something to be answered by the historians themselves and not by the author of this chapter who happens to be a sociologist.

20 See also Knöbl 2012.

Works Cited

Agamben, Giorgio (2013). Que l'Empire latin contre-attaque! *Libération*, 24.03.2013. URL: http://www.liberation.fr/monde/2013/03/24/que-l-empire-latin-contre-attaque_890916

Almond, Gabriel (1980). The Intellectual History of the Civic Culture Concept. In Gabriel A. Almond and Sidney Verba (eds.). *The Civic Culture Revisited. An Analytic Study*. Boston and Toronto: Little, Brown & Company.

Almond, Gabriel, and Sidney Verba (1989 [1963]). *The Civic Culture. Political Attitudes and Democracy in Five Nations*. Newbury Park, London and New Delhi: Sage.

Anderson, Charles W. (1992 [1964]). Toward a Theory of Latin American Politics. In Howard J. Wiarda (ed.). *Politics and Social Change in Latin America. Still a Distinct Tradition?, 239–54*. Boulder: Westview Press.

Baklanoff, Eric N. (1968). Spain and the Atlantic Community: A Study of Incipient Integration and Economic Development. *Economic Development and Cultural Change*, 16: 4, 588–602.

Banfield, Edward C. (1963 [1958]). *The Moral Basis of a Backward Society*. Chicago: The Free Press.

Barrett, Richard A. (1974). *Benabarre: The Modernization of a Spanish Village*. New York et al.: Holt, Rinehart and Winston.

Borutta, Manuel (2010). *Antikatholizismus. Deutschland und Italien im Zeitalter der europäischen Kulturkämpfe*. Göttingen: Vandenhoeck & Ruprecht.

del Campo, Salustiano (1992). Sozialstruktureller Wandel und die Modernisierung Spaniens. In Wolfgang Glatzer (ed.). *Entwicklungstendenzen der Sozialstruktur. Soziale Indikatoren XV, 183–92*. Frankfurt and New York: Campus.

Casanova, José (1982). The Modernization of Spain. *Telos 53*: Fall, 29–43.

Casanova, José (1983). Modernization and Democratization: Reflections on Spain's Transition to Democracy. *Social Research, 50*: 4, 929–73.

Dahrendorf, Ralf (1968 [1966]), *Gesellschaft und Demokratie in Deutschland*. München: Piper.

Dunnage, Jonathan (2002). *Twentieth-Century Italy: A Social History*. London: Pearson Education.

Elkins David J. and Richard E.B. Simeon (1979). A Cause in Search of Its Effect, or What Does Political Culture Explain? *Comparative Politics*, 11: 3, 127–45.

Garcia-Petit, Jorge, and Bernhard Schäfers (1979). Sozialer Wandel in Spanien. Über einige Prozesse der Modernisierung und sozialen Mobilmachung. *Schweizerische Zeitschrift für Soziologie*, 6, 87–108.

Käsler, Dirk (2004). Sonnig, gegenwartsfroh und katholisch. Max Webers Italien. In Friederike Schönemann and Thorsten Maaßen (eds.). *Prüft alles, und das Gute behaltet! Zum Wechselspiel von Kirchen, Religionen und säkularer Welt. Festschrift für Hans-Martin Barth zum 65. Geburtstag*, 271–96. Frankfurt/Main: Lembeck.

Knöbl, Wolfgang (2001). *Spielräume der Modernisierung. Das Ende der Eindeutigkeit.* Weilerswist: Velbrück.

Knöbl, Wolfgang (2012). Beobachtungen zum Begriff der Moderne. *Internationales Archiv für Sozialgeschichte der Deutschen Literatur,* 37: 1, 63–78.

Lepsius, Rainer M. (1990 [1965]). Immobilismus: das System der sozialen Stagnation. In Rainer M. Lepsius (ed.). *Interessen, Ideen und Institutionen*, 170–210. Opladen: Westdeutscher Verlag.

Lerner, Daniel (1958). *The Passing of Traditional Society. Modernizing the Middle East.* New York: Free Press.

Levy, Carl (1996). From Fascism to 'post-Fascists': Italian Roads to Modernity. In Richard Bessel (ed.). *Fascist Italy and Nazi Germany. Comparisons and Contrasts,* 165–96. Cambridge: Cambridge University Press.

Lewis, Martin W., and Kären E. Wigen (1997). *The Myth of Continents. A Critique of Metageography.* Berkeley et al.: University of California Press.

Lipset, Seymour Martin (1988 [1959]). *Political Man. The Social Bases of Politics.* Baltimore: Johns Hopkins Universtiy Press.

Macry, Paolo (1997). Rethinking a Stereotype: Territorial Differences and Family Models in the Modernization of Italy. *Journal of Modern Italian Studies,* 2: 2, 188–214.

Mason, Tim (1988). Italy and Modernization: A Montage. *History Workshop, 25*: Spring, 127–47.

McClelland, David (1961). *The Achieving Society.* New York and London: The Free Press.

Morse, Richard (1964). *The Heritage of Latin America.* In Louis Hartz (ed.). *The Founding of New Societies.*, 123–77. New York: Harcourt, Brace, and World.

Moss, David (1995). Patronage Revisited: the Dynamics of Information and Reputation. *Journal of Modern Italian Studies,* 1: 1, 58–93.

Pateman, Carole (1980). The Civic Culture: A Philosophic Critique. In Gabriel Almond and Sidney Verba (eds.). *The Civic Culture Revisited. An Analytic Study.* Boston and Toronto: Little, Brown & Company.

Payne, Stanley G. (1972). Political Ideology and Economic Modernization in Spain. *World Politics, 25*: 1, 155–81.

Payne, Stanley G. (1986). The Concept of 'Southern Europe' and Political Development. *Mediterranean Historical Review,* 1: 1, 100–17.

Putnam, Robert D. (1993). *Making Democracy Work. Civic Traditions in Modern Italy.* Princeton: Princeton University Press.

Roseman, Mark (2011). AHR Roundtable: National Socialism and the End of Modernity. *The American Historical Review,* 116: 3, 688–701.

Rostow W. W. (1955). Marx Was a City Boy or, Why Communism May Fail. *Harper's*, February, 25–30.

Rostow, Walt (1971 [1960]). *The Stages of Economic Growth. A Non-Communist Manifesto.* Second Edition. Cambridge: Cambridge University Press.

Rueschemeyer, Dietrich (1970). Partielle Modernisierung. In Wolfgang Zapf (ed.). *Theorien des sozialen Wandels*, 382–96. Cologne and Berlin: Kiepenheuer & Witsch.

Sapelli, Giulo (1995). *Southern Europe Since 1945. Tradition and Modernity in Portugal, Spain, Italy, Greece and Turkey*. London and New York: Longman.

Sarti, Roland (1970). Fascist Modernization in Italy: Traditional or Revolutionary? *American Historical Review, 75*: 4, 1029–45.

Schachter, Gustav (1968). Regional Development in the Italian Dual Economy. *Economic Development and Cultural Change*, 15: 4, 398–407.

Schneider, Peter, Jane Schneider and Edward Hansen (1972). Modernization and Development: the Role of Regional Elites and Noncorporate Groups in the European Mediterranean. *Comparative Studies in Society and History*, 14: 3, 328–49.

Singh, Bhagwant (1967). Italian Experience in Regional Economic Development and Lessons for Other Countries. *Economic Development and Cultural Change*, 15: 3, 315–22.

Smelser, Neil J. (1960 [1959]). *Social Change in the Industrial Revolution. An Application to the Lancashire Cotton Industry 1770–1840*. London: Routledge & Kegan Paul.

Somers, Margaret R. (1995). What's Political or Cultural about Political Culture and the Public Sphere? Toward an Historical Sociology of Concept Formation. *Sociological Theory*, 13: 2, 113–44.

Tezanos, José Félix (1984). Cambio social y modernizazión en la España actual. *Revista española de investigaciones sociologicas*, 28, 19–61.

Véliz, Claudio (1980). *The Centralist Tradition of Latin American*. Princeton: Princeton Universtiy Press.

Wagley, Charles (1992 [1968]). A Framework for Latin American Culture. Howard J. Wiarda (ed.). *Politics and Social Change in Latin America. Still a Distinct Tradition?*, 25–39. Boulder: Westview Press.

Waisman, Carlos H. (1987). *Reversal of Development in Argentina. Postwar Counterrevolutionary Policies and Their Structural Consequences*. Princeton: Princeton University Press.

Wiarda, Howard J. (1973). Toward a Framework for the Study of Political Change in the Iberic-Latin-Tradition: The Corporative Model. *World Politics, 25*: 2, 206–35.

Wiarda, Howard J. (2009). Research Note: The Political Sociology of a Concept: Corporatism and the 'Distinct Tradition'. *The Americas*, 66: 1, 81–106.

Manifold Discourses. Mapping the South in Contemporary European History

Patricia Hertel

Portugal, Spain, Italy and Greece hold a marginal position in Western European historiography after 1945. In comparison to the historiographical attention paid to their neighbors Great Britain, France and Germany, these countries have been of little concern for historians beyond their national boundaries. In their marginalization, they share a common destiny with other regions such as Scandinavia, the Benelux, the Balkans or smaller countries in the former Soviet Bloc. The geographical distribution of articles in historiographical journals in the past decades or the denomination of history departments or professorships are just indicators of a considerable imbalance of historiographical attention in European, or more specifically, in Western European history.

In the context of several important shifts in recent historiography, historians have become aware of this marginalization, not just of the South, but of geographical and analytical imbalances in general. Political changes such as the Fall of the Berlin Wall, the enlargements of the European Union and the processes of globalization contributed to a new historiographical consciousness. Historians have called for decentralization of European history on different levels: Transnational approaches have questioned the old West-East divide and a nation-centered historiography (Budde et al. 2006; Clavin 2010; Cole and Ther 2010; Gassert 2012; Middell and Roura y Aulinas 2013). These approaches challenged also European History as a historiographical discipline (Dejung and Lengwiler 2015, forthcoming).[1] This has had various consequences: Different new overview works have explicitly broadened the geographical frame of analysis by integrating regions in Southern, Eastern and Northern Europe which had often been overlooked or treated with less attention (Mazower 1998; Judt 2005). Approaches of the postcolonial studies have abolished classical sender-receiver models by investigations on cen-

1 I thank the authors for facilitating access to the manuscript of their forthcoming article.

ter-periphery dynamics, not just for colonial, but also for European history (Feichtinger 2003). Peripheries—both geographical and analytical ones—became explicitly objects of research in order to decenter European history (Dejung and Lengwiler 2015, forthcoming; Paulmann 2013; Bösch et. al. 2012; Mishkova et. al. 2013). However, despite strong methodological claims among European historians to overcome imbalances in European history, the empirical basis of such studies is still quite thin.

How did it come to this marginalization? Asking for the reasons might be a first step in overcoming centralist narratives. This article offers one line of explanation —there might be many more—by analyzing the complex relation between historical and historiographical discourses around 'the South'. This spatial metaphor was used in the last centuries to express differences and hierarchies. Its semantic connotations were often ambiguous or even contradictory. Scholarship on such 'mental maps' emerged especially after the end of the Cold War and of the Soviet Union, when the political changes questioned the semantic images that were coded in spatial metaphors. These studies, most of them referring directly or indirectly to the deconstruction of the 'Orient' by Edward Said (Said 1995 [1978]) have shown that mental maps are powerful discursive concepts in politics, economy, culture, and also historiography (Wolff 1994; Todorova 1997; Schenk 2002). While the processes of mental mapping have first been investigated in depth about 'Eastern Europe', 'South-Eastern Europe', 'Western Europe' and 'Northern Europe', the 'South' did not receive comparable attention for some time (Schenk and Winkler 2007b, 10–11). In the last years, significant research has been done for the 'mental mapping' of the South from the early modern period until the twentieth century (Schenk and Winkler 2007a). These mappings of the South had also an impact on the postwar period. Some of them just re-write older narratives, some of them break clearly with them. The article defends the argument that discourses of historical actors had often influenced the historiographical discourses. In order to offer an explanation for the marginalization of the South in European historiography, it is helpful to analyze the origins of the structures and discourses that led to the establishment of spatial hierarchies and to perceptions of 'centers' and 'peripheries'.

This article distinguishes three of these discourses that are discussed separately for analytical reasons. In fact, one has to imagine them as interwoven in their historical contexts. Due to necessary limits, the study takes a focus on Western European history and historiography. It concentrates on Portugal, Spain and Italy. The first part of the article analyzes the discourse "A backward South", probably the most ancient and most famous of these discourses. It deals with the perspective of foreigners who described the Southern countries from outside, scrutinizing spatial images of 'backwardness' versus 'modernity'. This discourse can be drawn back to the eighteenth century and beyond; however, after 1945, it gained once again especial importance in the creation of a Southern European periphery in political and economical terms. The second part, "A South re-mapped", takes into account an internal perspective. It shows how spatial codes were also used in Spain, Italy and Portugal to describe internal differences. In particular, it deals with changes in self-images during decolonization. The third part, "An overshadowed South", takes a closer look at the reasons for the marginalization of the South in postwar historiography mentioned above. It analyzes semantic codes of 'North and South' versus 'East and West' in the postwar era and the emergence of the discourse of 'Southern Europe' in European history.

"A Backward South": Spatial Perceptions of Tradition and Modernity

In terms of centuries, the perception of the South as a periphery is quite a recent one. Historians of Antiquity and the Middle Ages referred to the South as the cradle of civilization in contrast to a barbarian North. Even when the center of political power in the Holy Roman Empire moved towards the North, the South was still seen as the center of culture and religion (Hildermeier 2006, 118; Wolff 2007, 212). Renaissance Italy embodied the notion of European high culture, fifteenth and sixteenth century Spain and Portugal, as the first European maritime empires, could claim for themselves the role of pioneers and of hegemonic powers. Other European countries regarded them as important partners who could facilitate a share in the benefits of overseas expansion.

The Enlightenment is an important moment for processes of mental mappings everywhere in Europe, as political and cultural perception of peoples and countries changed significantly in this period (Dipper 2011, 41). This was not the first but an important historical moment from which on the South was placed in a new dimension and connoted with backwardness (Baumeister 2007, 34; Dainotto 2011, 39; Dipper 2011, 43–44; Wolff 2007, 223–224; Briesemeister 2004, 3; Briesemeister 2007, 18–22; Kaelble 2006,

110). This was a consequence of a new thinking in concepts of borders. Older constructions of difference between 'European freedom' and 'Asian despotism' were abolished. The substitute was, as Roberto Dainotto has argued, "an internalization of difference, namely of Asia, within Europe's own south" (Dainotto 2011, 47). At the same time when Europe, according to Edward Said (Said 1995 [1978]), started to discover the Orient as a central Other, this paved also a way for the construction of the South as an 'Orient', an 'Other' within Europe (Dainotto 2000, 379).

This shift in discourse, however, must be considered in its connection and its interference with political developments that stimulated it. In the same way as the discursive "invention" of the Orient by Europeans was fostered by a loss of power in the Islamic world, the discourse of Southern backwardness was linked to the loss of political power in the European South. By the eighteenth century, Spain had lost the maritime pioneer role to Britain, and the formerly great empire seemed itself to be reduced to a colony (Baumeister 2007, 38–39). During the nineteenth century, the successive independence of the former Spanish colonies in America and Asia until 1898 only intensified this tendency. Portugal could maintain large parts of its colonial empire in Africa and Asia. However, the independence of the most important colony, Brazil, in 1822 and the British ultimatum in 1890 that stopped further dreams of expansion of Africa made clear that the climax of colonial power was definitively over. Italy, too, was of no major concern for its neighbors. The national movements and later the establishment of the kingdom served as a role model for the German nationalist movement and the struggle for a nation-state between 1859 and 1870. However, the fascination for Italy as a political pioneer was of short and limited duration. (Dipper 2011, 46–49).

French, British or German travellers, diplomats and intellectuals could therefore easily describe the South as a poor and backward region. Southern Italy was not considered to be European, but a "part of Africa" (Baumeister 2007, 35). Negative stereotypes towards Spain could refer to what the Spanish intellectual Julián Juderías would, in retrospective, in 1914 call "*leyenda negra*", "Black Legend": a set of negative images derived from the Age of Reformation that had promoted the image of a fanatically catholic, intolerant, despotic and therefore hopelessly antimodern Spain (Juderías 1914). The term "Black Legend" has become since then a prominent expression to describe other negative attributes beyond the Spanish case (Pérez 2009, 9). Foreign images of the South in the nineteenth and early twentieth century were, however, not just purely negative, but ambiguous and multiple. The positive counterpart of a Southern backwardness was that of an exotic world and a genuine place not alienated by civilization. Travellers inspired by ideas of Romanticism could find in Southern Spain a piece of the 'Orient' without having to travel to North Africa (Raquejo 1989, 16; Viñes Millet 2007). In the works of French intellectuals on the Mediterranean region, the older image of the South as the "cradle of civilization" could be actualized. The Mediterranean was presented, in different ways and contexts, as a significant place for the development of mankind or as a place of tolerance, cosmopolitanism and dialogue (Baumeister 2007, 29–34).

These discourses of backwardness, or more specifically of exoticism, were also crucial for the postwar era. In fact, the images of the South after 1945 cannot be understood without them. Older stereotypes could be maintained slightly updated or even completely unchanged. For example, a prominent stereotype circulating in West Germany during the postwar era described Italy as the "country of the donkey stables" and as a region dominated by a corrupt and violent mafia (Sala 2012). In contrast, the "Italia docet" narrative, which emerged in leftist circles after 1969, was much more limited (Dipper 2011, 54–56, 59). Exoticism as the internal counterpart of backwardness became especially important, as the Mediterranean South became the most important destination of the emerging mass tourism in the sixties and seventies. The region was poorer in economic terms than the Northern neighbor countries, but could offer sun, sea and exoticism in abundance. Tourists from abroad could find "La dolce vita" in Italy and enjoy that "Spain is different"[2] (Manning 2011; Pack 2006; Crumbaugh 2009). Thanks to foreign currency, the countries in the South could, maybe for the first time, convert consequences of the backwardness discourse into economic benefit.

"A South Re-Located": Postcolonial and Post-Dictatorial Historiography in Portugal

The mechanism to use the semantic code 'South' to express an internal difference was not a simple projection from 'Northerners' onto 'Southerners'. Intellectuals and politicians in Italy, Spain and Portugal referred to similar

2 This was a slogan that the Spanish Ministry of Tourism successfully employed from 1964 to 1979.

patterns, though adapted each time to the national particularities: The Italian Risorgimento was based on a narrative of national unity, which contrasted with the economic and cultural differences in the regions that were now united in the new state. While the North was perceived as the pioneer of progress and modernity, the *mezzogiorno* became the incorporation of anti-modernity and backwardness. (Vögle 2012; Petri and Stouraiti 2007, 163–167; Baumeister 2007, 34–38). In Spain, the emergence of the peripheral nationalisms that questioned the national cohesion in the Basque Country, Catalonia, and Galicia was, in the opinion of their representatives, fostered by their economic success as well as by linguistic and cultural particularities (Núñez Seixas 2001). In contrast, the promotion of folkloristic elements, such as Flamenco music and gypsy culture in Andalucia, helped to fix this region's role as a picturesque and backward Southern counterpart. At the same time, it was considered an incarnation of the nation in images inspired by Romanticism (Baumeister 2007, 43). To a lesser extent and without deeper political implications, North-South patterns in Portugal were expressed in a dualism between the 'Christian North' and the 'Islamic South', nicknamed as *mourolândia* (Sobral 2004, 280). The term expressed an ancient rivalry between the region of Porto, claimed to be the genuine "cradle of the nation", and the capital Lisbon.

Spatial metaphors were, however, not just used to describe internal differences within the national communities. When decolonization questioned the national community as a whole, the use of spatial metaphors and the related discourses show the search for a new identity and a new position towards Europe and the world. This, for example, was true for Spain when it lost its most important remaining overseas colonies in 1898 and for Italy after the Second World War, and for Portugal, the longest lasting colonial empire in Europe. The Portuguese case study provides a striking example in terms of a re-location of identity along a North-South axis. While the colonial empire had defined itself as a European power in a self-attributed mission of civilization towards the Asian, African and American colonies, without them, Portugal saw itself reduced to a small poor and powerless country at the edge of Europe, a Southern periphery. The loss of the colonial empire was closely linked to a political change, as in the two years of political instability and disorder after the Revolution of April 25, 1974 when the weakened motherland lost all overseas territories except Macao. Accordingly, there was an urgent need for a relocation of Portugal's self-image in space and time.

With its long Atlantic coastline and the Mediterranean features of wide parts of its landscape, there existed already a tradition of discussing geographical and cultural features for Portugal. In 1945 the geographer Orlando Ribeiro stressed the entanglement of these two influences and differentiated the dualism of a simple dichotomy between an Atlantic North and a Mediterranean South (Ribeiro 1967 [1945]; Sobral 2004, 257). But the dominating self-image of Portuguese historiography during the Estado Novo was that of an 'Atlantic' empire. 'Atlantic' in this sense was not just a geographical denomination, but a code of political, cultural, and to a certain extent, also religious relevance. Historians of the Estado Novo celebrated the time of the overseas expansion in the fifteenth and sixteenth century as the Portuguese Golden Age. Especially in the 1930s when the young state needed historical legitimation, historians and politicians promoted the image of Portugal as a global empire with a historical mission to civilize other parts of the world. This was not only done in history textbooks, but also on different occasions in the public sphere: The "Exposition of the Portuguese World" in 1940 and even the famous children's leisure park *Portugal dos Pequenitos* claimed an unbroken continuity from the Portuguese empire in the Age of Explorations to the Estado Novo as its successor (João 2002; Corkill and Pina Almeida 2009; Herold-Schmidt 2010). Portuguese politicians cultivated this 'Atlantic' image that was repeated over and over in the official rhetoric. In all these historical interpretations, Portugal had a clear position: the face towards the Atlantic and, as a consequence of this, the back towards Europe. This was even true for intellectuals opposed to the dictatorship of Salazar like the most famous modern poet Fernando Pessoa. In his often-cited first poem of the anthology *Mensagem* ("Message"), he described Portugal as "the face with which Europe looks" towards the Occident (Pessoa 2004 [1934]).

After the revolution and the breakdown of the colonial empire, the Atlantic vision had no more physical basis except nostalgia of a past gone by. Political events, such as the admission to the European Economic Community, forced Portuguese historians to come to terms with the dictatorial and colonial heritage of the past and to relocate the nation's position. Long-lasting myths about the position of Portugal in Europe were revisited, such as the famous dictum of Salazar on 18 February 1965 in which he had described the Portuguese as "*orgulhosamente sós*" ("proudly alone") in their colonial fights in Africa, disguising the political pressure from the international arena. This metaphor of international isolationism had stressed the Atlantic image of Portugal and a defiant attitude towards other countries. Historiography after the dictatorship deconstructed these myths of exceptionalism and demonstrated that Portuguese colonial policy was in many ways similar to that applied by other European states (Alexandre 1997, 87). It analyzed Portuguese colonial policy in the frame of its international relations and deconstructed the black and white picture that the regime painted of its international position (Costa Pinto 2001, 13). This relocation of Portugal and its history did not only take place in historiography of the recent past, but also for more remote centuries such as the Middle Ages. A group of researchers started with excavations around the city of Mértola in the Alentejo region to investigate the Roman, Paleochristian, Islamic, and Jewish heritage in 1978. The initiators of this project, Cláudio Torres and António Borges Coelho, imprisoned during the Estado Novo for being opponents of the regime, chose explicitly these periods, as they had been neglected during the dictatorship. (Borges Coelho [1971] 1989; Macias 2003, 38–39). This valorization of Antiquity and the Middle Ages went along with the promotion of the Mediterranean heritage of Portugal. In this historical interpretation, Portugal's role as pioneer of the Atlantic Discoveries was countered with the enhancement of an older Mediterranean past with close connection to the neighboring regions of Spain, Italy, and North Africa. The same tendency was visible in publications that promoted the Medieval Islamic roots of Lisbon and the Algarve region (Hertel 2015, 67). This narrative stressed the perception of the Mediterranean South with its Hellenic, Roman and Arabic heritage as a milestone in the history of human civilization—and that Portugal could be proud to be part of it.

Of course, these tendencies did not erase completely the ancient 'Atlantic' narratives. The colonial empire was, as shown above, a central *lieu de mémoire* for the Estado Novo, and continues to be that in the Portuguese democracy. This results in competing and heterogeneous forms of memory (Pinheiro 2010). Nevertheless, several shifts in focus can be seen. When Lisbon hosted the World's Fair in 1998, the theme "The Oceans, a Heritage for the Future" converted the importance of the sea in Portuguese history into a commitment for the present and future generations. The newly constructed bridge across the Tagus river, a look-out tower and the shopping mall in the form of a caravel received the name of the Portuguese explorer and national hero Vasco da Gama who had discovered the sea route to India 500 years before. The surrounding area, however, was baptized *Parque das Nações* (Park of the Nations), showing in a literal and symbolical sense Portugal's firm location in Europe and the world. With regard to the self-image of Portugal during the Estado Novo, this can be seen as a counterpart of the old "proudly alone" narrative. All these historiographical and symbolic relocations contributed in different ways to new paradigms in Portugal's self-images: They made it more 'European', but also more 'Southern'.

"An Overshadowed South": The Cold War as a Mainstream Narrative

In the postwar era, processes of mental mapping became a geopolitical tool, interwoven with new constellations and conflicts. Spatial metaphors expressed new perceptions on a worldwide level. Transnational discourses of the Cold War profoundly shaped the contemporary perceptions and influenced also historiographical perceptions of these decades. As a consequence, the European South was overshadowed in a double way: by a West-East divide and by the global North-South divide. These two paradigms were closely interwoven.

The East-West paradigm was neither an exclusive nor a new phenomenon of the postwar period. It can be traced back at least until the eighteenth century, where the shift in the perception of 'North' and 'South' mentioned above brought with it the rise of a new dichotomy between 'West' and 'East' and the "invention" of Eastern Europe (Wolff 1994; Wolff 2007, 212; Schenk 2002, 499–500). This imagination preceded the political East-West conflict of the twentieth century. However, the political tensions of the so-called Cold War created an unprecedented culminating phase of this confrontation. Accordingly, this conflict absorbed not just most of the political attention, but also the historiography of that time. Research on Eastern Europe was overshadowed by the ideological confrontation with the USSR—and also fostered in economic terms (Kappeler 2001, 233; Engerman 2011).

In this new constellation, the European South fell in-between. Especially the dictatorships of Spain, Portugal and Greece were a "central anomaly" for their Western European neighbors (Graham and Quiroga 2012, 505). The anticommunism of the dictators, the strategic importance of their territories and colonies made them allies of the West, as visible for example in the NATO membership of Portugal. However, the Western governments were well aware of the fact that the authoritarian regimes in Greece and the Iberian Peninsula did not fit well within the Western rhetoric of a free world.

Western politicians were very aware of that and had to maneuver carefully in their diplomatic, economic and military relations between these ambiguities (Balfour and Preston 1999; Aschmann 1999; Aschmann 2000; Farré 2006; Lehmann 2006; Fonseca 2007; Lopes 2014; Schroers 1998). However, compared with the constant concern that the Soviet Union caused for Western Europe, the Southern countries were certainly important, but not the biggest political problem of that time. This was interwoven with a historiographical negligence. Historians working on nineteenth and twentieth century political history in Europe who tried to analyze the historical roots of the landmark political conflicts concentrated on the main actors. Italy as the birthplace of fascism certainly had relevance, but in order to analyze World War One, World War Two and the Cold War, Southern Europe was not the first region to turn to.

Parallel to the Cold War confrontation, a new concept of a 'global South' emerged. With the Bandung conference of 1955, the formula of a 'Third World' became not only a counter-concept to the "East versus West" narrative. It also prepared the way for the narrative of a North-South divide that gained political importance in the context of decolonization. With it, the idea of a 'global South' in opposition to a developed 'North', including Japan as well as Australia, gained importance. However, this did not diminish the historiographical marginalization of the European South—to the contrary, it was literally caught in the middle. The southern part of Europe was neither a typical representative of the rich industrial European countries nor did it belong to the 'global South.'

This also had a counterpart in a historiographical negligence. When the new academic concept of interdisciplinary area studies emerged in the USA after 1945 and found its way to Europe, it was the birth of Latin American studies. One of the reasons for this academic trend might also be found in the societies of the time: not only the 1968 movement, but also socialist European politicians showed interest and solidarity with Latin America and iconic figures such as Che Guevara and Salvador Allende. It is not surprising that this fascination for Latin America corresponded with a promotion of Latin American studies in Europe in the sixties and seventies (Potthast and Bodemer 2002, 7; Craske and Lehman 2002, 62 and 74). In the frame of such studies, Spain and Portugal did not occupy a relevant place as well. As case studies on Latin American Studies in West Germany show, amongst these area studies on Latin America, only some of them covered also Iberian, de facto mostly Spanish, history (Pietschmann 1994, 302–305; Sáez-Arance

2003, 192). Neither Spain and Portugal nor Italy and Greece benefitted, in terms of historiographical attention, from the new interest that the new keyword 'South' aroused.

After the end of the Cold War, the category 'Southern Europe' as a new pattern of description for Portugal, Spain, Italy and Greece emerged in scholarship. The term, used since the seventies in social sciences, was adopted by historians from the mid-eighties to the nineties (Payne 1985; Malefakis 1992; Sapelli 1995). In these works, Southern Europe was characterized as a region with historical particularities such as late industrialization, interventionist but administratively weak states, a low degree of political institutionalization, and a widespread system of clientelism that distinguished it from its Northern neighbors (Sapelli 1995, 20). Apart from using 'Southern Europe' as an analytical concept whose suitability is discussed in this volume, the term can be also read as a new discourse in the mapping of the South. In such a reading, the connection of geographical, economical, cultural and geopolitical factors becomes clear. This is visible in the discussions over whether Turkey should be part of 'Southern Europe', as Sapelli had argued, or not, or the exclusion of the Balkan countries, as they followed different political and social patterns due to the Soviet influence (Pedaliu 2013, 9). The discourses around the concept 'Southern Europe' show processes of negotiating belonging. The emergence of 'Southern Europe' itself was also a reaction to Cold War historiography, as the concept pointed to the limits of the East-West dichotomy and the corresponding marginalization in historiography (Malefakis 1992, 2–3). In this way, the emergence of the category of 'Southern Europe' for Portugal, Spain, Italy and Greece in the eighties and nineties is not a contradiction to their marginalization in the Cold War era, but rather the consequence. Until today, the concept of 'Southern Europe' is used far more in social sciences than in historiography (see the theoretical chapter of Baumeister and Sala in this volume). It is not clear, and maybe not very probable, whether the "regional deepening" (Pedaliu 2013, 14) fostered by the economic crisis in Portugal, Spain, Italy and Greece will produce some new historiographical discourses on 'Southern Europe' in the long term. However, it shows that older discursive patterns are not pure relics of the past. They might still reappear, adapted to new circumstances. The 21st century is again, or better yet, still a time of mental mapping.

Concluding Remarks

In his book about the Black Legend, Juderías polemically asked whether Shakespeare would have been "as famous, placed at the side of Homer or Dante if he would have been Polish, Romanian or Swedish instead of English?"(Juderías 1914, 36). Beyond Juderias's clear intention to expose foreign prejudices towards Spain, this rhetorical question points, in a broader context, to the selective and often accidental mechanisms of core-periphery dynamics. What is considered marginal or central—an author, a culture, or also historiographic interest—is submitted to various and complex preconditions.

This is also true for the three discourses on the South discussed here. They did not exist separately next to each other, nor were they pure black and white pictures. Rather, they were interwoven and incorporated a wide range of nuances, even opposed images could co-exist in the same periods. All of them were not pure intellectual phantasies, but had a complex relation to the historical structures, processes or events of their time. Discourses on a "backward South" were a response to ideas and processes of modernity by the historical actors. Discourses of the "South re-mapped" in Portugal were a reaction to decolonization. The "overshadowed South" can be explained with both the Cold War and globalization.

The starting point of this article was the marginal place of the South in European history after 1945. But this marginal position makes the South at the same time a highly interesting topic for European history. The genesis of these spatial metaphors that contributed to marginalization allows a consciousness of tendencies in historiography. It offers insight in cycles of historiographical interest and indifference. This might also help to overcome teleological models of a European modernity that have often been influenced by normative narratives. In this way, nation-states or region within nation-states that have been claimed to be marginal, offer good examples for a decentered European history (Paulmann 2013, 27; Dejung and Lengwiler 2015, forthcoming). The South offers the chance to reconsider master narratives of European history, not only, but especially for the postwar period. Central topics of European history, such as the end of fascist or authoritarian regimes, appear differently if the geographical frame is widened: the cesura of 1945 does not have the same impact for Greece, Spain and Portugal than for Germany or Italy. Just as the countries of the former Soviet block, the South offers many perspectives for new approaches to European history (Kaelble 2006,

111). Furthermore, throughout history, the South shows that it was a place where the borders of 'Europe' were discussed in many ways (Dainotto 2011). Examining the postwar experience of the European 'South' on its own terms offers, therefore, a good case study for historical negotiations of belonging: both within Europe, but also, pars pro toto, of the global connections with Europe and the world. Such perspectives might enrich European history beyond the classical North-South or West-East paradigms.

Works Cited[3]

Alexandre, Valentim (1997). Der Estado Novo und das Kolonialreich. In Fernando Rosas (ed.). *Vom Ständestaat zur Demokratie: Portugal im 20. Jahrhundert*, 75–88. Munich: Oldenbourg.

Aschmann, Birgit (1999). *"Treue Freunde…?" Westdeutschland und Spanien 1945–1963*. Stuttgart: Franz Steiner.

Aschmann, Birgit (2000). "Stolz wie ein Spanier": Genese und Gestalt des deutschen Spanienbildes in der Nachkriegszeit. In Birgit Aschmann and Michael Salewski (eds.). *Das Bild "des Anderen": Politische Wahrnehmung im 19. und 20. Jahrhundert*, 90–108. Stuttgart: Franz Steiner.

Balfour, Sebastian, and Paul Preston (eds.). (1999). *Spain and the Great Powers in the Twentieth Century*. London: Routledge.

Baumeister, Martin (2007). Diesseits von Afrika? Konzepte des europäischen Südens. In Frithjof Benjamin Schenk and Martina Winkler (eds.). *Der Süden: Neue Perspektiven auf eine europäische Geschichtsregion*, 23–47. Frankfurt am Main: Campus.

Bösch, Frank et. al. (eds.). (2012). *Europabilder im 20. Jahrhundert: Entstehung an der Peripherie*. Göttingen: Wallstein.

Briesemeister, Dietrich (2004). *Spanien aus deutscher Sicht. Deutsch-spanische Kulturbeziehungen gestern und heute*. Tübingen: Max Niemeyer.

Briesemeister, Dietrich (2007). Spanienbilder im Wechselrahmen. In Anne-Katrin Becker und Margarete Meggle-Freund (eds.). *¡Viva España! Deutsche Reisen nach Spanien*, 16–26. Karlsruhe: Badisches Landesmuseum.

Budde, Gunilla et. al. (eds.). (2006). *Transnationale Geschichte: Themen, Tendenzen und Theorien*. Göttingen: Vandenhoeck & Rupprecht.

3 Spanish authors are listed under the first family name, Portuguese authors under the last family name.

Clavin, Patricia (2010). Time, Manner, Place: Writing Modern European History in Global, Transnational and International Contexts. *European History Quarterly*, 40, 624–640.

Coelho, António Borges (1989 [1971]). *Portugal na Espanha Árabe*. Lisbon: Caminho.

Cole, Laurence, and Philipp Ther (2010). Current Challenges of Writing European History. *European History Quarterly*, 40, 581–592.

Corkill, David, and José Carlos Pina Almeida (2009). Commemoration and Propaganda in Salazar's Portugal: The Mundo Português Exposition of 1940. *Journal of Contemporary History*, 44: 3, 381–399.

Craske, Nikki, and David Lehmann (2002). Fifty Years of Research in Latin American Studies in the UK. *Revista Europea de Estudios Latinoamericanos y del Caribe*, 72, 61–80.

Crumbaugh, Justin (2009). *Destination Dictatorship: The Spectacle of Spain's Tourist Boom and the Reinvention of Difference*. Albany: SUNY Press.

Dainotto, Roberto (2000). A South with a View: Europe and Its Other. *Nepantla: Views from South*, 1:2, 375–390.

Dainotto, Roberto (2011). Does Europe Have a South? An Essay on Borders. *The Global South*, 5: 1, 37–50.

Dejung, Christoph, and Martin Lengwiler (2015). Ränder der Moderne: Neue Perspektiven auf die Europäische Geschichte (1850–1950)—Einleitung. In Christoph Dejung and Martin Lengwiler (eds.). *Ränder der Moderne: Neue Perspektiven auf die Europäische Geschichte (1850–1950)*. Cologne et al.: Böhlau (forthcoming).

Dipper, Christof (2011). Traditionen des Italienbildes in Deutschland. In Oliver Janz and Roberto Sala (eds.). *Dolce Vita? Das Bild der italienischen Migranten in Deutschland*, 39–61. Frankfurt am Main: Campus.

Engerman, David C. (2011). Die Ursprünge der amerikanischen Sowjetologie im Zweiten Weltkrieg. In Bernd Greiner et. al. (eds.). *Macht und Geist im Kalten Krieg*, 50–67. Hamburg: Hamburger Edition.

Farré, Sébastien (2006). La Suisse et l'Espagne de Franco: de la guerre civile à la mort du dictacteur (1936–1975). Lausanne: Antipodes.

Feichtinger, Johannes et. al. (eds.). (2003). *Habsburg postcolonial: Machtstrukturen und kollektives Gedächtnis*. Innsbruck: Studien-Verlag.

Fonseca, Ana Mónica (2007). *A força das armas: O apoio da República Federal da Alemanha ao Estado Novo, (1958–1968)*. Lisbon: Coleccao Bibliotheca Diplomatica do Ministerio dos Negocios Estrangeiros.

Gassert, Philipp (2012). Transnationale Geschichte, Version: 2.0. In *Docupedia-Zeitgeschichte*, 29.10.2012. URL: https://docupedia.de/zg/Transnationale_Geschichte_Version_2.0_Philipp_Gassert.

Graham, Helen, and Alejandro Quiroga (2012). After the Fear was Over? What Came after Dictatorships in Spain, Greece and Portugal. In Dan Stone (ed.). *The Oxford Handbook of Postwar European History*, 502–525. Oxford: Oxford University Press.

Herold-Schmidt, Hedwig (2010). Die Feste der iberischen Diktaturen: Portugal und Spanien in den 1940er Jahren. In Michael Maurer (ed.). *Festkulturen im Vergleich: Inszenierungen des Religiösen und Politischen*, 291–319. Cologne et al.: Böhlau.

Hertel, Patricia (2015). *The Crescent Remembered: Islam and Nationalism on the Iberian Peninsula*. Brighton: Sussex Academic Press.

Hildermeier, Manfred (2006). Osteuropa als Gegenstand vergleichender Geschichte. In Gunilla Budde et. al. (eds.). *Transnationale Geschichte: Themen, Tendenzen und Theorien*, 117–136. Göttingen: Vandenhoeck & Rupprecht.

João, Maria Isabel (2002). *Memória e Império: Comemorações em Portugal (1880–1960)*. Lisbon: Fundação Calouste Gulbenkian.

Juderías, Julián (1914). *La leyenda negra y la verdad histórica*. Madrid: Tip. de la "Rev. de arch., bibl. y museos."

Judt, Tony (2005). *Postwar. A History of Europe Since 1945*. New York: Penguin Press.

Kaelble, Hartmut (2006). Europäische Geschichte aus westeuropäischer Sicht? In Gunilla Budde et. al. (eds.). *Transnationale Geschichte: Themen, Tendenzen und Theorien*, 105–116. Göttingen: Vandenhoeck & Rupprecht.

Kappeler, Andreas (2001). Osteuropäische Geschichte. In Michael Maurer (ed.). *Aufriss der Historischen Wissenschaften*. Volume 2: *Räume*, 198–265. Stuttgart: Reclam.

Lehmann, Walter (2006). *Die Bundesrepublik und Franco-Spanien: NS-Vergangenheit als Bürde?* Munich: Oldenbourg Verlag.

Lopes, Rui (2014). *West Germany and the Portuguese Dictatorship, 1968–1974. Between Cold War and Colonialism*. Basingstoke: Palgrave Macmillan.

Macias, Santiago (2003). Entrevista a António Borges Coelho. In Santiago Macias (ed.). *Historiador em discurso directo: António Borges Coelho*, 15–42. Mértola: Campo Arqueológico de Mértola.

Malefakis, Edward (1992). Southern Europe in the Nineteenth and Twentieth Centuries: An Historical Overview. Working papers Instituto Juan March de Estudios e Investigaciones. Madrid: Centro de Estudios Avanzados en Ciencias Sociales. URL: http://digital.march.es/ceacs-ir/es/fedora/ir:3928.

Manning, Till (2011). *Die Italiengeneration: Stilbildung durch Massentourismus in den 1950er und 1960er Jahren*. Göttingen: Wallstein.

Mazower, Mark (1998). *Dark Continent: Europe's Twentieth Century*. New York: Vintage.

Middell, Matthias, and Lluis Roura y Aulinas (eds.). (2013). *Transnational Challenges to National History Writing in Europe*. Basingstoke: Palgrave Macmillan.

Mishkova, Diana et. al. (2013). Regional History as a "Challenge" to National Frameworks of Historiography. The Case of Central, Northeast and Southern Europe. In Matthias Middell and Lluis Roura y Aulinas (eds.). *Transnational Challenges to National History Writing in Europe*, 257–314. Basingstoke: Palgrave Macmillan.

Núñez Seixas, Xosé Manoel (2001). The Region as Essence of the Fatherland: Regionalist Variants of Spanish Nationalism (1840–1936). *European History Quarterly*, 31, 483–518.

Pack, Sasha D. (2006). *Tourism and Dictatorship: Europe's Peaceful Invasion of Franco's Spain*. New York: Palgrave Macmillan.

Paulmann, Johannes (2013). The Straits of Europe. History at the Margins of a Continent. *Bulletin of the German Historical Institute Washington*, 52, 7–28.

Payne, Stanley (1986). The Concept of "Southern Europe" and Political Development. *Mediterranean Historical Review*, 1, 100–116.

Pedaliu, Effie (2013). The Making of Southern Europe. A Strategy for Southern Europe (LSE Ideas, Special Report 17), 8–14. URL: http://www.lse.ac.uk/IDEAS/publications/reports/pdf/SR017/Pedaliu.pdf.

Pérez, Joseph (2009). *La légende noire de l'Espagne*. Paris: Fayard.

Pessoa, Fernando (2004 [1934]). *Mensagem*. Ed. Fernando Cabral Martins. Lisbon: Assírio & Alvim.

Petri, Rolf, and Anastasia Stouraiti (2007). Raummetaphern der Rückständigkeit: Die Levante und der Mezzogiorno in italienischen Identitätsdiskursen der Neuzeit. In Frithjof Benjamin Schenk and Martina Winkler (eds.). *Der Süden: Neue Perspektiven auf eine europäische Geschichtsregion*, 151–174. Frankfurt am Main: Campus.

Pietschmann, Horst (1992). Geschichte. In *Handbuch der deutschsprachigen Lateinamerikakunde*, 297–331. Freiburg im Breisgau: Arnold Bergstraesser Institut.

Pinheiro, Teresa (2010). Facetten der Erinnerungskultur—Portugals Umgang mit dem Estado Novo. *Neue Politische Literatur*, 55, 7–22.

Pinto, António Costa (2001). *O fim do império português: A cena internacional, a guerra colonial, e a descolonização, 1961—1975*. Lisbon: Livros Horizonte.

Potthast, Barbara, and Klaus Bodemer (2002). La investigación sobre América Latina en Alemania: un balance del último decenio. *Revista Europea de Estudios Latinoamericanos y del Caribe*, 72, 7–24.

Raquejo, Tonia (1989). *El palacio encantado: La Alhambra en el arte británico*. Madrid: Taurus.

Ribeiro, Orlando (1967 [1945]). *Portugal—o Mediterrâneo e o Atlântico*. Lisbon: Livr. Sá da Costa.

Sáez-Arance, Antonio (2003). Constructing Iberia: National Traditions and the Problem(s) of a Peninsular History. *European Review of History*, 10: 2, 189–202.

Said, Edward (1995 [1978]). *Orientalism*. London: Penguin.

Sala, Roberto (2012). Das Land der Eselställe? Das populäre Italienbild in der Bundesrepublik. URL: http://www.europa.clio-online.de/2012/Article=561.

Sapelli, Giulio (1995). *Southern Europe since 1945. Tradition and Modernity in Portugal, Spain, Italy, Greece and Turkey*. London: Longman.

Schenk Frithjof Benjamin, and Martina Winkler (2007b). Einleitung. In Benjamin Schenk Frithjof and Martina Winkler (eds.). *Der Süden: Neue Perspektiven auf eine europäische Geschichtsregion*, 7–20. Frankfurt am Main: Campus.

Schenk Frithjof Benjamin, and Martina Winkler (eds.). (2007a). *Der Süden: Neue Perspektiven auf eine europäische Geschichtsregion.* Frankfurt am Main: Campus.

Schenk, Frithjof Benjamin (2002). Mental maps: Die Konstruktion von geographischen Räumen in Europa seit der Aufklärung. *Geschichte und Gesellschaft*, 28, 493–514.

Schroers, Thomas (1998). *Die Außenpolitik der Bundesrepublik Deutschland: Die Entwicklung der Beziehungen der Bundesrepublik Deutschland zur Portugiesischen Republik* (1949–1976). Hamburg [no place of publication given].

Sobral, José Manuel (2004). O Norte, o Sul, a raça, a nação—representações da identidade nacional portuguesa (séculos XIX–XX). *Análise social*, 39, 255–284.

Todorova, Maria (1997). *Imagining the Balkans.* New York et. al.: Oxford University Press.

Viñes Millet, Cristina (2007). La Alhambra que fascinó a los románticos. Granada: Patronato de la Alhambra y Generalife.

Vögle, Theresa (2012). *Mediale Inszenierungen des "Mezzogiorno": Die "Südfrage" als Prüfstein der Einheit Italiens und der Idee Europas.* Heidelberg: Universitätsverlag Winter.

Wolff, Larry (1994). *Inventing Eastern Europe. The Map of Civilization on the Mind of the Enlightenment.* Stanford: Stanford University Press.

Wolff, Larry (2007). Dalmatische und italienische Reisen: Das Paradies der mediterranen Rückständigkeit. In Frithjof Benjamin Schenk and Martina Winkler (eds.). *Der Süden: Neue Perspektiven auf eine europäische Geschichtsregion*, 207–228. Frankfurt am Main: Campus.

IV. Political Entanglements

Southern Europe and International Politics in the Post-War Period

Guido Franzinetti[1]

The distinction between South and North is firmly rooted in European intellectual history 'from time immemorial'. In Pre-Modern and Early Modern European history the dichotomy had worked as a distinction between the 'barbaric' Northerners *versus* the 'refined' Southerners (Thompson 1957). It is, in fact, intimately connected to the development of climate theory in European intellectual history, from Ibn Khaldun to Bodin (Tooley 1953; Gates 1967). A key shift took place with Montesquieu's climate theory in 1748, which created the basis for the conceptualization of a 'backward' (Catholic) South *versus* an 'advanced' (Protestant) North (Shackleton 1955; 1960; Berry 1974; Rotta 1974). This dichotomy was further elaborated and expanded, especially after the defeat of Napoleon, with the rise of the North-Western European powers in all fields, whether economic, military or political. A key aspect was the *religious* divide between Protestant or secular-oriented Europe and Catholic Europe. This divide could cut across countries (e.g. unified Germany) or societies (secular elites versus Catholic rural populations).

However, until the First World War there was not much inclination to discuss the South as a European region. The focus was, rather, on 'Turkey-in-Europe' (a quite accurate and pertinent label), and later the 'Balkans' (Todorova 1997). The Great Power dreams of Italian Fascism did not lead to the construction of a 'Southern European' identity–not even at a cultural level- as Italy was more inclined to orient itself towards the Balkans and the Southern shores of the Mediterranean rather than towards Spain and Portugal.

As we shall see, categorizations of Southern Europe (which could include Italy, Spain, Portugal, but also Greece and even Turkey) were to emerge only gradually, as a consequence of a series of successive shifts in European pol-

1 This paper reflects discussions connected with the research project *European Regions and Boundaries. A Conceptual History* coordinated by the Centre for Advanced Studies of Sofia. I would also like to thank the editors for their helpful commentaries.

itics in the post-war period, ranging from the outbreak of the Cold War, to Southern European democratic transitions, and to European integration. This paper will first illustrate some key developments of the Cold War which affected the Southern European region. It will then focus on the consequences of the end of the Cold War. It will also analyze some key social science debates which concern specifically Southern Europe.

The South in Cold War Europe

The premises that made Southern Europe a political framework referring to Italy, Spain, Portugal and Greece (as well as partly Turkey) emerged, quite literally, with the Cold War. This was the natural consequence of the redefinition of strategic interests at the end of World War II, and was already evident in the well-known Churchill-Stalin conversations in Moscow in October 1944. The so-called 'percentages agreement' involved a re-definition of the borders of Eastern Europe. The 'percentages agreement' has been endlessly interpreted and discussed (Resis 1978; Tsakaloyannis 1986; Sfikas 1999; Roberts 2003; 2006). In this context, what matters is the actual meaning of the presumed agreement. The only substantive point of the agreement was that Greece was going to be left to the Western Allies. The rest of the agreement concerned countries which were already destined to end under Soviet control, and Churchill was well aware of that. As he said to Stalin: "Let us settle about our affairs in the Balkans. *Your armies are in Rumania and Bulgaria.*" (Churchill 1954, 198; italics added). It would have made little difference if Churchill had tried to formally oppose Stalin's decisions on Rumania and Bulgaria. Even stopping Tito in Triest in 1945 proved to be difficult enough. The percentages agreement represented a tentative ratification of the new balance of power in Europe, which the military outcome was creating on the ground.

As a main consequence, Greece was *excluded* from Eastern Europe (to which it had always belonged, at least since the Byzantine era). Todorova has pointed out Churchill's accommodating attitude towards a Communist takeover in Yugoslavia. "When Fitzroy Maclean…warned about Tito's open allegiance to communism and his pro-Soviet orientation, Churchill calmed him down with the infallible argument: 'Do you intend…to make Jugoslavia your home after the war?…the less you and I worry about the form of government they set up, the better'" (Todorova 1999, 135). When it came instead to Greece, Churchill had no qualms about resorting to military intervention to prevent a Communist takeover. Hugh Seton-Watson (1975) was one of the few who challenged this exclusion of Greece from its Eastern European historical context.

The case of Turkey was more complex. It had been marginalised during the interwar period, but immediately after the end of the Second World War it suddenly acquired a key strategic role because of the Soviet requests for access to the Bosphorus. Together with Greece, Turkey was an immediate beneficiary of the launching of the Truman doctrine in 1947. The subsequent entry of the two countries into NATO in 1952 ratified a pre-existing strategic alliance with the emerging Atlantic bloc.

Henceforth, Turkish membership of the Atlantic alliance remained crucial to US geo-political interests, but was always problematic. On the one hand, the Turkish Republican Secular establishment (especially the military) willingly adopted the political, economic and military package offered by the USA. On the other hand, since 1960 the relationship became more awkward, for a variety of reasons. In its initial phase the Turkish military coup of 1960, before the higher echelons of the Turkish military reined in, appeared to have a 'Nasserist' inclination. The Cuban crisis of 1962 was in effect solved through the US decision to withdraw missiles from its Turkish bases. The Cyprus issue repeatedly involved the possibility of conflict between Greece and Turkey, two NATO members. In any case, from the beginning of the sixties US administrations strove to orient Turkey towards a 'European' destination (Bali 2010).

As is well known, the political integration of these two countries into Western Europe was consolidated by their inclusion into NATO in 1952 when they came to establish the 'Southern Flank' together with Italy (Hatzivassiliou and Triantaphyllou 2012; Chourchoulis 2015). Even the inclusion of Italy into NATO in 1949 was by no means as smooth as it might seem in retrospect. Truman was extremely reluctant to accept Italy in the first wave of NATO members (after all, Italy was neither Northern nor Atlantic) (Smith 1983). The inclusion of Italy involved the enlargement of NATO responsibility to the Mediterranean, without bringing any significant contribution in exchange (Romano 1993, 58–59). France played a role in supporting Italian entry, stressing the *Mediterranean* dimension of the military alliance, since at the time it had the *Département français d'Algérie* on the southern shores of the Mediterranean (ibid., 60).

The creation of the Southern Flank did not mean the emergence of a clearly defined area called 'Southern Europe'. This was due not only to the most obvious diversities (starting from Roman, Hellenic and Ottoman cultural heritage) but first of all because the Southern Flank always remained within strictly strategic horizons, and never expanded into the political and economic sphere. Furthermore, by 1955 the divergence of interests of the three pillars of the Southern Flank was manifest: for Greece and Turkey, this was made evident by the Cyprus rebellion and the anti-Greek riots in Istanbul in 1955; for Italy, the talks which were to lead to center-left governments revealed an orientation which was quite different from that of the other two pillars. As Dionysios Chourchoulis has pointed out, "the Southern Flank in the 1950s was a political situation rather than a military strategy of the alliance" (2015, 223).

Moreover, Spain and Portugal—the two other countries becoming a main component of the region called Southern Europe at a later stage—were *left out* from the Southern Flank. Spain was an embarrassing partner which was kept out of NATO, and constituted a marginal player in international post-war politics (Guirao 1998). Portugal was a different case, since it had a great importance from a strategic point of view, as a founding member of NATO. However, the country was (historically and economically) more connected with Great Britain than with any other part of Western Europe, let alone the Southern Flank (Kiernan 1973).

In the mid-fifties further developments initiated the progressive convergence—in terms of the international perception as a common area—of the countries of the Southern Flank with the Iberian dictatorships. Firstly, Spain's international isolation, that had also deeply affected its economy, began to be questioned, initially through the US-Spanish rapprochement sanctioned by the Treaty of Madrid in 1953, then in 1955 with the admission of the country as a member of the United Nations together with other countries, including Portugal and Italy (Black 2010, 22, 33). In particular, Spain gradually began to acquire more acceptability. In 1959 it became a full member of the Organization for European Economic Co-operation (Ellwood 1992, 222). This then led to the first agreements with the European Economic Community (EEC) in the early sixties (Hierro Lecea 2015; Guirao 1998).

In the light of several further turning-points—the Austrian *Staatsvertrag*, the Soviet-Yugoslav partial reconciliation, the anti-Greek riots in İstanbul (Stourzh 1998; Rajak 2010; Vryonis 2005), the effects of the 'thaw' in Moscow in the satellite regimes of Eastern Europe —another key event was the beginning of a new balance of power in the Middle East, which emerged with the Czechoslovak-Egyptian deal and the beginning of the Algerian and Cypriot rebellions. As it happens, the crucial French decision to go ahead with the plans for the creation of the European Economic Community — taken in the aftermath of the Suez debacle (Hitchcock 2002) or, perhaps, in consideration of structural economic factors even before (Wall 2001, 62–63; Milward 1993)—corresponded to the partial downsizing of French ambitions as a European power.

This was the moment in which there was a decisive shift from a trans-'Mediterranean' framework to a neo-'Carolingian' one (in which a Franco-German hegemony was rapidly and irreversibly defined, even in terms of administrative practice of emerging European institutions).

These developments facilitated the further normalization of Spain in the context of international relations and the EEC. The Portuguese case was slightly different, not least because of the strength of the British connection. Portugal had made some initial attempts to achieve associate membership with the EEC, but after the first French veto to British entry, it followed Great Britain in joining the European Free Trade Agreement (EFTA). When Britain finally did manage to join the EEC, Portugal began to reorient itself in the same direction (Leitão 2001; 2006; Geary 2009; Cunha 2012; Coppolaro and Lains 2013).

The rise of a military regime in Greece in 1967 appeared to define a new constellation, linking Iberian right-wing dictatorships with the Southern Flank (Greece, if not Turkey). The US together with the two major Western European powers, France and Federal Germany, were quite pragmatic about this aspect (Del Pero 2011). In fact, in December 1973 Henry Kissinger made a point of stopping over in Portugal while flying to Geneva for peace talks "to show appreciation for Portugal's help, almost unique in Europe, during the airlift to Israel" at the time of the Arab-Israeli war of 1973 (Horne 2009, 361). On the other hand, the survival and emergence of right-wing dictatorships, three decades after the defeat of Nazi Germany and Fascist Italy, always remained a source of embarrassment and unease at an international level, at least for some North-Western European countries, e.g. the Netherlands, if not for the EEC as a whole.

Italy also appeared vulnerable, if not to a right-wing coup, quite possibly to a left-wing takeover, given the presence of the largest Communist Party in Western Europe. If a Southern European categorization was emerging, it would have been as an area of instability, marked by right-wing dictatorships, countries inclined to military coups, and, in the case of Italy, a very shaky parliamentary democracy.

The End of the Cold War

The wave of democratic transitions in Spain, Portugal, and Greece did not come entirely unexpectedly. What was unexpected was the speed of these transitions, and their virtually peaceful outcome. Although the three 'transitions' reflected three quite *different* processes, they were telescoped into a reassuring narrative of democratization (Linz and Stepan 1996). This outcome allowed, in the eighties, a new phase of enlargement of the European Community, which was now to include 'Southern Europe' in its entirety. European integration was therefore instrumental in establishing and consolidating Southern Europe as a category.[2]

Although the subsequent conflicts for resources in Brussels consolidated the idea of 'Southern Europe' as a common area, other events weakened it, at least in the medium-term: the end of the Cold War and, more specifically, the emergence of Italy and Greece as Cold War 'orphans'. All of a sudden, at the end of 1991, those countries lost their strategic relevance in the eyes of the remaining super-power. Henceforth, some old clients and beneficiaries of the Cold War lost their value. This also happened in South-Eastern Europe, in the Yugoslav Federation, where the consequences proved to be dramatic (Zimmermann 1999; Danner 1997).

Preventing the Italian Communist Party from coming to power was no longer relevant. For that matter, the acceptance in a government coalition of the *Movimento Sociale Italiano*, which at the time was still loyal to its Fascist heritage, could also take place without much of a reaction from Washington or Brussels. In fact, following the collapse of the established party system, Italy began a period of two decades of virtually continuous neo-populist hegemony in 1994. At an international level Italy began to be seen as a fragile and unreliable democracy.

In Greece, the end of the Cold War also produced a disruption of the existing political alignments. This was made evident by the successive changes

2 As regards the consequences of European integration, see Massimo Piermattei in this volume.

in governments in 1989–1993. After this phase, it appeared that the Greek political system was back to business as usual, starting from the continuation of a dynastically-based leadership (the surnames were Papandreou and Karamanlis). At an international level, Greece continued to extract maximum benefit by resorting to the use of its veto power (as it had in the eighties, in threatening to veto Spanish and Portuguese accession to the EEC). This was made evident in the dispute over the recognition of what came to be known as the Former Yugoslav Republic of Macedonia (FYROM), and, later, over the admission of Cyprus to the European Union (EU), which was successfully made into a precondition for the admission of the other countries in 2004. The entry of Greece into the European Monetary Union (EMU) was by no means a foregone conclusion. As David Close has pointed out, from 1985 to 1998 Greece was repeatedly given a low rating by International Financial Institutions (IFIs) and by Brussels. Indeed, "[d]uring the most of the 1990s Greece was under the humiliating supervision by the European Commission and IMF, which both tried to ensure reduction of the budget deficit" (Close 2002, 169). It was the only 'Southern European' country to be excluded from the EMU. Entry was sanctioned by Brussels in 2000, and the drachma was replaced by the euro in 2002.

The end of the Cold War was thus profoundly destabilizing in Italy and Greece. This was not made immediately apparent, not least because of the immediate outbreak of the Wars of Yugoslav Dissolution (1991–1999), followed by the acceleration of democratic and economic transitions in East-Central Europe.

Spain and Portugal had a much smoother transition into the post-Cold War world. This was due to a variety of factors. Distance from the dissolved Soviet bloc and the Socialist Federation of Yugoslav Republics (SFRY) helped. In the case of Spain, the process of political and economic transition had been prepared and nurtured for many decades, so the end of the Cold War had already taken place by the early eighties. This was already apparent at the time of the attempted military coup in February 1981, when the political elite reacted firmly and cooperatively. The election of a Socialist government marked a definitive normalization of the Spanish political system. In the case of Portugal, the political turbulence of the 1974–75 period together with the fallout of the loss of the African colonies had been rapidly overcome, with the consolidation of a stable political system. Moreover, in Spain and in Portugal the post-Cold War shift had already been factored in before 1989. This was definitely not the case in Italy. Furthermore, the Spanish and Portuguese party systems proved quite resilient in the two decades which followed the end of the Cold War. In fact, at the beginning of the two-thousands Spain was seen as politically and economically healthier than Italy.

In other words, although it had played a significant role within the debates on the monetary union in the nineties[3], at the very beginning of the 21st century the concept of Southern Europe appeared to be about to lose its relevance. The 'Southern European' countries seemed to follow quite different paths of economic and political development. While some had become a model (Spain), others seemed to be stuck in a never-ending political–as well as latently economic–crisis (Italy).

The picture changed radically after the beginning of the Great Recession following the collapse of Lehman Brothers in 2008. The chain of financial, economic, and debt crises led to the immediate invention of the acronym PIGS (Portugal, Italy, Greece and Spain). Commentators in the international arena eagerly adopted this unfavourable label, while Southern European governments struggled to distance themselves from their neighbours, arguing that their national crises were quite different. In particular, Spain and Portugal (which had begun to be considered success stories in the EU) found themselves saddled with the negative images which Italy and Greece had already acquired throughout the nineties.

Echoes in Scientific Studies

In 1958 an American political scientist published a short study of 'Montegrano', a locality in Basilicata, in Southern Italy. Its basic thesis was that what characterised Montegrano was what he designated as 'amoral familism', which he defined in the following terms: "maximise the material, short-run advantage of the nuclear family; assume that all others will do otherwise" (Banfield 1958, 85). This text has been endlessly debated (see e.g. Pizzorno 1966; Ginsborg 1990a; 1990b; Cafagna 1994). It is sometimes taken as a crude exemplar of theories of modernization, while it was in fact a conservative critique of these (Gilman 2003). As it enhanced aspects such as family, honour, patronage or clientelism, Banfield certainly touched a raw nerve. The book anticipated some key elements that have characterized the scien-

3 See again Piermattei in this volume.

tific reflection on 'Southern European' societies, as made particularly evident by Giulio Sapelli's synthesis (1995). However, in the fifties and sixties 'Southern Europe' did not represent a relevant analytical framework for social sciences, and it was no coincidence that Banfield's study focused on a national case study. In the first decades of the post-war period, Southern Europe was still emerging as a regional categorization within international relations and was too weak to influence the scientific reflection.

Quite soon, however, the democratic transitions in Spain, Portugal, and Greece led to the emergence of a specific field of research related to 'Southern Europe', i.e. transitological studies. Linz and Stepan (1996) summarized the debate, which can also be gauged from some of the more general studies (Gunther et al. 1995; Morlino 1998; Diamandouros and Gunther 2001). These studies all represented a significant effort to establish an actual field of Southern European studies. At the same time, the consolidation of Southern Europe as a regional categorization in the context of the European integration process offered new perspectives for a 'Southern European' research agenda. In this context, since the late seventies a broad number of scientific studies emerged.[4] The field of Social Policy was very fertile. In the nineties Ferrera (1996) and Rhodes (1997) produced extremely insightful studies of the 'Southern Model' of Welfare. This is not just because their analyzes turned out to be all too accurate, but also because it provided a workable model which could be usefully applied, even outside the borders of Southern Europe as traditionally understood. The comprehensive analyzes produced by Turkish scholars such as Burğa and Keyder (2006) on the Turkish version or adaptation of the 'Southern Model' point in that direction.

However, at the end of the nineties, with the reorientation of European and NATO enlargement towards the Eastern European countries of the former Soviet bloc, debates and analyzes of Southern Europe in the social sciences lost much of their resonance. The post-2008 developments led to a rediscovery of Southern Europe as a field of research. The need for a sustained analysis of what may be termed the 'Southern European Debt Crisis' has now come to the fore (see e.g. Simonazzi et al. 2013).

4 Malefakis (1992) provided a useful overview of Southern European studies in the social sciences as a whole.

Conclusions

As a regional categorization, Southern Europe, due to its peripheral or semi-peripheral position, has been particularly influenced by international settings. After World War II, there existed no categorization of Southern Europe as a feature of international relations. However, several factors—that partially had quite different origins—soon collectively began to promote the perception of Southern Europe as a common area embracing Italy, Spain, Portugal, Greece, and partially Turkey: the emergence of the 'Southern Flank', the gradual process of normalization of relations between Western Europe and the Iberian peninsula, the shift towards a Franco-German axis, and, crucially, the European integration process. After the Spanish, Portuguese, and Greek democratic transitions had eventually led to 'Mediterranean Enlargement', Southern Europe advanced to an influential category within European relations.

Nevertheless, it faded into the background, as the European integration proceeded eastwards and the 'Southern European' countries appeared to follow quite different paths of development at the end of the nineties and at the beginning the two-thousands. The post-2008 revival of the label 'Southern Europe' shows how exceptionally flexible and volatile this category has always been. It is a spatial concept that can be activated to negotiate power relations within Europe, or rapidly forgotten if not needed. This is likely to remain the case in the foreseeable future.

Works Cited

Banfield, Edward C. (1958). *The Moral Basis of a Backward Society*. Glencoe, Illinois: Free Press.

Berry, Christopher J. (1974). "Climate" in the Eighteenth Century: James Dunbar and the Scottish Case. *Texas Studies in Literature and Language,* 16:2, Summer, 281–292.

Bali, Rıfat N. (ed.). (2010). *Turkey in the 1960's and 1970's through the Reports of American Diplomats*. İstanbul: Libra Kitapçılık ve Yayıncılık.

Black, Stanley (2010). *Spain Since 1939*. New York: Palgrave Macmillan.

Buğra, Ayşe, and Çağlar Keyder (2006). The Turkish Welfare Regime in Transformation. *Journal of European Social Policy*, 16:3, 211–228.

Cafagna, Luciano (1994). Riflessioni su qualche libro. In Luciano Cafagna. *Nord e Sud. Non fare a pezzi l'unità d'Italia*, 89–94. Venezia: Marsilio.

Chourchoulis, Dionysios K. (2015). *The Southern Flank of NATO, 1951–1959: Military Strategy or Political Stabilisation*. Lanham, Boulder, New Yor, and London: Lexington Books.

Close, David H. (2002). *Greece Since 1945. Politics, Economy and Society*. London: Pearson.

Churchill, W. S. (1954). *Triumph and Tragedy* (*The Second World War*, vol. VI). London: Cassell.

Coppolaro, Lucia, and Pedro Lains (2013). Portugal and European Integration, 1947–1992: an Essay on Protected Openness in the European Periphery. *e-journal of Portuguese History*, 11:1, 61–82.

Cunha, Alice (2012). The European Economic Community's Third Enlargement. *The Jean Monnet/Robert Schuman Paper Series*, 12:6.

Danner, Mark (1997). The US and the Yugoslav Catastrophe. *New York Review of Books*, November 20, 44:18, 56–64.

Del Pero, Mario (2001). *The United States and the Crises in Southern Europe*. In Guia Migani and Antonio Varsori (eds.). *Europe in the International Arena During the 1970s*, 301–316. Bruxelles: Peter Lang.

Diamandouros, Nikoforos, and Richard Gunther (2001*). Parties, Politics and Democracy in the New Southern Europe*. Baltimore: Johns Hopkins University Press.

Ellwood, David W. (1992). *Rebuilding Europe. Western Europe, America and Postwar Reconstruction*. London and New York: Longman.

Ferrera, Maurizio (1996). The "Southern Model" of Welfare in Social Europe. *Journal of European Social Policy*, February, 6:1, 17–37.

Gates, Warren. E. (1967). The Spread of Ibn Khaldûn's Ideas on Climate and Culture. *Journal of the History of Ideas* , 28:3, July-September, 415–422.

Geary, Michael J. (2009). *The Third Enlargement: Spain's and Portugal's Access to the EEC: Report on the Council of Ministers Archival Material*. Brussels: Council of the European Union.

Gilman, Nils (2003). *Mandarins of the Future. Modernization Theory in Cold War America*. Baltimore: Johns Hopkins University Press.

Ginsborg, Paul (1990a). Family, Culture and Politics in Contemporary Italy. In Zygmunt G. Baranski and Robert Lumley (eds.). *Culture and Conflict in Postwar Italy: Essays on Mass and Contemporary Culture*. London: Macmillan.

Ginsborg, Paul (1990b). *A History of Contemporary Italy. Society and Politics 1943–1988*. Harmonsworth: Penguin Books.

Guirao, Fernando (1998). *Spain and the Reconstruction of Western Europe, 1945–57: Challenge and Response*. Basingstoke: Macmillan.

Gunther, Richard, P. Nikiforos Diamandouros, and Hans-Jurgen Puhle (1995). *The Politics of Democratic Consolidation : Southern Europe in Comparative Perspective*. Baltimore: Johns Hopkins University Press.

Hatzivassiliou, Evanthis, and Dimitrios Triantaphyllou (2012). Apropos NATO's First Enlargement. *Southeast European and Black Sea Studies*, 12:4, 467–469.

Hierro Lecea, Pablo del (2015). *Spanish-Italian Relations and the Influence of the Major Powers, 1943–1957*. Basingstoke, New York: Palgrave Macmillan.

Hitchcock, William I. (2002). Crisis and Modernization in the Fourth Republic: From Suez to Rome. In Martin Alexander and Kenneth Mouré (eds.). *Crisis and Renewal in France, 1918–1962*, 221–241. Oxford: Berghahn Books.

Horne, Alastair (2009). *Kissinger's Year: 1973*. London: Weidenfeld & Nicolson.

Kiernan, Victor G. (1973). The Old Alliance: England and Portugal. *The Socialist Register*, 261–281.

Leitão, Niculau Andresen (2001). Portugal's European Integration Policy, 1947–1972. *Journal of European Integration History*, 7:1, 25–35.

Leitão, Nicolau Andresen (2006). Alice in Wonderland? Portugal and the Attempt to Enlarge the EEC, 1961–1963. Helsinki: XIV International Economic History Congress.

Linz, Juan, and Alfred Stepan (1996). *Problems of Democratic Transition and Consolidation. Southern Europe, South America, and Postcommunist Europe*. Baltimore: Johns Hopkins University Press.

Malefakis, Edward (1992). *Southern Europe in the 19th & 20th Centuries: An Historical Overview*. Madrid: Estudio/Working Paper 1992/35, January 1992.

Milward, Alan (1993). Conclusions: The Value of History. In Alan Milward et al. (eds.). *The Frontier of National Sovereignty: History and Theory, 1945–1992*. London: Routledge.

Morlino, Leonardo (1998). *Democracy between Consolidation and Crisis : Parties, Groups, and Citizens in Southern Europe*. Oxford : Oxford University Press.

Pizzorno, Alessandro (1966). Amoral Familism and Historical Marginality. *International Review of Community Development*, 15, 55–66.

Putnam, Robert D. (1993). *Making Democracy Work: Civic Traditions in Modern Italy* (with the assistance of Roberto Leonardi and Raffaella Y. Nanetti). Princeton: Princeton University Press.

Rajak, Svetozar (2010). *Yugoslavia and the Soviet Union in the Early Cold War: Reconciliation, Comradeship, Confrontation, 1953–1957*. London and New York: Routledge.

Resis, Albert (1978). The Churchill-Stalin Secret "Percentages" Agreement on the Balkans, Moscow, October 1944. *American Historical Review*, 83:2, 368–387.

Rhodes, Martin (1997). Southern European Welfare States: Identity, Problems and Prospects for Reform. In Martin Rhodes (ed.). *Southern European Welfare States: Between Crisis and Reform*, 1–22. London: Frank Cass.

Roberts, Geoffrey (2006). *Stalin's Wars: From World War to Cold War, 1939–1953*. New Haven: Yale University Press.

Romano, Sergio (2002 [1993]). *Guida alla politica estera italiana. Da Badoglio a Berlusconi,* Milan: Rizzoli.

Rotta, Salvatore (1974). *Il pensiero politico francese da Bayle a Montesquieu*. Pisa: Pacini.

Sapelli, Giulio (1995). *Southern Europe Since 1945. Tradition and Modernity in Portugal, Spain, Italy, Greece and Turkey*. London: Longman.

Seton-Watson, Hugh (1975). Intelligentsias in East-Central Europe. *Times Literary Supplement*, May 2, 483.

Sfikas, Thanalis D. (1999). Toward a Regional Study of the Origins of the Cold War in Southeastern Europe: British and Soviet Policies in the Balkans, 1945–1949. *Journal of Modern Greek Studies*, 17:2, 209–227.

Shackleton, Robert (1955). The Evolution of Montesquieu's Theory of Climate. *Revue Internationale de Philosophie*, 9, 317–329.

Shackleton, Robert (1960). *Montesquieu. A Critical Biography*. Oxford: Oxford University Press.

Simonazzi, Annamaria, Andrea Ginzburg, and Gianluigi Nocella (2013). Economic Relations between Germany and Southern Europe. *Cambridge Journal of Economics*, 37, 653–675.

Smith, E. Timothy (1983). The Fear of Subversion: The United States and the Inclusion of Italy in the North Atlantic Treaty. *Diplomatic History*, 7:2, 139–156.

Stourzh, Gerald (1998). *Um Einheit und Freiheit: Staatsvertrag, Neutralität und das Ende der Ost-West Besetzung Osterreichs: 1945–1955* 4. Auflage. Wien: Böhlau.

Thompson, E. A. (1957). Christianity and the Northern Barbarian. *Nottingham Medieval Studies*, 1, 3–21.

Todorova, Maria (1997). *Imagining the Balkans*. New York: Oxford University Press.

Tooley, Marian J. (1953). Bodin and the Medieval Theory of Climate. *Speculum*, 28:1, 64–83.

Tsakaloyannis, Panos (1986). The Moscow Puzzle. *Journal of Contemporary History*, 21:1, 37–55.

Vryonis, Jr, Speros (2005). *The Mechanism of Catastrophe: the Turkish Pogrom of September 6–7, 1955, and the Destruction of the Greek Community of Istanbul*. New York: Greekworks.com.

Wall, Irvin M. (2001). *France, the United States, and the Algerian War*. Berkeley: University of California Press.

Zimmerman, Warren (1999 [1966]). *Origins of a Catastrophe. Yugoslavia and its Destroyers*. New York: Times Books.

Ptolemaics and Copernicans. Southern Europe and the European Integration Process

Massimo Piermattei

This contribution aims to retrace the milestones, actors and peculiarities of the building of the concept of Southern Europe in the framework of the European integration process. This is because the underlying assumption is that it is increasingly difficult to fully understand the evolution of the vicissitudes of Southern Europe in the second half of the 20th century without considering the perspective of European integration. Indeed, from the point of view of historical disciplines, the European integration process was a matter purely for a restricted community of academics for a long time. However, in the last twenty years, the enlargement, the depth and the complexity of the European integration process has meant that an increasing number of researchers and scholars, not only coming from the field of social sciences, began to deal with questions concerning European Union (EU) issues. This process of involvement started in the early nineties during the period between the Single European Act (SEA) and the Treaty of Maastricht (TEU) when, as political scientists argued, a new area of politics, previously only partially defined, become more evident and stronger.[1] An area clearly separated from the other two, traditional domestic and foreign politics, representing the repercussions of EU membership: domestic and foreign politics of a country, in other words, are profoundly influenced and redefined by the European integration process (Cotta et al. 2005, 8). This process led to the coinage of the term "Europeanization" to represent this action of transformation (Featherstone and Redaelli 2003). The main consequence of Europeanization is the difficulty to focus on any one country during a given period—from a economic, social, political or institutional perspective–without considering the "EU factor". Just some simple examples: How it is possible to study the transition and the crisis of the Italian Republic in the early nineties without considering Maastricht? How can we focus on the transformations of Spanish and Italian

1 Though the relevance of the seventies in the history of the European integration process should not be undervalued.

societies without studying the impact of EU policies in fields such as those of equal opportunities (Di Sarcina 2015) or human rights? How can we understand the transition to democracy and its stabilization in Spain, Greece and Portugal without considering their entry into the European Economic Community (EEC)? Or the migration and environment issues in the Mediterranean Sea? These examples simply confirm the way through which the European integration process gradually penetrated so many fields requiring new attention from researchers coming from the disciplines that intersect topics touched by EU action. For these reasons, although very briefly summarized, a broad reflection on Southern Europe in post-war Europe has to deal with the EU and its process of integration.

Approaches and Historical Background

The first question to be addressed is: what does Southern Europe mean in the context of European integration? It might seem a purely academic discussion, but it is actually crucial when discussing a given region and its development in the long term, because it involves defining exactly what this region is and is not. And this is particularly difficult in the case of Southern Europe because its configuration continuously changes depending on the approach adopted. It is also difficult because it is not easy to separate the issues related to the European integration process from those studied by the ample literature on Southern Europe in the 20th century: it is a complex interweaving in which the contribution of European studies is becoming increasingly relevant. So in order to understand the "EU factor" and the development of the idea of Southern Europe in the European integration process, it is necessary to begin with some introductory remarks to show how the idea of Southern Europe changed in the past century.

Studies on the late 19th and early 20th centuries suggest an idea of Southern Europe focused on a group of countries comprising France, Italy, Spain and Portugal: the interchanges between the Republican movements in Spain and Italy, following the path traced by the French, are one example (Ridolfi and Suarez 2010; Thomson 2007, 21–54; Ridolfi 2011). However, elements of dichotomy of two different viewpoints seem to arise after this period, reflecting two different approaches: Southern Europe and Mediterranean Europe. The renowned Italian journal *Memoria e Ricerca*, for example, has published four special issues on this question in recent years: three of them focused on Mediterranean Europe and included Greece (Noiret 2001; Tonizzi 2002)—and even Croatia (Ridolfi 2012)–while the last one centered on Southern Europe and excluded Greece (Ridolfi 2002). The well-known work by Fernand Braudel on the Mediterranean space had already mapped this duality: the famous French historian stated that if someone drew a boundary line from Corfu and the channel of Otranto through Sicily until the coastlines of Tunisia, Mediterranean Europe would be split in two, into Western and Eastern Mediterranean Europe, "in the full and classic meaning of both the terms" (Braudel 2010, 12).

The exportation of the fascism/anti-fascism dichotomy to the Iberian Peninsula in the thirties seems to reinforce the link between Spain, Portugal and Italy, increasing the distance with France. In the early post-war period, the problematic search for a shared conceptualization of Southern Europe grew even further thanks to the Cold War. There was Southern and Mediterranean Europe, of course, but the most relevant cleavage was that between Eastern and Western Europe, both of them with a boundary in their own South.

In the mid-nineties, Giulio Sapelli published his interesting book *Southern Europe since 1945: tradition and modernity in Portugal, Spain, Italy, Greece and Turkey*, breaking the cleavage described above (Southern and Mediterranean Europe) and substantially proposing a new definition. Starting from an analysis focused on economic development and growth and on the building of democratic systems after the end of dictatorships (Sapelli 1995), Sapelli developed an idea of Southern Europe as the set of states named in the subtitle of his book: Portugal, Spain, Italy, Greece and Turkey. It seemed a more "modern" and interdisciplinary definition, influenced by the end of the regimes in Spain and Portugal and, probably, by the fall of the Berlin Wall. The relevance of Sapelli's approach consists, from the perspective of this contribution, in three main points: 1) the clear interdisciplinary approach, with an adroit mix of economics, politics, anthropology and history; 2) the fulcrum on contemporary issues as a new paradigm to approach the European Mediterranean region; 3) the corroboration of the French detachment from "the others". However, even in that work, the dimension of European integration, as an interpretative key to study Southern Europe, was not particularly present and this fact is even more significant if we think that the work of Sapelli was developed while the EEC was enlarging to the South and the first contrapositions with Germany were emerging.

The conclusions which may be drawn from the results of these historical processes and approaches underlined two problems to solve: the controversial role of France (part or not of Southern Europe?) and the relationship of Greece with the historical core of the idea of Southern Europe (Italy, Portugal and Spain). However, the fall of the Berlin Wall suddenly changed the context and setting of the problem of the relationships between Western and Eastern Europe after the end of the Cold War. For Southern European countries this means, among other things, the need to deal with the Balkan countries and the dramatic repercussions of Yugoslavian dissolution. This also means the need to build a new relationship with Ankara and Turkey once the process of reunification of Europe started. However, to deal with these issues the time has come to introduce into this perspective the "EU factor".

Milestones and Junctures of Southern Europe Countries' Involvement in the EU

The central role of many Southern European countries in the early post-war period emerged relatively early: the civil war in Greece and the subsequent formulation of the Truman doctrine, the Labour Day massacre in Portella della Ginestra (Sicily) in 1947; the problematic collocation of Spain as an undemocratic regime, however necessary for the security and stability of Western Europe as a whole, are the first examples to confirm it. However, the first European community—The European Coal and Steel Community (ECSC)—was born and developed around the Rhine border, representing a historical reconciliation between France and Germany, with Italy alone representing the South of the ECSC. Why this marginality of the South? There are four reasons: 1) *scarce French interest*: since the beginning of the European integration process, it was clear that Paris was mainly interested in assuming the leadership of the new Community and forging a strong relationship with Bonn; it was less interested in building a common approach to European integration with Italy. Since the beginning of the Fifth Republic, this strategy was strengthened (Valette 2004, 108)[2]; 2) *an undemocratic Iberian*

2 The strong link between the French position towards the European integration development and the conflictual relationship between De Gaulle and US governments (Wall 1989; Jauvert 2000) has to be mentioned.

Peninsula: Spain and Portugal aimed to join the ECSC but the end of their dictatorships, and the beginning of a new season of freedom and democracy, was posed as prerequisite to join; therefore, they had to wait until the seventies to apply (Samaniego Boneu 2004; Tavares Ribeiro 2004; Powell 2011; Porto 2005); 3) *the withdrawal of Greece*: Athens wanted to join the ECSC and was on the point of doing so when the Colonels revolted and negotiations to enter the European Community ground to an abrupt halt for exactly the same reasons as those preventing Spanish and Portuguese membership; 4) *the Turkish dilemma*: Turkey was, together with Greece, the first country to apply to join the EEC. In the early sixties the so-called *Ankara agreement* was signed with the aim to promote a closer relationship between the Community and Turkey to better prepare the path towards full membership (Ankara Agreement 1963): the Turkish Government is still waiting for a definitive answer, in or out, to their application.

As already mentioned above, it was necessary to wait until the end of the dictatorships in Greece, Spain and Portugal to see these countries of the South join the EEC[3]. If, on the one hand, this meant a strong enhancement both of the EEC's self image and of the external projection of it as a means dedicated to building freedom and democracy across Europe, on the other hand it also meant that the EEC had come a long way and passed through some crucial events such as the Treaties of Rome, the so-called empty-chair crisis, the re-launch of The Hague and the first direct election of the European parliament without a relevant presence from the South of Europe. Therefore, the significantly different starting point of Greece, Spain and Portugal and that of the other countries of the EEC towards the European integration process has to be underlined. With the enlargement to Greece in 1981 (Papastratis 2005) as well as to Spain and Portugal in 1986 (Blanco Sío-López and S. Muñoz 2013; Cunha 2014), the centre of gravity of the EEC seemed to shift towards the Mediterranean Sea.[4] However, the new line-up had no time to come to bear before the fall of the Berlin Wall suddenly led to a new European framework. Indeed, after that event, another enlargement comprising Denmark, Finland and Austria (1995), sanctioned the rebalancing of the

3 In this perspective, those countries afterwards become a model for the Eastern block countries after the Berlin wall fall (Bielanski 2013).

4 A confirmation of the renewed attention of the EU to the South was the beginning of the so-called Barcelona process, a strategy for the Mediterranean area to promote dialogue between the different banks of the Sea (Shlaim and Yannopoulos 1976; Laschi 2011; Gomez 1998; Calandri 2009).

center of gravity Northwards, and initiated the troubled accession path to the Central and Eastern European countries (CEEC). In the enlargement of 2004 mainly to the CEEC, three other (small) Southern countries of Europe joined the EU: Malta, Cyprus and Slovenia. Then, it was the turn of Croatia, the twenty-eighth member as of July 2013.

However, the main interesting point is that while the enlargement of the EU to the East, North or West is virtually complete,[5] the involvement of other countries which could claim to belong to Southern Europe, due to their geographical collocation, is an open issue and an on-going process (Anderson and Bort 1998). Many states are currently on track to join and many others aspire to do so: the *candidate countries* are Albania, Macedonia, Montenegro, Serbia, Turkey, while the *potential candidates* are Bosnia-Herzegovina and Kosovo. Although this is not the right forum to discuss the status of each candidate or the enlargement process as a whole in depth,[6] three points have to be mentioned: 1) with the involvement of the Balkan Peninsula in the EU, Europe will finally come to terms with the dramatic history of the 20th century, which had such a dramatic coda in the area (Bideleux 2005; Privitera 2011); 2) the controversial role of Turkey that, between political problems (the relationship with Cyprus[7]and the respect of the minority groups and human rights) and social-cultural issues (namely, the role of women and the entry of more than 75 million people, most of them Muslims), remains unsolved.

Nevertheless, in the perspective of this article, the main (and third) point to be mentioned is France's limited interest in developing an idea of Southern Europe and the exclusion, for different reasons, of Turkey and the Balkan countries for such a long time, which has consolidated a definition of Southern Europe as the set of countries comprising Spain, Portugal, Greece and Italy, thanks to her geographical collocation and the vicissitudes that will be

5 It being understood that with the determination of Switzerland and Norway not to join the EU, the only open issues for an enlargement outside the South are Ukraine and perhaps Belarus and Moldova. Iceland definitively decided to stay out of the EU on March 2015 (http://euronews.it/en/302077, accessed on March 13, 2015).

6 See the webpage of the EU Enlargement policy to find details about each situation. See http://ec.europa.eu/enlargement/ (see March 12th 2015).

7 The problematic accession negotiations with this country are actually on hold: "until Turkey agrees to apply the Additional Protocol of the Ankara Association Agreement to Cyprus, eight negotiation chapters will not be opened and no chapter will be provisionally closed". (URL: http://ec.europa.eu/enlargement/countries/detailed-country-information/turkey/index_en.htm, accessed on March, 11 2015).

illustrated in the following paragraph–about the difficult path of those countries in the EEC/EU, especially in the nineties.

The consequence of this mere geographical conceptualization is increasingly calling into question the idea of Southern Europe in the EU once the enlargement process is achieved (Dolghi and Horga 2011). In that case there will be three macro regions that could claim the designation of "Southern Europe": the *historical set* comprising Italy, Portugal, Spain and Greece (extended to Malta and Cyprus); the *Balkan wedge*, a connecting hinge between the Mediterranean Sea, the CEEC and Germany; the *Turkish frontier* limited to Turkey and her problematic role in Northern Cyprus, as a double interface between Europe and Asia, Europe and the Middle East.

However, these considerations are not the only reason to define the geographical approach to Southern Europe as limited in the European integration process. Indeed, since the institution of the European Regional Development Fund in 1975, the EEC/EU, following the approach of subsidiarity, increasingly developed a strong regional policy—especially through the SEA and TEU—and many common policies to provide a decisive role for regional institutions (Grazi 2012; Bachtler et al. 2013).[8] This focus on the infra-national level–in particular, on a regional level–led over time to an erosion of the sovereignty of the member states (Bitsch 2003; Keating and Jones 1995; Zucca 2012): the implications of this process is the need to supersede the definition of Southern Europe in the EU, strictly focused on the classic model of nation states, to embrace a new framework which takes the regional dimension into greater account. While France as a whole may feel little association with Southern Europe, some French regions are closely related to the area.[9] Without wanting to enter into the merits of the north-south divide which characterises a number of countries such as Italy, Spain, Greece and, in the perspective described above, France itself, the emphasis on the regional issue and on infra-national levels has at least the repercussion of enhancing the idea of a Southern Europe in the EU that could continually change in its configuration depending on the point of view. It changes, as will be illustrated in the following paragraph, mainly due to the effects of the political dynamics of the integration process: the development of the European

8 The EU regional policy produced controversial results. The research of Robert Leonardi in the time span 1981–1995 has shown how Italian and Spanish regional disparities, contrary to the German ones, have increased instead of decreased (Leonardi 1998, 161).

9 Corsica, Languedoc-Roussillon, Provence-Alpes-Côte d'Azur and Rhône-Alpes (the latter most only partially).

construction, in other words, has significantly contributed to a concept of Southern Europe in the EU.

The First Steps in the EU's Control Room Between Rivalries and Contrapositions

As can be easily deducted from the evolution of the enlargement process briefly described in the paragraph above, the involvement of the countries included in the different ideas of Southern Europe in the European integration process is a relatively recent fact, first mooted in the early eighties. The period between the eighties and nineties is interesting when investigating two aspects: 1) the pre-membership relationships between the acceding countries and the member states of the EEC and the preparation of the latter for the European and domestic repercussions that these enlargements would provoke; 2) the development of the relationships with the other partners, particularly Germany.

Regarding the former aspect, the first consideration that has to be addressed is that usually the neighbours looked at an enlargement to a Southern country as a threat to their national interests and not as an opportunity. They feared that the acceding countries could attract more investments, more EU funds or erode their position acquired within common institutions and the EEC/EU. Therefore, they try to pre-empt the effects by strengthening their position and their status to maintain the gap with the acceding countries after the completion of the enlargement.

It is possible to glimpse this approach in the years before the entry of Greece[10]- with the birth itself of the regional policy–and especially in the mid-eighties when the time came for Spain and Portugal to join the EEC. Indeed, the clearest example were the Integrated Mediterranean Programmes (IMP) claimed by Greece, Italy and France when the Iberian enlargement

10 Introducing the common policy for the Mediterranean, vice president of the European Commission, Natali, stated: "Geopolitical reasons in themselves make an impressive case for the necessity of a coherent European community policy on the Mediterranean. A glance at the map proves it. Look first at the Balkans and then at the mouth of the Atlantic. Take in the Dardanelles and the petrol-producing region of the Near East; remember too that the Mediterranean is the inescapable North-South axis for links between Europe and Africa" (Commission of the European communities 1982).

was approaching. The European Council of Brussels (March 1985), on the basis of a proposal advanced by the European Commission since 1982 (Grazi 2014), finally adopted the support program for the "southern regions of the present Community [...] to improve the economic structures of those regions to enable them to adjust under the best condition possible to the new situation created by enlargement" (European Council 1982, 2). The failure to extend the IMP to Spain and Portugal after their accession was a confirmation of the real purpose of that tool: preparing Italy, Greece and France for the Iberian enlargement and maintaining their advantage towards those countries. It also confirms the relevance of the regional level in the institutional architecture of the Community, and the action of variable geometries in the development of a concept of Southern Europe in the European integration process: France suddenly supported Greek and Italian claims in a decisive way just because it had an obvious national interest in doing so.

The first steps were not a good debut mostly because the first answer adopted by the newcomers, obviously, was to strike back at the less-than-friendly welcome received as soon as possible. Indeed, Portugal and Spain had not forgotten the vicissitudes of the IMP. Therefore, during the Maastricht negotiations they promoted an alliance, together with Greece and Ireland, mainly against Italy, on the issue of the Cohesion Fund. The protocol on "Economic and Social Cohesion", annexed to the treaty, established a cohesion fund in the fields of environment and trans-European networks in the member states "with a per capita GNP of less than 90 percent of the Community average which have a program leading to the fulfilment of the conditions of economic convergence" (Tue, No C 191/94). This last sentence made two shots against Italy, like the mention of the convergence program, a particularly thorny issue for the government in Rome. However, the real master stroke was to adopt the national per capita GNP and not a regional one—as would have made more sense in the context of cohesion–to access the fund: Italy, a country with huge regional disparities, but also with significant levels of economic wealth thanks to its industrialization and economic development in the North, had a GNP higher than the fixed limit of 90 percent of the Community average. Thus, Italy and its poor Southern regions were excluded from the Cohesion Fund. It was a clear point in favour of Spain which was able to take full advantage of the negotiation weakness of Italy (Dyson and Featherstone 1999; Piermattei 2012; Mechi 2009).

The considerations about the IMP and the Cohesion Fund lead to the conclusion that the countries of Southern Europe in the EU rarely try to build common positions, or to elaborate their own approach during potential opportunities such as the Maastricht negotiations: on the contrary, they continuously build, destroy and re-build again a series of shifting alliances, depending on the situation and aimed mainly at grabbing the largest possible slice of the structural funds pie. So engaged were they in this self-referential struggle, that they failed to take account of the implications of the convergence program for them and, above all, the determination of Germany and its Central bank, which they failed to respect to the letter.[11] Italy, Greece, Portugal and Spain, while sharing some structural weaknesses and problems, were divided in Maastricht and thus facilitated the linking of the path towards a single currency union with the monetarist approach of Germany–parameters such as unemployment and, regional disparities were not taken into account—and the postponing, once again, of the development of a common Southern Europe space within the EU.

Indeed, in September 1994 there was a step forward when the CDU-CSU parliamentary group published a paper on European integration issues to influence the German Presidency of the Union.[12] In this document, they strongly called for a two-speed Europe through the establishment of a "hard kernel" to create "a consolidated fulcrum to counteract the centrifugal forces caused by a continuous enlargement, and to prevent a further divergent development between a South-East group more inclined to protectionism, headed by France, and another group based on the North East in favour of direct and global free trade, led by Germany" (CDU-CSU 1994, 180). Members of the "Core Europe" had to be Germany, of course, together with France, Belgium, Luxembourg, the Netherlands, Denmark and Ireland, according to Kohl's party. No space for countries of Southern Europe that, on the contrary, were marked as one of the main causes of the lack of integration:

> "The Kernel has to persuade all the other members of the EU, particularly Italy, a founder member, but also Spain and obviously Great Britain about its determination to integrate them once they have resolved their problems […] The building of the kernel is not a goal in itself, but a way to balance two other conflicting goals, the enlargement and the deepening of the EU" (Cdu-Csu 1994, 181).

11 German minister Theo Waigel liked to say that 3 percent means 3 percent, and not 3,01 percent.

12 The official paper in German is available on https://www.cducsu.de/upload/schaeublelamers94.pdf (accessed on March 17, 2015).

What makes this document interesting, from the perspective of this contribution, was the decision to include Belgium, with its huge public debt—higher in percentage than Italy's, in the Kernel. This inclusion seemed to confirm that the document aimed to break the EU down and not to build a strong Union which was able to manage the enlargement and the deepening of the integration process, but in a seeming attempt to detach the South from the North. The two-speed Europe proposed by the CDU-CSU was structured according to a geographical approach.

Thus the first definition of Southern Europe was not a positive one and while the deadline for the beginning of the third phase of the Economic and Monetary Union was approaching, conflict increased. Spain, Italy, Portugal and Greece began to be called the poor relatives of the family; German political and economical elites called Southern Europe countries by the offensive acronym of PIGS—from their initials—or the "Club-Med" countries, to highlight their role as mere providers of sun, sea, good food and wine.

The only attempt to build a common position in the EMU and the development of the integration process, with the support of the British Labour party and the German Green party, was held in Lisbon in May 1997 ahead of the European Council of Amsterdam which would close all the open issues in order to sign the new treaty. On this occasion when the Communist parties of France, Italy, Spain, Greece and Portugal convened for a huge demonstration, trying to build a front to renegotiate the Maastricht criteria or to place the issue of the dramatic rise of unemployment beside the monetarist pillar (Minniti 1997).

The contraposition with the other EU partners and particularly with Germany did not lead Spain, Italy, Greece and Portugal to unite or to elaborate a common approach to the EMU or the integration process as a whole. On the contrary, they began another struggle to try to establish better relationships with Brussels and Berlin. The litmus test of this approach, for example, was the Italian and Spanish summit of Valencia in September 1996, just four months before the deadline for the convergence program, which related to the European Monetary System (EMS). In that situation Italian prime minister Romano Prodi tried to establish an alliance with José Maria Aznar to call for a postponement of the third phase of the EMU:[13] Aznar abruptly blocked the Italian attempt by reaffirming Spanish *clarísima determinación*

13 The Italian perspective was clear: Italy did not respect at that time four out of five criteria.

to join the Euro at the first stage. There are different reconstructions of this summit: Prodi himself, even afterwards, strongly rejected the relevance of Valencia (Prodi 2010). The fact is that after that summit the Italian effort towards the EMU became Herculean, starting with the (new) entry into the EMS that followed just a few weeks after Valencia. Italy, Portugal and Spain joined in the third step of the EMU as fully paid-up members in the spring of 1998 without resolving their domestic economic problems,[14] while Greece was excluded and joined later in 2001. The problematic path of those countries towards the single currency union, German distrust of Spain, Italy, Portugal and Greece's ability to achieve safe financial consolidation; and the lack of a shared proposal for the development of the European integration process from those countries, laid the foundations which were to maintain the division between the member states associated with the concept of Southern Europe developed in the mid-nineties by third countries—as shown above– and the partners. Such a division, therefore, intended to worsen relationships and the very essence itself of the European project, namely, the overcoming of the divisions prevalent in Europe's traumatic 20thcentury. And this is what happened with the outbreak of the economic and financial crisis in the last few years.

The Need for a Copernican Revolution

The analysis both of the involvement of Southern European countries in the European integration process and the vicissitudes in the EU after their accession, especially concerning the path towards the single currency union, have provided a unsatisfactory conceptualization of Southern Europe in the EU. The former because it is based purely on a geographical approach and the latter because it is a result of the political dynamics and the contraposition between Germany and the group of countries represented by Italy, Spain, Greece and Portugal. These two approaches have some points of interests and one great limit. The interesting items are: 1) The existence, once the process of enlargement is complete, of three macro regions which can claim the appellative of Southern Europe or to be a part of it–the *Balkan wedge*,

14 Italy, for example, did not respect all the criteria: Italian public debt stood at 106 percent instead of the percentage established in the Tue (60 percent).

the *historical set* and the Turkish *frontier*. This process will enhance the relevance of the dimension of the South in the EU and the Mediterranean area as a whole; 2) The need to overtake an approach rigidly anchored to the idea of the nation state; the rising relevance of the regional level of government within the European integration process calls into question the membership of some French regions and the problem of regional contraposition in Spain and Italy.[15] From this perspective, the time has come to call for a new season of studies on the interconnections between the macro-regions and the raising of the relevance of the regional level in the European integration process (actors, policies, relationships); 3) A certain *quarrelsome attitude* among the countries of the South and particularly between Italy and Spain[16] that has certainly not encouraged the development of good relationships on difficult issues such as the EMU or the construction of a shared approach to the future of the EU; 4) The outbreak of the contraposition in the nineties between the North and the South of the EU. The two geographical areas, in other words, became two political fields; 5) the controversial role of Italy, a founding member of the EEC/EU and a cornerstone of the integration process, but rarely able to influence the development of the integration process at the crucial period starting from the end of the eighties and finally ending in the "ballast group" of the EU–in light of the previous paragraph.

However, the approaches described above have one great limit in common: they try to understand what Southern Europe is in the European integration process by focusing on the Member states. This is a Ptolemaic perspective where the countries are at the center and all the vicissitudes related to the EU turn them around, changing the countries defined as being Southern Europe from time to time in a complex game of variable geometries. Any attempt to define Southern Europe in the EU through these approaches is destined to remain unsatisfactory because there will be another point of view that could change the composition of the countries that may be called Southern Europe.

---

15 In Italy, for example, the Northern League was strongly opposed to the idea of Southern Europe because it felt like part of the Kernel Europe. During the electoral campaign of 1996, the Northern League's MEP Mario Borghezio stated: "If the two Roman-based political poles of Italy want to continue to sail sportingly towards the Mediterranean Sea, *Great Padania* wants to stay, and will stay, in Europe. Even if it has to do so alone" (Borghezio 1996).

16 Just think of the dispute over the GDP between Berlusconi and Zapatero in the early 2000s.

Therefore, it is necessary to completely capsize the perspective by passing from Ptolemy to Copernicus, namely, putting in the centre of the investigation not the member state, but the European integration process itself, leaving the member states free to turn around it. Through a multi-level investigation with an interdisciplinary approach that is able to intersect the studies on the European integration process, it is possible to understand what Southern Europe means in the EU, and which countries comprise it exactly. It is necessary to merge together, for example, research on: 1) the elaboration, implementation and domestic impact of common policies, the transformation of national societies due to EU membership of their country; 2) the contamination between the different political cultures in the European parliamentary political groups and in the trans-national federation of the European parties; 3) the different national debates about the treaties to be approved, the development of the integration process, the position on the different EU issues, and the national interests to preserve. A Copernican revolution will serve to better define Southern Europe in the EU and to better understand the evolution of Southern Europe in the second part of the 20th century as a whole.

Works Cited

Anderson, Malcolm, and Eberhard Bort (1998). *The Frontiers of Europe*. London and Washington: Pinter.

Bachtler, John, Carlos Mendez, and Fiona Wishlade (2013). *EU Cohesion Policy and European Integration. The Dynamics of EU Budget and Regional Policy Reform*. Aldershot: Ashgate.

Bideleux, Robert (2005). The Balkans and the European Union: a Difficult Road. In Landuyt Ariane and Pasquinucci Daniele (eds.). *Gli allargamenti della Cee/Ue 1961–2004*, 659–683. Bologna: il Mulino.

Bielansky, Stefan (2013). La importancia del proceso de democratización y europeización en España para las transformaciones de la forma de gobierno en Polonia. In Cristina Blanco Sío-López and Susana Muñoz (eds.). *Converging pathways. Spain and the European integration process*, 339–348. Brussels: Peter Lang.

Bitsch, Marié Térese (ed.). (2003). *Le fait régional et la construction européenne*. Bruxelles: Bruylant.

Blanco Sío-López, Cristina, and Susana Muñoz (eds.). (2013). *Converging Pathways. Spain and the European Integration Process*. Brussels: Peter Lang.

Borghezio, Mario (1996). Sen. Stefani e On. Borghezio: bisogna essere europeisti nei fatti. *AgeLega*, 59.

Braudel, Fernand. (2010). *Il Mediterraneo. Lo spazio, la storia, gli uomini, le tradizioni*. Milano: Bompiani.

Calandri, Elena (ed.). (2009). *Il primato sfuggente. L'Europa e l'intervento per lo sviluppo (1957–2007)*. Milan: Angeli.

Cdu-Csu (1994). Riflessioni sulla politica europea. In Enrico Letta, *Passaggio a Nord-Est*, doc. X. Bologna: il Mulino.

Commission of the European communities (1982). *The Community and the Countries and Region of the Mediterranean*, File 19/82, 1. In Archives of the European integration. University of Pittsburgh. URL: http://aei.pitt.edu/14644/1/Eur_File_19–82.PDF.

Costa Pinto, António, and Nuno Severiano Teixeira (eds.). (2002). *Southern Europe and the Making of the European Union 1945–1980s*. Boulder: Social Science Monographs; Columbia University, Press.

Cotta, Maurizio, Pierangelo Isernia, and Luca Verzichelli (2005). *L'Europa in Italia*. Bologna: il Mulino.

Cunha, Alice (2014). Mediterranean Europe and the Portuguese Accession Negotiations to the European Economic Community. *Officina della Storia*, 11.

Di Sarcina, Federica (ed.). (2015). *Cultura di genere e politiche di pari opportunità. Il gender mainstreaming alla prova tra Ue e Mediterraneo*. Bologna: il Mulino.

Dolghi, Dorin, and Ioan Horga (2011). The Relationship between Political Europe and Cultural/Geographical Europe. In Giuliana Laschi (ed.). *Oltre i confini: l'Ue fra integrazione interna e relazioni esterne*, 73–86. Bologna: il Mulino.

Dyson, Kenneth, and Kevin Featherstone (1999). *The Road to Maastricht. Negotiating Economic and Monetary Union*. Oxford: Oxford University Press.

European Council (1985). Conclusions of Brussels Summit 29 and 30 March 1985. *Bulletin of the European Parliament*, 6.

EU delegation to Turkey (1963). *Ankara Agreement*. URL: http://avrupa.info.tr/en/eu-and-turkey/history.html.

Featherstone, Kevin, and Claudio M. Redaelli (2003). *The Politics of Europeanization*. Oxford: Oxford University Press.

Gomez, Ricardo (2008). The EU's Mediterranean Policy: Common Foreign Policy by the Back Door? In John Peterson and Helene Sjursen (eds.). *A Common Foreign Policy for Europe? Competing Vision of the Cfsp*. London-New York: Routledge.

Grazi, Laura (2012). The Long Road to a Cohesive Europe. The Evolution of the EU Regional Policy and the Impact of the Enlargements. *Eurolimes*, 14, 80–96.

Grazi, Laura (2014). L'allargamento della Cee e i nuovi strumenti di riequilibrio regionale (1977–1985). *Officina della Storia*, 11.

Jauvert, Vincent (2000). *L'Amérique contre de Gaulle*. Paris: Seuil.

Keating, Michael, and Barry Jones (eds.). (1995). *The European Union and the Regions*. Oxford: Clarendon Press.

Mechi, Lorenzo (2009). Abilità diplomatica, insuccessi economici, progressi amministrativi. Appunti per una storia dell'Italia e i fondi strutturali. In Pietro Crave-

ri Pietro and Antonio Varsori (eds.). *L'Italia nella costruzione europea*. Milan: Angeli.
Minniti, Marco (1997). "Esaurito il ciclo conservatore. La parola è ora alle sinistre europee". *L'Unità*. June 2.
Noiret, Serge (ed.). (2001). La campagna elettorale nell'Europa mediterranea (secoli XIX-XX). *Memoria e Ricerca*, 8, Special Issue.
Papatratis, Procopis (2005). Opening the Gates to Enlargement. The Debate on the Entry of Greece. In Ariane Landuyt and Daniele Pasquinucci (eds.). *Gli allargamenti della Cee/Ue 1961–2004*, 289–301. Bologna: il Mulino.
Laschi, Giuliana (2011). I vicini del Sud: le relazioni tra la Cee e i paesi mediterranei. In Giuliana Laschi (ed.). *Oltre i confini: l'Ue fra integrazione interna e relazioni esterne*, 347–379. Bologna: il Mulino.
Leonardi, Robert (1998). *Coesione, convergenza e integrazione nell'Unione europea*. Bologna: il Mulino.
Piermattei, Massimo (2012). *Crisi della repubblica e sfida europea. I partiti italiani e la moneta unica*. Bologna: CLUEB.
Porto, Manuel (2005). L'allargamento dell'Unione europea. La prospettiva portoghese. In Ariane Landuyt and Daniele Pasquinucci (eds.). *Gli allargamenti della Cee/Ue 1961–2004*, 327–349. Bologna: il Mulino.
Powell, Charles (2011). The Long Road to Europe: Spain and the European Community, 1957–1986. In Roy Joaquín and Maria Lorca-Susino (eds.). *Spain in the European Union: the First Twenty-five Years 1986–2011*, 21–44. Miami: Thomson-Shore.
Privitera, Francesco (2011). Le frontiere (o i limiti?) dell'allargamento: l'Ue di fronte ai Balcani. In Giuliana Laschi (ed.). *Oltre i confini: l'Ue fra integrazione interna e relazioni esterne*, 207–242. Bologna: il Mulino.
Prodi, Romano (2010). Per l'Euro scrissi a Kohl e Chirac. *Corriere della Sera*, 20 May.
Ridolfi Maurizio (ed.). (2002). Repubbliche e repubblicanesimo. L'Europa meridionale (secoli XIX-XX). *Memoria e Ricerca*, 9, Special Issue.
Ridolfi, Maurizio (2011). Republicanesimo, democrazia e classi popolari nel XIX secolo: dal caso italiano alla penisola iberica. *Bulletin d'Histoire contemporaine de l'Espagne*, 46, Special Issue.
Ridolfi, Maurizio (ed.). (2012). Destre e sinistre. Le culture politiche del Novecento nell'Europa mediterranea. *Memoria e Ricerca*, 41, Special Issue.
Ridolfi, Maurizio, and Manuel Cortina Suárez (eds.). (2010). *Democrazia e repubblicanesimo in Spagna e in Italia nell'età liberale*. Rome: Nutrimenti.
Samaniago Boneu, Mercedes (2004). Prospettiva storica dell'integrazione ispanico-comunitaria: un gioco di interessi politici ed economici. In Ariane Landuyt (ed.). *Idee d'Europa e integrazione europea*, 343–393. Bologna: il Mulino.
Sapelli, Giulio (1995). *Southern Europe Since 1945. Tradition and Modernity in Portugal, Spain, Italy, Greece and Turkey*. London: Longman.
Shlaim, Avi, and George Nicolas Yannopoulos (eds.). (1976). *The EEC and the Mediterranean Countries*. Cambridge: Cambridge University Press.

Tavares Ribeiro, and Maria Manuela (2011). Il portogallo e la nuova sfida dell'Europa. In Ariane Landuyt (ed.). *Idee d'Europa e integrazione europea*, 395–414. Bologna: il Mulino.

Thomson, Guy (2007). Mazzini y España. *Historia social*, 59: 3, 21–55.

Tonizzi, Elisabetta (ed.). (2002). Porti dell'Europa mediterranea (secoli XIX e XX). *Memoria e Ricerca*, 11, 23–40.

Treaty on European Union (1992). *Official Journal of the European Communities*, 191/92.

Valette, Jacques (2004). La Francia ovvero il rifiuto della federazione europea. In Ariane Landuyt Ariane, (ed.). *Idee d'Europa e integrazione europea*, 103–118. Bologna: il Mulino.

Wall, Irvin R. (1989). *L'influence américaine sur la politique française 1945–1956*. Paris: Balland.

Zucca, Fabio (2012). *Autonomie locali e federazione sovranazionale. La battaglia del Conseil des Communes et Regions d'Europe per l'unità europea*. Bologna: il Mulino.

Notes on Authors

Martin Baumeister is Director of the German Historical Institute in Rome, Italy, and Professor of Contemporary European History at the University of Munich, Germany.

Guido Franzinetti is Research Fellow and Lecturer in Contemporary European History and in East European History in the Department of Humanistic Studies, University of Eastern Piedmont, Italy.

Andrea Ginzburg, now retired, was Professor of Economic Policy at the University of Modena and Reggio Emilia, Italy.

Patricia Hertel is a researcher in the Department of History, University of Basel, Switzerland.

Russell King is Professor of Geography, School of Global Studies, University of Sussex, UK.

Wolfgang Knöbl is Professor of Sociology and Director of the Hamburg Institute for Social Research, Germany.

Claude Martin is Research Professor at CNRS (National Centre for Scientific Research) and Director of the Research Centre on Political Action in Europe, Rennes, France.

Martin Rhodes is Professor of Comparative Political Economy, Josef Korbel School of International Studies, University of Denver, USA.

Massimo Piermattei is Adjunct Professor in the Department of Economics and Business, University of Tuscia, Italy.

Roberto Sala is a researcher in the Department of History and Coordinator of the Basel Graduate School of History, University of Basel, Switzerland.

Annamaria Simonazzi is Professor of Economics in the Department of Economics and Law, Sapienza University of Rome, Italy.